# WAS IT *my* FAULT?

AN ABUSE SURVIVOR'S STORY AND GUIDE
FOR NAVIGATING NARCISSISTIC RED FLAGS

## ALANA SHARPS

The purpose of sharing my story is to help others currently in toxic relationships seeking a way out and need a guide to follow. It's also for the survivor currently experiencing post-separation abuse feeling they are alone in a society who only views physical abuse as domestic violence. Lastly, this book is for friends and family to recognize the signs of abuse and to assist and provide support to their loved ones.

**Author Photography**
Kimberly Metz
www.kimberlymetz.com

**Book Creation & Design**
DHBonner Virtual Solutions LLC
www.dhbonner.net

ISBN for Paperback: 978-0-578-33113-3
ISBN for eBook: 978-0-578-33501-8

Published in the United States of America

*This book is dedicated to my former self:*
*you are worthy, you are strong,*
*you are a "SurThriver"*

*Disclaimer:* This content is based on actual events captured from memories, conversations, experiences and personal journals. For the purposes of anonymity, names, locations, and other identifying characteristics have been changed. This book is intended to portray the author's healing journey through emotional and psychological abuse. It is not intended to offer legal or medical advice. The author is not responsible for personal decisions and/or negative consequences derived from the experiences contained in this novel. The reader is advised to seek professional advice for their own personal situations requiring therapeutic, medical or legal advice.

"I'm thankful for my struggle because, without it,
I wouldn't have stumbled across my strength."

—Alex Elle

# TABLE OF CONTENTS

# ACKNOWLEDGMENTS

To my children—Michael, Makenzey, and Maddox, thank you for inspiring me to be the best mother, provider and teacher.

To my dearest friends—Sonja, Angela, Toni, Tammy, Gloria, Jamie, Tia, and Amy, thank you for being that listening ear, praying with me, providing me shelter, as well as providing advice and encouragement while giving me strength during my darkest times.

# INTRODUCTION

As I glanced at myself in the mirror, I didn't recognize the woman I had become. The woman who stared back at me was a stranger. She was sad, disheveled, worn down and lifeless. She was broken.

She had married a psychological and emotional abuser — a charming, charismatic man to the outside world, who demeaned and abused behind closed doors. She was a strong, independent, ambitious and vivacious woman who was broken by her intimate relationship with someone who vowed to love her. Someone she would do anything for and love unconditionally. Someone she willingly gave up her own wants, likes, relationships, dreams and goals while losing herself in the process. Someone she molded herself to in order to please and received nothing in return. More than a decade had passed and the woman I saw before me was not someone I wanted to be anymore...

After being in a chaotic, emotional and psychologically abusive relationship for sixteen years, I finally found the strength to leave. The moment I first stepped foot into my tiny two-bedroom apartment after I had finally left, was life altering. I closed the door and leaned my back against the wall, as tears rolled down my face, releasing years of fear, frustration, confusion, low self-esteem, self-doubt and anger. I was finally free and stood in silence enjoying the peace. It was one of the most uplifting experiences of my life and it was as if two hundred pounds had been lifted from my shoulders . . . and I could finally breathe again.

As I collected my thoughts and cleared my head over the days that followed, I discovered therapeutic journaling as a way to heal from my experience. Throughout everything I endured during my relationship, I learned several things:

- Love does not control.
- Love does not manipulate.
- Love does not demean.
- Love does not condemn.
- Love is not cruel.
- Love is not hypocritical.
- Love is not passive aggressive.
- Love does not isolate.
- Love does not disrespect.
- Love does not break your spirit.

As the cloud of confusion lifted from my mind, I took a step back and realized it wasn't me with the problem, as my abuser had so frequently told me, it was him.

*It actually was not my fault.*

He was never happy, nor ever satisfied, no matter what I did to please him. He wasn't interested in taking accountability for his actions or changing his behavior, although he would often portray otherwise to family, friends and marital therapists. He was overly critical, controlling, demeaning, passive aggressive, and a hypocrite. He was, and is, a narcissist.

Surviving this relationship led me to the study of Narcissistic Personality Disorder, Post Traumatic Stress Disorder, as well as the practices and understanding of how to stay calm in high stress situations. While journaling my experience, I felt compelled to help other women who are enduring the same trauma. Women who may not realize they are in an abusive relationship. Women who may not realize that psychological and emotional abuse is domestic violence — a form of domestic violence that does not result in outward physical scars as our scars are hidden within our brains. Women who are caught up in the "FOG" of fear, obligation and guilt:

- The fear of being a failure as a mother, girlfriend, or wife
- The obligation being to stay in a psychologically and emotionally abusive relationship due to faith, societal perception, commitment to their kids, or finances.
- The guilt of contemplating breaking up the family unit and the consequences of that decision on children overwhelmingly convinces you to stay, despite every red flag that goes up, every transgression that occurs, despite everything.

Domestic abuse can happen to anyone, and it need not be the stereotypical violent abuse. Abuse can and does happen to people who are talented, independent, confident, educated, with or without happy childhoods and loving parents. It is often their devotion to family that binds victims to their abusers. Many people ask victims, 'why didn't you just leave?' A question easier said than done.

Victims stay for a multitude of reasons:

- Victims are conditioned to believe that everything that goes wrong in the relationship is their fault.
- Victims love their partners and believe that if they can make their partners happy, their partner will return to the loving and affectionate person they once were.

- Victims fear societal stigmas of breaking up a family and subjecting their children to a "broken home."
- Victims are embarrassed and ashamed.
- Victims are fearful of what may occur once they leave the relationship.
- Victims do not believe they can financially survive without their partner.

And again, it is important to understand that abuse does not always equate to hitting. Psychological and verbal abuse are considered domestic violence. Studies have shown that psychological abuse is more mentally debilitating in the long term than physical violence. Most people think that if you aren't being physically hit, you aren't being abused. However, a punch to the face and a verbal attack are perceived the same way by the brain.

Both experiences endured over long periods of time can lead to and often do lead to Post Traumatic Stress Disorder (PTSD). Being trapped in your own mind, reliving a traumatic experience over and over in your head, unable to escape is the hardest thing to experience and endure.

If this resonates with you, here are a few questions to ask yourself:

- Does your partner/spouse isolate you from friends or family?
- Do you constantly feel belittled and overly criticized in your relationship?
- Do you often feel tense and anxious around your intimate partner, constantly walking on eggshells?
- Do you often feel jittery in everyday situations or find yourself crying for no reason?
- Do you find yourself apologizing for things you're not at fault for in your intimate relationship to avoid conflict?

- Does your partner/spouse constantly blame you for everything that goes wrong in their life?
- Do you find yourself dismissing things that would indicate something is wrong or *off* and rationalize it as something else?

These reasons and many more often culminate into one overarching premise — they collectively become an invisible restraint or a force that emotionally and physically prevent you from leaving, despite any logic or rationale under any other circumstances that would cause you to leave a situation like this. There is nothing normal about how convoluted the web of deception, manipulation, control completely eradicates your will and your sense of reason. It is without question, a force that no one is ever prepared for.

Which is why this book not only portrays my story, but also provides insight into the signs of abuse for victims as well as friends and family, the neurological and physical effects of abuse, and the barriers to leaving an abusive relationship. I hope you learn from my healing journey and find the strength to begin yours.

**FOG:** *Fear, Obligation, and Guilt. A term coined by Susan Forward and Donna Frazier in the book Emotional Blackmail to explain the emotions most commonly used by emotional manipulators to gain and keep control over others and certain situations. When emotions are being exploited, a fog of confusion sets in and the person in the fog has a hard time sorting out what's really going on and who has the problem. One of the many reasons why victims stay in the abusive relationship for so long.*

*Chapter 1*

# PRINCE CHARMING

**Idealization Phase:** *The first phase of the narcissistic abuse cycle, also known as the grooming stage or love bombing. A stage of immense flattery, gifts, and excessive attention to appeal to your heart, weaken your defense mechanisms, and allow you to be drawn into a whirlwind romance without even realizing it.*

## TOO GOOD TO BE TRUE

I was introduced to online dating by a coworker. I had recently split from my husband and was raising a one-year-old son named Elijah. I wasn't seriously looking to meet anyone. I figured, why not create an online dating profile and see what happens. Worst case scenario, I wouldn't meet anyone. No loss there. Or I'd meet someone to hang out with every once in a while. That didn't seem like a bad idea. Of course, I had my standards for the ideal suitor, he had to have a professional job, make equivalent to my income, be my height or taller, and attractive.

It was my second week of scrolling through the online profiles of possible suitors when Jon popped up in my list of matches; a young attractive guy, tall in stature with an athletic build. He was still in college, but currently in a cooperative program working full-time for a semester. He didn't meet any of the dating standards listed in my profile ▶, but I gave him a chance anyway when he sent me an online message. We chatted by phone a few days later and he piqued my interest during our phone conversation.

Our first conversation occurred while Jon was driving to North Carolina from Indiana, a ten-hour drive and we spoke for four of them. I didn't have high expectations for our initial phone call since Jon was just some random guy who reached out to me online. I decided to get a few chores done around the house while we talked on the phone. I figured the call would be quick, thirty minutes at the most.

I grabbed a dust cloth to begin dusting my living room and dialed Jon's number. After the initial, "Hey, it's so and so from Love.AOL," I decided to ask Jon a few questions.

I began wiping down my fireplace mantle, cleaning around my TV.

"So, where do you go to school?"

"I'm currently doing a co-op with a small company. Since I plan to move to North Carolina, I'm applying to NC State University's Engineering program."

"Oh really? What major?"

Intrigued by what I was hearing, I stopped dusting and leaned on the mantle, listening intently.

"Electrical Engineering."

"What!? That was my major. What a coincidence!"

"I like to tinker with things. I love math and I'm always analyzing things."

I sat down in my glider chair in my living room, shifting the phone in my hand to get comfortable. He had piqued my interest and I was interested in learning more about him.

"I'm not practicing engineering anymore, but it was a great foundation for me to do other things. I'd really like to own my own business one day. It's been my dream since I was a little girl."

"What a coincidence! I, too, have always been interested in owning a business. It sounds like we're off to a great start," ▶ Jon said.

It was during our conversation that Jon received a call from his dad, informing him his mom was in the hospital. She had a horrible peanut allergy and had been exposed at work while eating lunch in her school's cafeteria. I got a glimpse into Jon's soft side as he explained his mother's condition.

"Sorry about that, my mother is in the hospital for an allergic reaction. She passed out at school and had to be transported to the hospital," Jon said, choking back tears. ▶

I jumped out of my chair, gripping the phone tightly.

"Oh my God! Is she ok?" I gasped.

"She's doing better, but still having difficulty breathing. They gave her epinephrine in the ambulance."

I slowly slid back into my chair, propping my feet up on the cushion to get comfortable as a flood of emotions came over me.

"I'm so sorry to hear this. I'm sure it's tough to hear being so far away right now and unable to see her."

I could tell by the tone of his voice, the long pauses in conversation and how he struggled to choke back tears, how concerned he was about his mother's well-being and not being able to be by her side. I suddenly felt knots in my stomach feeling what Jon felt. I sympathized with him and his mother as he pulled at my heartstrings, telling me her current situation. I wished he was by my side so I could give him a hug and let him know that she would be okay.

After Jon arrived in North Carolina, we went on our first date a day later. I was excited for the date after a few phone conversations. He was so easy to talk to; I felt like I could open up and talk to him about any and everything. He had a charm ▶ about him that made you feel comfortable enough to relax your inhibitions.

We planned a great dinner at a high-end restaurant based on the recommendation of Jon's boss. Jon picked me up from my home and we headed to downtown Cary. It was a beautiful fall evening in the middle of October when the leaves were just beginning to change. We arrived at the restaurant and double-checked the address to make sure we were at the right place. The restaurant was located in an old decrepit building that appeared to have been neglected for years. We decided to take a chance and walked inside to take a look at the menu. *Escargot? Duck Liver?* Jon and I both looked at each other, trying to figure out if either one of us were interested in the menu items.

"How about Ruby Tuesday?" I suggested, looking over at Jon for a response.

"I didn't see anything on the menu I liked but didn't want to hold you back from enjoying it if you were interested," Jon said, grimacing at the menu.

The restaurant was way too fancy for us. We gave the hostess back the menus, got back in the car and drove to the local bar and grill not far down the road. Prior to our date that night, I was very upfront with Jon about my thoughts and feelings on dating him. I reiterated I was not looking for anything serious. I didn't see him as someone I would be with long term, due to the six-year age gap, and the fact that he was still in college. I didn't need someone else to take care of in addition to my young son. I already had a one-year-old child to raise. Jon sat quietly in the booth and listened with a somber look on his face. He nodded his head in agreement as if he understood where I was coming from but didn't let that stop his pursuit of my heart.

"I'm very mature for my age, you know? My parents are both educators so I'm great with kids. I'm also completely in tune with women and their moods, especially when it's that time of the month and you need extra sensitivity. Some men get offended easily when women are moody. I tend to take a step back and think about what is currently going on that may affect a woman's mood." ▶

Jon paused for a moment, looking down at the table.

"Oh, and I've never cheated and would never cheat on someone. I've been cheated on and know the pain it causes." ▶

I shifted around in the booth I was sitting in, trying to find a comfortable position as Jon spoke. I listened intently, although I never intended to change my stance on where the relationship was going. The waitress brought our food to the table after thirty minutes of waiting. We sat and ate quietly before sparking up conversation again.

As the night continued, Jon started to draw me in. The conversation began to flow as easily as it did during our very first phone conversation. He seemed to fit perfectly ▶ into where I was in life with my goals, ambitions and view of the world. I found myself being mesmerized by his words and his calm demeanor as he spoke. I looked at him and thought to myself, *this is the guy I'm going to marry. Is he really the one?* We had the same interests in music, movies, activities, and entrepreneurial pursuits. He enjoyed traveling, he loved kids, and he was majoring in the same thing I majored in during college. He seemed so in tune to my thoughts and my feelings.

It was as if God had finally answered my prayers and brought this man to me — the man I had been searching for my entire life. The man I dreamt about when I was a child. My prince charming.

I'd never met a man so in sync with my interests and goals in life. *Was he my soulmate?* I couldn't imagine feeling so strongly about anyone else the way I felt about Jon that night. However, there was still that six-year age gap tugging at me.We had so much fun at dinner, neither of us wanted the date to end. As Jon paid for our dinner, he looked up at me and asked, "Interested in a movie? I'm really enjoying your company and would like to spend more time with you, if you don't mind."

"Sure! I'd love to see a movie. There's a great Michelle Pfeiffer movie out right now I've wanted to see for a while, but I just haven't gotten around to it."

We drove to the nearby movie theater after leaving Ruby Tuesday. Jon purchased our movie tickets and concession items. As we sat down in our chairs to be seated, he grabbed my hand and held it throughout the movie.

After the movie ended, Jon drove me home, holding my hand the entire drive to my house. The night was calm with a few dimly lit stars illuminating the sky as I looked up from the car window. Once we arrived and pulled into the driveway, Jon leaned over and whispered, "Sit still." I watched as he walked around the front of the car. He opened my car door and grabbed my hand helping me up out of my seat and slowly walked me to the front door, caressing my hand with every step. As I gathered my keys to open the door, he leaned in to kiss me goodnight. His lips were soft, supple and so electrifying that it sent chills down my spine.

"Goodnight, Jon," I whispered as I walked into the house.

"Goodnight," he replied, waving as he walked back to his car.

I shut the door and closed my eyes reflecting on the evening. I found myself hypnotized by his words, his soft tone, his innocent behavior. I had never met someone so in tune with myself and it was scary and exciting at the same time. ▶However, he was still six years younger than me. I really was not in the mood for teaching a man how to start up a career and all the other life lessons I already experienced as a young adult straight out of college.

In the days that followed, I repeatedly expressed to Jon my inhibitions with moving forward with the relationship in light of his age. He went full steam ahead with trying to convince me otherwise. ▶ For every reason I had for not pursuing the relationship, he had a rebuttal. A reason why I should give him a chance. He sent me a poem he wrote in high school about children and how they needed to be nurtured and loved. He doubled down on all the ways he's supported and cared for women in his life.

He often told me stories of how he and his mom were extremely close and how she taught him the proper way to treat a woman. The more I pushed back, the more he pursued until I eventually succumbed to giving him a chance. I had developed an emotional bond with him that I couldn't deny, no matter how much I tried to convince myself the relationship would never work.

Two weeks into our relationship, Jon asked me to remove my profile from the dating board so that we could be in an exclusive relationship. After giving it some thought, I obliged with his wishes.

We began to see each other every other day after that, and I started tearing down the wall I built around my heart. He was the first person I thought of when I woke up in the morning and the last person I spoke to when I went to bed. He came into my life and caught me by surprise. He had swept me off of my feet and elevated me on a pedestal with his focus and attention solely on me. I couldn't imagine life without him. He was the perfect mate. ▶He gave the best sentimental hugs and the sweetest tender kisses. I loved the feeling of his arms wrapped around me while I lay my head on his chest, listening to his heartbeat and feeling the warmth of his body next to mine as we watched TV.

He was filling a hole in my heart with unconditional love and affection often sought, but not always found. I no longer thought about my insecurities and no longer had self-doubt. I was on a euphoric high, and I didn't want it to end.

Jon sent flowers to my job every week, called me all day every day, texted me throughout the day and sent me beautiful love poems every week. My coworkers repeatedly asked what the occasion was for the flowers or what he did wrong. Most people get flowers for special occasions. Jon was sending flowers *just because*; and I was caught up in the romance of it all. He was my prince charming. The one I had been dreaming about since I was a little girl. *Where had this man been all my life?* I became so enamored with him that I never wanted to ever have an argument and ruin the intense bond we had with one another.

As we lay together on the couch watching a television show one night, I turned to Jon and said,

"Let's always communicate about our feelings, whether they are good or bad,

to avoid arguments and misunderstandings."

"We will never argue, honey," Jon said with conviction. "We're too perfect for one another to argue about anything." ▶

Not completely convinced an argument would never ensue over spilled milk or something else frivolous, I sent Jon articles on nurturing relationships and how to communicate more effectively with your partner. Articles he took to be nice, but showed no true interest in. He placed the articles on the kitchen table, walked into the living room and sat on the couch.

Not only was Jon great with me, but he was also great with my son. He played with him all the time, took him to parks and museums, and read to him constantly. He was the perfect mate, and the perfect father. My son took some time warming up to him in the beginning. However, he eventually thought Jon was the greatest gift, and I loved seeing my son so happy.

One month into the relationship, Jon moved into the single-family home I owned ▶ in Cary. He often expressed how much he hated living so far away from me. He wanted to see me every day and living in Wilson was too far to travel every day. I wasn't fully onboard with Jon moving in so quickly, but I eventually gave in. I know it seemed sudden to our families. He lived an hour away with his boss and the constant driving back and forth became too much for him and me with a small child driving to see him. It was also during this time that Jon told his family about me.

Jon was from a small town in Arkansas, population of 1,666, with very little diversity. In fact, the town was so small it was considered a village. It didn't even make it to town or city status. Jon was the oldest of two, he had a younger brother who still lived at home. His family was very close knit and did everything together during his childhood and early adulthood. The closest living relative lived in California, so his family developed a strong bond as a four-person family. Almost too close by some opinions. Since I'm African American and Jon is Caucasian, German American to be exact, his family was not in favor of the relationship, and they made sure we knew it.

To make matters worse, I had a small child. Two things they didn't agree with or accept. Their biggest concern, what would their friends think of the relationship? His parents were well-respected educators, and this relationship would most definitely put a scar on their perfect image. This led to multiple tear-filled conversations with his family telling him to end the relationship or they would disown him.

His mom sent him numerous long, drawn-out emails with multiple reasons why the relationship would not work on top of weekly phone calls that eventually ramped up to daily. She started with the stigma of interracial relationships. When she realized that wasn't working to convince him to end the relationship, she moved onto the children and how society would never accept them. While I was preparing to give Elijah a bath one Sunday evening, Jon's mom called. Jon put her on speakerphone in order for me to hear the conversation.

"How was your day, honey?"

"Good, how was yours?" Jon replied.

"Have you considered what we talked about?"

Jon started pacing around the bedroom. "Yes, and I'm not changing my mind, Mom. It's my decision," he declared.

"I really wish you would reconsider. The kids will have a hard life. I'm a teacher. I've seen what these kids go through."

"Mom, it's my decision," Jon shouted, frustrated by his mother continuing to pressure him.

I heard enough. I began to gather Elijah's night clothes and get him ready for his bath. When I returned, Jon was in tears, as he typically was at the end of every call. ▶ Jon's father would often get on the phone as well during family conversations. He's not much of a talker and wouldn't say much. He didn't put pressure on Jon like Jon's mother. However, according to Jon, when he first saw a picture of Elijah, he made degrading comments about his appearance and compared him to a Latino baseball player — unnecessary and offensive comments.

The brother would call Jon on separate occasions to talk Jon out of the relationship and explain the burden it was putting on their parents. His angle was more along the lines of "see what your relationship is doing to our parents?" He put the guilt trip on Jon for the parents nonstop arguing over Jon's relationship.

Although hard to hear and deal with, the constant disdain for our relationship actually pulled us closer together instead of tearing us apart. However, it still plagued Jon that his family refused to accept me and my son.

By the second week of calls, texts and emails, I could see the toll it was taking on him. "Jon, maybe we should consider ending the relationship," I said while folding clothes one evening. Jon had just gotten off the phone, listening to his mother cry again, telling him all the reasons why our relationship would not work and how our children would be victims of society's hate.

"No." Jon reached over to grab a towel to fold. "I'm not going to let her control my life. It's my life and I'm going to live it how I want. I'm not a kid that she can control anymore, and she needs to understand that." Tears started to trickle down Jon's face. I put down the sheet I had in my hand to walk over and give him a hug. He laid his head on my shoulder and began to cry.

I've always been a compassionate person, so watching Jon break-down broke my heart. As I listened to the turmoil-filled conversations occur between Jon and his mother on a daily basis, I felt the need to console him and ease his pain. I was his shoulder to cry on and his listening ear. There were many days and nights where he just intensely cried on my shoulder and looked at me with despair. I could see the confliction in his eyes with every tear.

In light of his family issues, Jon pulled himself together as best he could to get himself back in school to finish his degree. He had two years of school left and needed to get back to it. Without the support of his parents or brother, he relied on me to be his rock as he navigated through life without the family, he had been so close to until now. He enrolled back in school during the fall semester and things slowly began to change. He began to focus entirely on his studies and nothing else. ▶

He wasn't working or contributing to the household, and he didn't help out with my son as he had in the beginning of the relationship. He became very self-centered and self-absorbed. For weeks, I transported Elijah to and from daycare, cooked dinner for everyone after working long hours, and prepared Elijah for bed every night. Jon was no longer working his co-op job. Therefore, I financially supported him while he attended school full time, paid off his debts and co-signed on a loan for a car when his jeep broke down. I also researched and secured him a summer internship that would eventually lead to his first full-time job and career path. Every misgiving I had about starting a relationship with a man six years younger, was becoming my reality. ▶

Jon had the luxury of going to school ten minutes away and arriving home by 2 p.m. every day. I, on the other hand, left home at 6:30 a.m. to take Elijah to daycare and then drove the opposite direction for forty-five minutes to work. After work, I'd drive to pick up Elijah from daycare, come home and prepare dinner for everyone.

## THE MASK BEGINS TO PEEL AWAY

As Jon sat oblivious to everyone and everything around him, at the kitchen table doing homework one night, I exploded. My son had a cold and was tugging on my leg to pick him up while I frantically tried to prepare dinner. I turned to Jon in frustration and said, "Jon, I really need you to help out. You sleep and eat here, yet you do nothing to help out. I need you to get a part-time job, and I need you to help out around the house. *I can do bad all by myself.* What I was essentially trying to communicate was that I can struggle raising a child by myself, without the addition of an adult in the home not pulling their own weight. That adult being him.

Jon looked up as if to come out of a trance. "What, sorry," shaking his head to wake up. "What can I help you with?" He asked, grabbing my son off the floor.

"Can you please watch ⬤ m while I finish dinner?" I gave Jon the "look" a mother gives her child when they misbehave in public.

"Yes, I'll take him in the front room to play for a little bit."

Jon picked up Elijah and took him to the front room to work on a floor puzzle.

It was at that moment Jon knew I had reached my limit. After that night, he structured his study time around dinner and getting my son ready for bed. Even though I began to regret dating a younger man, I couldn't deny that I loved him and felt deep down that he loved me ▶. I was willing to accept him with all of his flaws and lack of knowledge on life skills.

After six months of living together, Jon proposed while on a vacation trip to Las Vegas. I arranged for my parents to watch Elijah while we took an adult vacation. We stayed at the MGM overlooking the hustle and bustle of the Vegas strip. The first two days of our trip, Jon was intensely ill. Everything he ate came right back up and his throat was swollen with huge nodules in the back of his throat. He was on heavy antibiotics for strep throat at the time, and we were hoping he would feel well enough to enjoy some of the trip by the time we arrived. The first few days, I ventured out on my own up and down the strip. However, I wanted to do some activities and it just didn't seem right to do them while he was in the room sick. I felt guilty. ▶

By the third day, I had given up hope of being able to enjoy anything with Jon. I settled into simply staying in the room and watching TV. However, Jon insisted he was well enough to go out on this particular night. I kept wondering why he was so adamant about going out that night when he felt so awful. To my surprise, he arranged for a limo to take us to Red Rock Canyon at dusk. As I grabbed some clothes to put on for our night out, I turned to Jon and said,

"We don't have to go out. Get some rest to heal your body."

"I'm fine," Jon said, pulling his sweater over his head.

"Just get ready. We will have a great time. I promise."

Jon held both of my hands in his while smiling from ear to ear.

"Ok, I hope you're not pushing yourself too hard."

We finished getting dressed and walked downstairs to the front of the hotel to meet the limo driver. As we approached the car, the driver opened our doors to let us in. We sat back in our seats and began our drive to Red Rock. After a twenty-minute drive, the limo stopped. I glanced out my window and saw nothing but empty desert. We were in the middle of nowhere. I couldn't figure out what was going on and why we weren't moving. It was at that point, Jon got down on one knee. I was shocked! My heart began to flutter.

"What are you doing, Jon?" My palms were sweaty, and my hand started to shake as Jon placed a beautiful heart-shaped diamond ring on my trembling finger.

"Will you marry me?" he asked.

"Yes," I replied, leaning over to give him a kiss. I was so excited and surprised! I was going to marry my soulmate.

On our drive back to the hotel, Jon took a terrible turn for the worse. We ended up taking a cab to the ER thirty minutes after arriving back at the hotel. Jon was in terrible shape. He felt warm, was pale, having excruciating throat pain and vomiting. Jon had severe strep throat. After we arrived at the ER, the triage nurse immediately took Jon back and the doctors placed him on IV antibiotics. Five minutes into the IV drip, Jon was gasping for air.

"What's wrong, Jon?" I yelled as I jumped out of my chair to go to his side. Red splotches and hives appeared on his neck. I pulled down his gown to get a clear view of his chest where there were even more, and they were spreading like wild fire. "Nurse!" I called out, yanking back the curtain. "He's having difficulty breathing!"

The nurse came running over to examine him.

"Something's wrong, he can't breathe, and he's broken out in hives!" I didn't know what was going on, and I thought he was seriously ill. I laid my head in my hands as I began tearing up.

"It's ok, honey, it's just an allergic reaction to the antibiotics. I stopped the drip, and he seems to be breathing better," the nurse said.

After ten minutes, he was stabilized. Jon's breathing returned to normal, and his hives began to subside. Jon was discharged four hours after, and we flew back to the east coast later that day. My parents picked us up from the airport and Mom was excited to see the ring.

"It's beautiful!" Mom said, looking at the intricacies in the custom design.

I began the early stages of wedding planning the week after our Vegas trip. My dream since I was a little girl was to get married in the month of May. Since Jon's parents were teachers and couldn't take a Friday off to drive down for a May wedding, I was pressured into moving the date to June when school was out. One of the many disappointments that went into planning. ▶

Planning a wedding is not fun and extremely stressful without a wedding planner. Especially when you work full-time and have the responsibility of supporting a family. I didn't realize how much work it was until I started keeping a spreadsheet of everything that needed to be done and when; from contacting florists, to wedding cakes, to calligraphers, to dress shopping. So much to do and so little time!

I tried including Jon in all of the decision-making. Some things he was interested in doing and other things he could care less about. That meant the success of our wedding day fell squarely upon my shoulders. It was also during this time that we began selecting our wedding party. I selected six of my closest friends from all facets of my life, whereas Jon had difficulty selecting groomsmen.

Two of his groomsmen were from his co-op job; men he had met one year prior. There was also drama with who would be the best man. Jon selected an older gentleman he referred to as his "best friend" from his hometown, named Bob. Bob apparently had a reputation of hanging out with younger men in the town, I would later find out. The town had suspicions of this man's intentions with men twenty years his junior, according to Jon, so of course, this set off red flags with Jon's parents.

First of all, he didn't pick his father to be his best man and that was expected by the family. Second of all, he selected a man with a negative reputation, which would further stigmatize the family in town. In the end, Jon rescinded his offer to have Bob be his best man and selected his father. He notified me of this information four weeks prior to us walking down the aisle.

"I decided to make Dad my best man," Jon said, walking into the kitchen as I was preparing dinner.

"Ok, do you think that's fair to Bob after you already selected him?"

"I know, it's not fair. I profusely apologized to him and now he's angry with me. He's demanding I pay him in full for the engagement ring. He loaned me the money," he said, staring at the floor, avoiding eye contact.

"Excuse me?" I inquired, glaring at Jon while pouring pasta into the pot of boiling water on the stove. "So basically, I have to pay for my own engagement ring because you don't have a full-time job and can't qualify for a bank loan," I stated, shaking my head in disgust.

"I know and I apologize. It wasn't supposed to happen like this. Can you call him and talk to him? Maybe he will talk to you and we can work something out with him."

I stopped cutting up the bell pepper I was mincing to look over at Jon. "No, Jon, he's not my friend. You said this man was your best friend. If he is truly your "best friend," he wouldn't demand that you pay him back immediately, knowing you're a full-time student."

Jon sat silently for a little bit, gathering his thoughts while I continued making dinner. One week later, things intensified between Jon and Bob, to the point that Bob threatened legal action. In the end, I paid for my own engagement ring to keep the peace.

So much drama and stress occurred while planning the wedding that I was relieved when it was getting close to time to walk down the aisle. Two weeks prior to the wedding, Jon and I sat on the bed in our bedroom, discussing the fun we planned to have on our honeymoon in Hawaii. We were excited about our trip and couldn't wait to be married. During our conversation, I told Jon that I wanted to refrain from intimacy until we were married. Jon went from laughing and smiling to a stern angered look in a matter of seconds. A look I had not seen since we had been dating, and quite frankly, a look I'd rather not have seen since it scared me. ▶

He was not happy with me at all. He was angry. His eyes dilated and turned dark. He jerked back with a gaping mouth and said, "I DON'T WANT to do that."

"Well, I do, and it's my choice." Shocked, I got up from the bed and walked toward the bedroom door. I stood in the doorway looking at Jon.

"I don't know why we have to do that. It's dumb," Jon sneered, as he stood up and began walking toward me.

"Because I want to do it, Jon."

I inched closer to the hallway in case I needed to make a quick escape. Jon stormed off, walking past me and heading to the stairs. I took a few minutes to compose myself and then sat back down on the bed, making a list of things to pack for the wedding and the honeymoon.

I was packing my bags for our trip to my parent's house when Jon entered the bedroom in a rage. At this point, he was in full-out temper tantrum mode and I was in shock that a grown man would act this way ▶. He clearly did not respect my wishes or my feelings. I stopped what I was doing, looked Jon straight in the eye and said, "Is this how it's going to be when we get married? Are you going to act like this when you can't have sex for a few days, or get your way, in general? Please let me know now because if it is, we don't need to get married. I'd rather end the wedding now than deal with this behavior throughout the marriage."

Suddenly, Jon's entire demeanor changed as if he had become someone else. His aggression subsided, his face relaxed and his voice became calm. ▶He returned to the angelic, innocent-looking man I fell in love with not long ago.

"No, no, no, it won't be like this at all once we're married." Jon lovingly kissed me on my forehead and gave me a hug while apologizing for his behavior.

## REFLECTION

Jon exhibited charming chameleon-like behavior on our first date. He was everything I wished for in a mate from my perspective, not realizing that he was mirroring me to give the perception he was the perfect soulmate. People with Narcissistic Personality Disorder (NPD) are very perceptive. They watch and listen very closely to every word you say for clues on what will charm and win you over. They will have your same beliefs and attitudes as they become everything you've ever wished for in a mate. They listen intently to your weaknesses and insecurities, gathering information to use against you as a form of manipulation at a later time.

Narcissists will shower you with excessive attention, love, and affection. Who doesn't want to feel special? They will manipulate your empathy, continuously compliment you (you're beautiful, intelligent, amazing, funny, sexy, gorgeous), and make you feel loved at all times. They may make comments similar to, "I've never met anyone like you," "You are my soulmate," "I love you so much." (within weeks or even days of meeting you). They maneuver their way into becoming the center of your world very rapidly without you even realizing it. They also may consistently tell you how loyal and honest they are, never cheating in a relationship. Narcissists want to immediately get close to you, not giving the relationship time to develop at a normal pace. Everything is expedited to test your boundaries. What I thought was the perfect once-in-a-lifetime whirlwind romance was actually a manipulation tactic to draw me closer to a pathological manipulator.

Jon showed a lack of respect for my boundaries. I repeatedly told Jon I was not interested in a serious relationship with him due to his age. Instead of respecting my wishes, he pursued me even more, disregarding my feelings. Because narcissists lack empathy, have a strong sense of entitlement and exploit others, boundaries are something that gets in the way of their goals.

Furthermore, I missed a very important red flag when Jon went into a rage over not having sex. In his view his wants and needs were more important than my wishes. Unfortunately, I did not follow my intuition and continued with the marriage.

*Chapter 2*

# FOREVER IS FLEETING

*"For I had just, for the first time, found the woman
I would call "My Love" forever."*

**Devalue Phase**: *The second phase in the narcissistic abuse cycle when the victim is essentially knocked off the pedestal that the abuser placed them on during the idealization phase. Love bombing and admiration ceases to exist and is replaced by verbal and emotional abuse. This phase is characterized by cruel, degrading, and condescending remarks often disguised as jokes and sarcasm used to demoralize the victim. Victims during this phase feel confused, doubt themselves, and develop low self-esteem. It's a stage where the abuser uses all of the information collected in the idealization phase on personal weaknesses and insecurities to emotionally manipulate, shame, humiliate, criticize and control. Abusers become distant during a victim's time of need and during times of sickness. The abuser is often noted as exhibiting a Dr. Jekyll and Mr. Hyde persona due to the way they flip back and forth between caring and abusive masks.*

## HONEYMOON "MISS" AS OPPOSED TO "BLISS"

We got married during the summer of 2002 in what most would believe to be a beautiful fairy tale wedding. I woke up the morning of our wedding excited to marry the man of my dreams, in the wedding I had dreamt about ever since I was a little girl. The day was sunny and clear, without a cloud in the sky to worry about the possibility of rain. *"Rain on your wedding day, tears in your marriage,"* they always say. Everything had gone according to plan, so my mind was worry free. All of the stress from planning the event had finally paid off. I could finally relax and enjoy the day.

My wedding party consisted of six of my closest friends, all dressed in fitted periwinkle dresses with silver high heel shoes, reminiscent of a fashion show lineup. The men wore black tuxes with periwinkle bow ties. I wore a strapless white, fitted, shimmery dress with an extra-long train and custom designed Ked sneakers I bedazzled the week prior. I had my bridesmaids arrive at my parent's house by 8 a.m. to prepare for the wedding, scheduled for 12:30 p.m. I had attended a number of weddings that did not start on time, so I was determined to have my wedding start exactly as stated in the program.

We arrived at the church at 11:45 a.m. ready to get the show on the road. As it got closer and closer to the time to walk down the aisle, I got more and more anxious. My palms started getting sweaty, I got hot, felt lightheaded and had to sit down. My bridesmaids began fanning me with programs as I sat down in a chair while waiting to walk down the aisle.

As 12:30 approached, I walked out of the waiting area toward my dad, who was waiting patiently for me at the back of the church. He grabbed my arm as I approached, and we walked down the center aisle of the church to meet Jon at the altar; butterflies fluttered in my stomach for the entire walk. Jon gently took my hand in his as my dad and I greeted him. Jon and I turned to the priest to begin the ceremony as our wedding guests sat back down in the pews. The aromatic smell of roses filled the air from my rose bouquet as Jon and I professed our love for one another during our nuptials. Jon grabbed my hand as he professed:

> *"Each and every day I learn more about what it means to love, to be loved and to share love. You are my best friend and you have shown me not only how to love you and Elijah, but how to love myself. From this day forward, I promise to hold you softly, love you tenderly, take care of and protect you and to always make you laugh and smile. I love you now and forever."*

After completing our vows, Jon knelt down beside Elijah and whispered, *"You have given me something that no one else possibly could... a chance to be your daddy. You are a true blessing to my life. I promise to take care of you, to teach you, to love you, and to always be your friend. I love you handsome."* ▶

My heart filled with joy as I was overcome with love for the man of my dreams. It meant a lot to me that Jon took the time to incorporate Elijah into the festivities — something he planned on his own and I had no knowledge of.

After the service ended, we took a few photos inside and outside of the church and then headed to the reception to party. We had 150 guests from all over the country attend the wedding. I had the best time celebrating with family and friends. We danced, we laughed, we partied. It was truly the best day ever. I couldn't have wished for anything more. I was happy Jon's family finally accepted our relationship once we were engaged and welcomed me into the family with open arms. A complete 360-degree turnaround from how they behaved one year prior. I was glad they were able to be a part of the wedding festivities for his sake. I know how much involving them in our life event was important to him.

Jon and I celebrated at our wedding reception for two hours before leaving to start our honeymoon. We went back to my parent's house, changed clothes and headed to a hotel close to the airport for an overnight stay prior to leaving for Hawaii. My parents booked us a suite with a romance package that included champagne and chocolate covered strawberries. Unfortunately, I was super exhausted at the day's end and immediately fell asleep once my head hit the pillow, while Jon was in the shower, to his dismay.

"Are you asleep?" Jon asked, nudging my shoulder. I turned over in the bed slightly groggy to face him.

"I apologize. I'm exhausted from all of the planning for today. I barely slept last night. I didn't realize how tired I was until my head hit the pillow."

Jon stared at me blankly, gave a smirk and rolled over, turning his back toward me with disgust as he forcefully ripped the covers off of me. ▶

## THE GREAT PRETENDER REVEALED

We left for Hawaii the next morning for a week-long honeymoon. We wore t-shirts that said 'husband' and 'wife', earning us an upgrade to first class on our flight. Once we arrived on the island of Maui, we rented a car and began exploring everything the island had to offer. Our first two days, we took a helicopter tour, drove to the black sand beaches and enjoyed the cuisine. By the third day on the island, Jon's compulsive sexual behavior took on a whole new persona. He felt we should have sex every single waking moment of the honeymoon, while I wanted to explore and enjoy the paradise we were in — a place we may never get to experience for many years to come.

As I was dressing to go on our second helicopter tour, Jon laid in bed refusing to get up, seething as he watched me run around the room getting ready. "Why do we have to do activities every day? Our honeymoon should be about us having sex all of the time, not exploring Fantasy Island." ▶Jon slammed his arms on the bed in frustration, stopping me in my tracks.

"Have you not enjoyed the helicopter rides, the black sand beaches, and laying by the pool? You sure seemed to enjoy it, based on the ear to ear smile you've had every day. This is a once in a life-time trip and your concerned about having sex all day?"

Annoyed, Jon jumped out of the bed, throwing the covers to the floor and stomped into the bathroom to get dressed, slamming the door behind him. "It's always about you and your stupid activities," Jon yelled through the bathroom door. "I wish I married someone that cared about me and what I wanted to do, instead of someone who only thinks about themselves all the time."

Jon eventually calmed down and went on the helicopter tour, but continued to complain for the remainder of the trip; something that was supposed to be fun and exciting. Something I had been looking forward to for over a year turned into a nightmare. This nightmare would only continue when a month after our wedding, I found out I was pregnant with our first child and I became brutally ill. Jon was elated by the pregnancy and excited to have our first child. He told everyone about it and couldn't wait for the child to be born.

## THE HONEYMOON WAS OVER BEFORE IT STARTED

The telecom company I was working for at the time filed for bank-ruptcy and began laying off the workforce. Unfortunately, I was selected to be let go in the third round of layoffs. Little did I know at the time . . . it was a blessing in disguise. Jon slowly began to change during this time. His personality seemed to shift from the lighthearted loving person I dated and fell in love with to someone who showed less interest in me. ▶

I was extremely sick during my pregnancy with a potentially life-threatening pregnancy disease called Hyperemesis Gravidarum (HG); a debilitating medical condition I wouldn't wish on my own worst enemy. HG is characterized by relentless nausea and vomiting for up to nine months of pregnancy, causing dehydration and malnutrition that do not respond to traditional remedies for morning sickness.

While pregnant with Elijah, I was given an anti-nausea medication typically prescribed to chemotherapy patients to relieve the symptoms. With this pregnancy, I had the worst obstetrician care. My doctor believed my symptoms were psychosomatic. It was all in my head; and I was exaggerating, even though she could clearly see from my chart I was losing weight. She encouraged me to attempt to eat small meals throughout the day, take sips of water, eat ginger and wear sea bands. The typical prescription for morning sickness. I repeatedly informed her with each prenatal visit nothing was staying down and I was miserable. She still refused to prescribe me medication.

I was depressed and felt like I was going to die. No one understood what I was going through. It's a rare disease with 1-3% of pregnant women experiencing the illness. Jon thought I was overreacting as well. ▶ I was dehydrated, frail, stressed and lifeless. Every hour of every day I felt horrible. Every smell made me sick, and I couldn't sip water without vomiting. I spent my days and nights vomiting with multiple trips to the ER to receive IV fluids, losing weight the entire time as opposed to gaining.

It was during this time that Jon's mother insisted I keep Elijah with me during the day instead of keeping him in preschool. *A woman who said vile things about my son and I while dating Jon is now interested in the well-being of my child?*

She believed, *"A child needs to be home in the early years. They have their entire lives to be in school."* To satisfy her and to take the pressure off of Jon, I took my son out of preschool to stay home with me. Jon conceded to his mother's advice and convinced me it was the best decision for Elijah. I disagreed and was disappointed in Jon's decision to choose her wishes over mine, especially considering, when we were dating, he was adamant he didn't want his parents to run his life.

I was puking my guts out throughout the day and trying to take care of a young child when I could barely take care of myself. One afternoon, it became so unbearable I called Jon at work and literally begged him to come home.

## NOT IN SICKNESS OR IN HEALTH

"Jon, I need you to come home. I'm so sick I can barely move. I need help!" I begged.

"Why do I need to come home? Can't you call your friend, Leslie, and ask her to come over?"

*Leslie... a woman I just met at Elijah's preschool two weeks ago. He wants me to ask a woman I barely know to come over and help me in my time of need rather than immediately deciding to come to my aid. His pregnant wife with his first child?* I slowly lay on the cold tile floor of the bathroom, choking back tears.

"Jon, I need YOU to come home. I'm in no condition to take care of a small child when I can barely move. I've been over the toilet for the last two hours. My stomach hurts, my throat is burning, and my head is pounding. I'm miserable."

Before I knew it, tears poured down my face, and I could barely speak. I hung up the phone and laid on the floor, praying to be relieved of the pain and discomfort I was suffering from. I was in a state of depression. I couldn't believe I had to beg Jon to come home and take care of me. *What happened to the loving, caring man I fell in love with? The man who wrote vows stating, "From this day forward, I promise to hold you softly, love you tenderly, take care of and protect you and to always make you laugh and smile." Was all of that a lie?*

As I lay on the floor, shocked and confused, my son called out to me.

"What's wrong, Mommy?"

"It's okay, baby. Mommy's okay," I yelled back, fighting back the urge to scream out in pain.

I laid on the floor for a while, trying to make sense of my phone conversation with Jon. *Why wouldn't my husband want to take care of his wife who is obviously in dire straits if she's calling him at work? How dare he ask me to call up an acquaintance, whom I barely know, and ask her to take care of me when my husband should be the first person to run to my aid. The same man I looked after during the week of his proposal when he ended up in the ER now seemed to have zero empathy for me.* I was confused. I was hurt. I was angry and I was horribly sick.

Needless to say, Jon never came home, nor did he call to check on me throughout the day. I continued to suffer alone, spending the majority of my day laying on the cold tiled bathroom floor in gut-wrenching abdominal pain, waiting for the next volatile spew of puke to hit my mouth while my young son watched cartoons all day. Luckily, I kept fruit and snacks within reach in the kitchen so Elijah could grab something when he got hungry. To make matters worse, Jon returned home that evening acting as if nothing happened. He walked jovially in through the front door, "Hey buddy," he said to Elijah. "Come give me a hug." As Jon hugged Elijah hello, I slowly emerged, crawling on my hands and knees through the bathroom door.

"How are you feeling?" Jon inquired, looking down toward me in disgust.

"Not good, Jon. It was a rough day and I really needed you to be here for me."

I looked up at him as he looked at me, confused by what I said.

"There are a couple of ladies at my job that are pregnant as well; they are always happy and excited about their pregnancies. Why are you always so sad and unhappy about yours? Why can't you be excited about your pregnancy like they are?"

I stared at Jon blankly as I began to get upset, trying to decide how to respond to such an insensitive remark. Disgusted and hurt by his comments, I pulled myself together, got up off of the floor and slowly walked up the stairs to lay down in the bed. He just didn't understand why I couldn't *"act like them". Are you freaking kidding me? What person would choose to suffer like this? It's not like I chose to be sick and unhappy during my pregnancy.* No matter how much I tried to explain how bad I was feeling, he really didn't seem to understand.

I vomited so much during my pregnancy that I went into mental despair. I was malnourished, fatigued, sleep deprived and chronically dehydrated. My esophagus and teeth began to erode from the vomiting. I started to sink deeper and deeper into chronic depression and began having irrational thoughts of harming myself and the baby to relieve my pain and discomfort. There was no one I could turn to for help or understanding.

Jon was more concerned about his own needs than meeting mine. He still expected me to perform my wifely duties with spark and enthusiasm as to not ruin his *mood*. Whenever I mentioned I didn't feel well enough to perform, he would make me feel guilty by telling me it was just an excuse and he didn't understand why I never wanted to have sex with him, for it was my duty as his wife.

## THE ABSENCE OF SUPPORT

I suffered day in and day out from relentless nausea and vomiting for the entire nine months of pregnancy. The remaining months of my pregnancy became a blur, as I slipped into survival mode just to get by, sleeping as often as possible. I lost twenty-five pounds off my tiny one hundred and twenty-five-pound frame, yet still gave birth to a healthy seven-pound seven-ounce girl. She was as perfect as a baby doll straight out of the box; she was born with beautiful brown silky hair, deep colored brown eyes and caramel colored skin. She was my God-given gift and instantly brought me joy. All those memories of unrelenting nausea and vomiting began to fade as soon as I saw her angelic face. Also diminished was the horrible way my husband treated me. Once I saw my daughter, all that was put aside — at least for that moment in time. We named her Jasmine after my favorite fragrance.

I chose to breastfeed Jasmine and was her primary caregiver during the day as a stay-at-home mom. My daughter favored me more than anyone else, causing Jon perpetual angst. Every time he held her, she would cry nonstop until he gave her back to me in disgust. He was deeply hurt by her reaction to him and felt rejected. It was also during this time that he began to pull away from Elijah and myself. The baby became his world and his focus, as if no one else mattered.

I began to see a shift in how Jon treated Elijah, who was now four years old. Jon stated in his wedding vows: *"I promise to take care of you, to teach you, to love you, and to always be your friend. I love you handsome." However, the vows Jon stated during the wedding were not Elijah's reality.*

After Jasmine, the attention Jon used to shower Elijah with no longer existed. He began to critique every aspect of Elijah's behavior. He blamed Elijah for the silliest things — such as the misplacement of a TV remote — and came down on him for the smallest things, such as picking up his room appropriately. Appropriately, meaning to Jon's high, unachievable standards for a four-year-old child. Whenever I mentioned my concerns over his attitude toward Elijah, he vehemently denied he was treating him differently, and I was accused of not letting him be a father to his son.

Ironically, Jon offered and willingly adopted Elijah to become his full-time caregiver once we were married. I agreed to allow Jon to adopt Elijah because of the love I saw he had for my son while we were dating. He even referenced Elijah in one of his early love poems to me, *"I have come to love him [Elijah] as my own and consider myself so fortunate to have been touched by his life."*

I didn't expect the sudden flip in behavior toward Elijah after Jasmine was born.

The love, attention and constant love bombing I experienced during our dating stage was completely gone; and the emotional intimacy between us had waned. No one else mattered except for Jasmine. It was as if my daughter had become my replacement, in some ways, and I felt awful for feeling somewhat jealous. I began to feel emotionally neglected and unwanted, dreaming of the days when I had someone who loved and cared about me. I began thinking back to a time before Jon when I was truly happy with someone. That time was six years ago when I was dating a guy from my hometown.

I gave him a call out of the blue one day, just to see how he was doing. We chatted for a little bit and decided to meet up and have lunch to talk further. He was married and so was I, so it was just two old friends having lunch. We met at TGIFridays and got caught up on each other's lives over the last six years. I felt relaxed. I felt noticed. I felt heard and I felt validated. It was refreshing to get out of the home and have a real conversation with someone who cared about what I was saying. After lunch, I drove back home to be accused of cheating, even though it was an innocent lunch meeting.

## IT'S ALL ABOUT HIM

One year after our marriage, I started to find it odd that Jon had zero relationships outside of family. *Why didn't he have friends he could spend time with outside of the home?* He had his college roommate from the school he attended in his hometown, whom he claimed was a friend. The guy was in our wedding as one of the groomsmen, yet he didn't keep in touch with him. He also had people he hung out with at NC State while attending, but they were no longer in the picture either. None of these people were ever mentioned again. He didn't make plans to hang out with anyone or communicate with anyone that wasn't a part of his immediate family and hated the fact that I had friends as far back as childhood.

My children are my pride and joy and I worked very hard to be a mom that was actively involved in their lives. Jon knew how important being a good mom to my children was to me, yet he took every opportunity to tell me how awful I was at it. Everyone who knew me knew my kids were my number one priority in life and they came before anyone or anything. However, like anyone else, I also enjoyed the company of my friends from time to time.

A girlfriend from college that I hadn't seen since I married Jon called one day and asked me to go out with her for her birthday. She wanted to try out a new restaurant downtown and to catch up, since we hadn't seen each other in months. I talked it over with Jon and he begrudgingly agreed to watch the kids while I was gone. I got dressed, kissed everyone goodbye and headed out to dinner. It was so refreshing to get out of the house and catch up with my friend. I hadn't laughed so hard in months. We caught up on each other's lives, we laughed, we joked and just had an all-around good time. I finally felt good for once in a long time. I headed back home after two hours to find Jon sitting in the family room with an angry look on his face. He was fuming as I walked through the door, completely killing my euphoria. My stomach dropped and I became uneasy, suddenly regretting going out to see my friend. ▶

"What's up?" I asked, walking in through the front door.

"Did you have fun?" Jon glared at me as I walked in the family room.

"I did. It was good to catch up and spend some time together." I walked over to the couch Jon was sitting on, sat down and started taking off my shoes.

"How were the kids?"

Jon stared at the TV and didn't say a word.

"Jon, how were the kids?"

Staring blankly at the TV, Jon responded, "You should spend time with your family. We should be your focus, NOT your friends."

"Jon, I never go out. I go out one time and you throw a fit."

"Good mothers don't NEED to spend evenings out with friends."

I got up from the chair, looked back at Jon and said, "Thanks for ruining an otherwise great night." I went upstairs to take a shower. Jon was upset the rest of the night and continued to complain about my evening out as we lay in bed that night.

"I don't understand why you felt the need to go out with your *friend*."

"I never go anywhere, and it was good to get out for a change of pace," I replied.

"Good moms DON'T leave their kids to hang out with friends. Why did you go out?"

"I wanted to spend time with my friend for her birthday. I haven't seen her in a long time," I replied, pulling the covers off of me as my body started to heat up.

"I still don't understand why you went out. Why did you go out?"

"Jon, I just explained why. I don't know how else to explain it to you." Frustrated, I rolled on my side in hopes the conversation would soon be over.

"So, why did you go out?"

I turned my head in Jon's direction and snarled, "I WANTED to see my friend for her birthday."

"I still don't understand why you went out." Jon questioned again, tapping his fingers on his chest as he lay on his back in bed.

Jon trapped me in a circular argument that had no end in sight. It was 3 a.m. by the time he chose to stop.

## THE PAIN OF SEX

Sex became a chore rather than a physical connection due to the lack of emotional intimacy between us and how he consistently demeaned me, impacting my self-esteem. I began to loath going to bed every night because I knew that meant being intimate. I still constantly sought the man I married who made me feel so special in the beginning. The man who would do anything for me and made me feel like the most special person in the world; the man I had a spiritual and mental connection with that I thought would never be broken.

All Jon ever wanted was SEX. Not physical intimacy, just sex. If I rejected him in any way, I was made to feel guilty, selfish and uncaring. I learned during my pregnancy that saying no was not an option. I found it easier to just give in and let him have his way, regardless of how bad I was mentally or physically feeling. Being exhausted or ill wasn't a legitimate reason to not have sex. It was as if I was his property to do with as he pleased no matter how horrible he was to me.

"There's always something wrong with you," Jon would often say in disgust. If you hear that enough times, you start to wonder if it's an accurate assessment of your character and if there really is something wrong with "you" as opposed to your offender.

Even when I tried to wait Jon out and stay up until he fell asleep, as soon as I turned off the light beside the bed, he was suddenly wide awake.

"So, you're just going to go to bed now?" Jon sat up in the bed angry.

"Yes, I'm tired and so are you since you were just snoring." I replied, looking over at him.

"I wasn't asleep." He shook his head in disagreement.

"Yes, you were Jon, and you have been for the past thirty minutes."

"No, I wasn't."

"Jon, yes you were."

"NO, I WASN'T. Are you just going to go to sleep now?" Jon fumed ripping the covers off the bed. "Typical, it's always all about you. You're always so selfish. You don't think about anyone but yourself," he snapped, rolling over on his side with his back toward me.

"Jon, you were asleep, and I am tired."

"Just another EXCUSE. You always have an excuse not to have sex," Jon said with contempt. "Ed's wife is always ready and willing to *please* her husband. I don't understand why MY WIFE is not like that."

I took a long deep breath, mentally preparing myself for the continued rant I knew was about to ensue. My muscles became tense all over my body and my heart began to pound, wondering how long the rant would last.

Jon's arguments over sex consistently followed the same pattern. First, he would interrogate me with "why, why, why?" While answering his question, I was often cut off mid-sentence and ignored. Then, he would rant about how awful I was as a wife and a selfish human being for not meeting his needs. Next, he would accuse me of cheating because, if I wasn't having sex with him, there had to be someone else. Then, he would say I was an awful wife and mother.

Conversations that just looped and looped for hours until three or four in the morning, leaving me sleep-deprived and tired the next day. No matter what I said, my words were often labeled excuses or not heard at all. I was left feeling exhausted and mentally battered after these gut-wrenching circular conversations.

> *Gaslighting:* Gaslighting is a manipulative tactic abusers use to deny or minimize abuse. The victim starts to believe that their perception of reality is false. The narcissist will deny their own words and actions. Over time, the victim starts to believe they are confused and going crazy (otherwise known as crazymaking).

## BUILDING A LIFE ON A BROKEN FOUNDATION

Not long after Jasmine turned two, we moved into a bigger home for more space. *New home, new beginning.*

I had started taking classes at the local community college for Respiratory Therapy, a recession proof profession, a year after Jasmine was born. I was going to school full-time and working part-time at a local Wellness center. Elijah was old enough to participate in recreational sport activities; therefore, I registered him for sports through the local community center. I tried to keep peace in the home while balancing the many facets of life, school, work, kids, and a husband. Jasmine was a daddy's girl and Jon made sure she stayed that way. She depended on him for everything, idolized him and never wanted to leave his side. Jon laid with Jasmine every night at bedtime, stroking her hair while singing "You are my Sunshine". ▶

Activities such as combing Jasmine's hair, teaching her how to braid and teaching her how to paint her nails, all typically considered mother-daughter bonding activities, Jon took joy in doing, intentionally leaving me out of the picture. I was deeply and profoundly hurt by this. To add insult to injury, he was teaching her how to make faces at the meals I prepared and would often whisper in her ear at the dinner table as they both looked in my direction. I was a healthy eater and encouraged my children to be healthy eaters as well. Every meal I prepared involved vegetables and/or fruit. Jon was a Kraft Mac and Cheese, Spaghetti O's, chicken nuggets type of guy, so he continuously complained about my meal selections, refusing to expand his palate and that of his children.

**Emotional Incest:** *a parent/child relationship where the parental lines are blurred, making it difficult for a child to establish the level of independence considered healthy by mental health experts. There is often a lack of privacy between parent and child, the child is considered "best friends" with the parent and the parent shares secrets with the child. The child often feels as though they are the caregiver of the parent. Jon also began grooming Jasmine. The grooming process is a stage where the manipulator molds the victim to become the person they want by using a variety of tactics. The narcissist wants someone who will cater to them, anticipate and fulfill their needs, but not have any needs of their own.*

At some moments, life just seemed like too much to bear, but I couldn't show or discuss my struggles with anyone. I put on a happy face while mentally struggling in silence. Struggle meant failure and I refused to be a failure.

Not only did I have to maneuver around Jon and his ways, but I also had to navigate his mother, who consistently tried to tell me how to parent my children. She used tears when she didn't get her way. She never called before she came over to our house and always seemed to pop up right before it was time to lay the kids down to bed, disrupting their nightly routine.

Traditions I wanted to start with my family turned into traditions Jon had with his parents, because that's what his mother wanted, and he didn't want to upset her. She had difficulty accepting the fact that her children were adults with their own families. I often asked Jon to talk to his mother about overstepping boundaries. This fell upon deaf ears. His family left me off of their group text conversations and plans for family events. It was obvious they didn't want my opinion on anything. I went along to get along, trying to have peace in the home.

## THIS IS NOT WHAT IT SEEMS

Not long after Elijah turned eight years old, we were invited to take a weekend trip to an indoor water park in Charlotte with Leslie and her family. She had two daughters who were around the same age as Jasmine and Elijah. We had become friends with her and her family over time and sometimes spent time at each other's houses.

We arrived at the water park and the kids immediately wanted to get in the water. Leslie and I sat by the pool while the men took the kids down the water slides.

"You're so lucky to have a man like Jon," Leslie said while taking a sip of her mimosa. "He's so into you. You can tell he loves you dearly by the way he looks at you and he's great with the kids. Look at him over there helping Elijah down the slide. He's so gentle and loving."

I sat there quietly, smiling, not saying a word while watching Jon play with the kids.

We let the kids play at the park for a few hours before heading up to our rooms to prepare for bed. Everyone took turns taking a shower. We were in a double occupancy room at the Lodge. Two queen beds. The kids slept in one bed with Jon and I in the other. We watched TV until 11 p.m. and then I told the kids it was time for bed. I fell asleep only to be awakened at 1 a.m. by Jon nudging me and whispering, "Are you asleep?"

"Yes, it's 1 a.m." I responded, barely awake.

"Why are you asleep?"

"What?" I said as Jon began pulling up my nightgown. "Stop Jon, I'm not fooling around with the kids right next to us."

Jon rolled on his back and huffed, "Typical, you don't care about me as USUAL." He laid there for a moment staring at the ceiling, sat up and put his clothes on that were lying beside the bed.

"Where are you going? It's 1 a.m.?" I sat up in the bed, looking over at Jon.

"What do you care?" Jon snapped back, staring down at me.

Jon left the room, and I went back to sleep. I was glad he didn't stay in the room to nag me with the kids there. When we woke up later that morning he was back. We got our swimsuits on and went downstairs to the breakfast buffet to join our friends as if nothing happened the night prior.

## A GLIMMER OF HOPE SLOWLY EXTINGUISHED

A few years after this incident, the movie "The Secret" came out and I thought it was the best thing in the world. It introduced me to John Assaraf and the power of mindset. The movie discussed how positive thinking and changing your mindset can change your world. It gave me inspiration. It gave me hope.

> *"Whatever your mind can conceive and believe, your mind can achieve."* —Napoleon Hill

I began writing a list of affirmations to state every morning before work to get my mind ready for the day. I even taped them onto the bathroom mirror so I wouldn't forget to recite them in the morning. It takes thirty days to develop a habit; and I desperately needed to uplift my mind and spirit. Jon attempted to jump on the bandwagon as well, but he didn't stick with it. For months, I stated positive affirmations, meditated, and worked on positive thinking, trying to maintain some sort of mental sanity.

I was on a path of self-enlightenment after five years of living in chaos, believing things might change, if not for my marital relationship, then at least for me. That all changed when I became pregnant with my third child and Hyperemesis Gravidarum hit me like a ton of bricks.

Having a third child was my decision and a planned pregnancy. Jon was happy, but not thrilled about having a third child. He promised to take better care of me during this pregnancy than with my pregnancy with Jasmine. By this time, Elijah was self-sufficient at the age of eight and Jasmine was four years old and in prekindergarten during the day. Luckily, I had found a new obstetrician by this time whose wife experienced HG with her two pregnancies. He was well aware of the debilitating disease and its effect on the body.

Once I became pregnant, he monitored my symptoms closely. As soon as I started going down the dark path of HG, he put me on home care until the vomiting was under control. I was back to working in an office setting at this time for an IT firm and was able to go on short term disability until I became stable. My obstetrician put me on a medicine pump for the remainder of my pregnancy to keep me stable. I knew exactly when it was time to refill the pump . . . every time the nausea returned. It was like clockwork. I literally had to stay medicated 24 hours a day, 7 days a week to feel normal.

Despite this being a better experience overall than I had with my pregnancy with Jasmine, the one constant was Jon's treatment of me ... again. Jon, fully aware of my experience with my second pregnancy, failed to provide the emotional support when I needed it the most. For the second time in our marriage during a crucial and important time, Jon was disconnected and felt no sense of responsibility or obligation to care for his ailing pregnant wife. ▷

I was able to finish my last pregnancy, ultimately gaining weight as opposed to losing. I gave birth to a healthy seven-pound boy we named Maxwell (Max). I experienced excessive bleeding during delivery, startling the doctor and requiring a blood clotting agent to be injected into my leg to get it under control. It took two weeks for my body to recover from the blood loss and for me to feel somewhat normal. It took only four weeks for Jon to start demanding sex knowing my body had not fully recovered from delivery.

I was sleep deprived, hormonal, and my body was sore all over. Yet none of that mattered to Jon. Max slept in our bed for the first few weeks after birth for convenience since I was nursing. Against my wishes, Jon still proceeded to have sex with my broken body with our newborn son laying in the bed beside us. His needs were more important than the safety and well-being of his child.

Max became a focal point, taking primary focus off of Jasmine to her dismay. Jasmine and Max were Jon's pride and joy. Instead of focusing on Jasmine 24/7, Jon now split his attention between the two children, leaving Elijah in the dark.

## WHAT ONCE WAS IS NEVERMORE

In the years that passed, the conflict and chaos in the home became our "normalcy." But, as Elijah approached his teen years, new conflicts and issues would arise. By the time Elijah turned twelve he began to experience more and more attacks from Jon. ▶It was as if Jon felt he was in competition with Elijah for attention from me.

I never understood this behavior from Jon and often questioned his inability to behave as an adult parent as opposed to a child. However, for some reason Jon couldn't recognize the immaturity of his actions and blamed Elijah. Jon believed all of his negative interactions with Elijah were Elijah's fault — the twelve-year-old. Elijah did nothing right in Jon's eyes, yet Jasmine did nothing wrong. My parents noticed the preferential treatment of Jasmine as well, yet Jon's family saw nothing wrong.

During the summer months, I had set up a working arrangement for my parents to keep Elijah until school re-opened (he had started staying summers with my parents when he was six to get him away from Jon's overly critical focus on him). I was excited for Elijah to go to free himself. He got to be an only child with them, and they treated him like a prince. He spent time with family, met new people and got to travel to new cities and states every summer.

One day before one of Elijah's summer breaks and our trip to my parent's house, Jasmine, who was eight at the time, called me at work in a panic, "Mom, come home quick!" My heart sank. *What was wrong with my baby?!* Jon was responsible for transporting the kids to and from school since their school was on his way to work. They hadn't been home that long when I received the call. *What could have possibly gone wrong?*

"What's wrong, honey?"

"Dad's fighting with Elijah." Jasmine's voice trembled on the phone.

"Put Daddy on the phone." I got up from my desk and began to walk outside of my office building. I could hear shuffling in the background as Jon picked up the phone.

"Yeah," Jon grumbled.

"What's going on? Jasmine called me, crying, saying you're fighting with Elijah."

"I'm just *asking* him to do his homework," Jon snapped.

"Is that all that's going on? Why would Jasmine call me panicked?"

Jon got silent. I could hear Elijah in the background crying.

"Can I speak to Elijah please?"

Jon put Elijah on the phone.

"What's going on Elijah?"

"Daddy came into my room and started yelling at me to come downstairs and do my homework. I told him I would come down and do it in a minute. He yelled at me to come and do it now. When I got downstairs, he threw my book down on the kitchen table, breaking it apart. Then, he kept yelling at me while I was sitting at the table trying to work."

I could hear Jon in the background yelling, "I didn't come into your room yelling. Stop lying, Elijah!" My son was in tears and it hurt me to listen to his pain as well as my daughter's. However, I was an hour away and there was no way I could leave work at that time. I had a meeting I was required to attend in thirty minutes.

After I finally left work and got home that evening, Elijah explained to me again what occurred. He said Jon was yelling at him for not doing his homework at the exact moment he wanted him to do it. He said Jon continued to yell and forced him to come downstairs to do it immediately, and then continued to yell at him about it while he was attempting to get his homework done.

When I confronted Jon about the situation, he said he didn't do anything out of line as a parent. "I was simply "disciplining" him," Jon said. I stared at Jon for a moment, trying to decide if I wanted to take the conversation further or let it go. I decided to just let it go and began packing for the weekend, since Elijah was on his way to Delaware for the summer.

## DIFFERENT PLACE, SAME GAME

We drove to Delaware every summer to drop Elijah off and my parents would drive him back at the end of summer. We left around 11 a.m. the next morning, after this incident, to drive up the east coast. Jon and I took turns driving. When I drove, he alternated between playing on his phone and taking a nap. When he drove, I was belittled and berated for falling asleep or playing on my phone.

"You're always on your phone. God forbid you actually have a conversation with someone," Jon griped.

"What would you like to talk about? I inquired.

"Never mind… just keep playing on your phone. My needs aren't important as usual," Jon muttered.

I rolled my eyes and continued to scroll through the news on my phone. Jon needed someone to talk to him while he drove and that was my job. He didn't want to initiate conversation, yet became angry when I didn't talk to him.

Once we arrived, my parents greeted us at the door, hugging us as we walked in. We put our things back in our bedrooms and then sat down with my parents to socialize. Jon sat in silence. Barely speaking to anyone and tried to occupy the time by talking to Jasmine in sidebar conversations.

"How's work, Jon?" my mom asked.

Jon looked up from Jasmine, "It's good. It's starting to slow down right now with summer approaching," Jon said, before returning his focus to Jasmine.

"Are your parents doing ok?"

Jon looked back up, "Yes, they're good. Working part-time and spending time with the grandkids."

We sat with my parents for a couple of hours before retiring to bed. After Jon's brief chat with my mother, he no longer engaged in the conversation and continued to play with Jasmine.

The next day, my girlfriend from college, Angela, stopped by to visit. We sat down in my parent's living room to chat and catch up. My mother had run out to the grocery store to grab a few things and my dad was in his man cave, otherwise known as the garage, tinkering. The kids played board games in the sunroom while we chatted in my parent's living room. Jon chose to sit with Angela and I while we socialized and caught up.

"So how have you been?" asked Angela, shifting her weight in her chair as she was looking over at me.

"Good, work has been busy, but I'd rather be busy than bored," I replied.

Angela looked over at Jon, who was sitting right beside me. "How have you been, Jon?"

"Good, good ... glad it's summer," he replied smiling, and nodding his head up and down in agreement.

Angela and I chatted for an hour, catching up on mutual friends and work while Jon sat next to me the entire time, listening, but not participating in the conversation.

Later that night, while lying in bed, Jon rehashed the earlier events of the day. "Who was that guy Angela was talking about from college? Jon inquired.

"What guy?"

"The one you apparently had a relationship with and never told me about."

"Really, Jon? We're going to have a conversation about a guy I dated in college that Angela ran into recently?"

"You never told me about him, so there must be something still there," Jon sniped.

"Are you serious? You're ridiculous," I muttered while rolling over to go to sleep, until Jon felt the need to harass me about sex.

By Sunday morning, it was time to head back to North Carolina. My mom prepared breakfast prior to us leaving. As we got ready to sit down at the table, we noticed Jasmine and Jon were not in the house and no one knew where they were. Twenty minutes later they emerged from the railroad tracks across the street from my parent's home. Apparently, Jon had taken Jasmine for a walk, leaving the other two kids behind and without informing anyone he was leaving.

We finally sat down for breakfast, ate, and then got up to head home. We hugged and kissed everyone goodbye and drove back down to North Carolina.

## REFLECTION

In the first few years, what presented itself differently than during our courting was Jon's increased demands and needs. Everything was an argument when he didn't get his way. It got to the point that

I felt nothing ever satisfied him, and I didn't know what to do. No matter what I said or did to meet his needs, he was never happy.

It was exhausting being in a relationship with someone who constantly put me down, yet required so much from me. However, I still tried to make him happy to keep our family unit. I didn't want to sacrifice my marriage and family because I couldn't make the marriage work. ▶ I kept waiting for the man I dated to return. The man that loved me unconditionally. The man I knew was in that body somewhere.

Sometimes I saw glimpses of that man, giving me hope. I just had to learn how to get the old Jon back and keep him around. ▶ Jon told me I never listened, so I tried to listen more. Jon complained about my friends and family, so I began to limit my contact with them. If I was invited to go out to lunch or dinner with a friend, I turned the invitation down. Jon would never tell me explicitly not to go out with friends, yet his attitude and demeanor spoke volumes when I did.

Over time, I found myself thinking about my actions and choosing my words very carefully to avoid confrontation with Jon. I also tried to shield my first son as much as possible, not leaving him alone with Jon if I could prevent it. No matter how much I tried or what I tried, I still endured his fits of rage. I spoke to my family a little bit about some of the small things I was experiencing with Jon by our fourth year of marriage. The second time, I considered leaving. However, I received responses like, *"He just needs to mature a little more,"* *"You have young kids, what will you do?",* *"It will get better over time,"* to *"All men behave like that."* ▶

All men do not behave like this. They wanted to believe the image Jon presented during the dating phase as well; the mask of a well-adjusted, outgoing, loving and caring man. To their defense, they really didn't understand the magnitude of problems I was going through at the time; and I had difficulty putting into words what I was truly experiencing. I began to believe that maybe all men did act like Jon and I just didn't know how to handle it. Jon already constantly alluded to the fact that I was the problem so it had to be my fault, right?

Maybe I WAS a bad mother and wife for wanting to spend time with friends and have a life outside of my family. Maybe I WAS being a bad wife for not giving into Jon's every want and need, no matter how ridiculous or delusional it sounded. Maybe if I just did everything he asked of me, life would return to how it was when we met. Maybe there was still a shred of hope, a small spark that could be reignited, and get us back to where we started. I could not have been more wrong.

## Chapter 3

# THE BEGINNING OF THE END

> **Discard Phase:** *The third phase of an abusive relationship where the victim's usefulness to the abuser has ceased. The abuser has found a new supply. Someone to replace the victim to fulfill all of their needs. The victim is tormented and thrown away as if the love shared between them never existed. It is typically sudden, catching the victim off guard and in a constant state of stress while trying to determine what went wrong. This is the phase where the most humiliation, name calling, projection, gaslighting and degradation occurs.*

## NEXT EXIT —THE ROAD TO RUIN

After years of trying to voice my feelings and needs within the marriage and not being heard or validated, I conceded. I became complacent, accepting the fact that my marriage would continue to be a soulless shell. ► An empty cold shell — empty of true love, respect or emotional intimacy. Whenever I attempted to express how I was feeling about our relationship, Jon immediately shut me down with what I was not providing him. I didn't pay him enough attention, I spent too much time on the computer, he wasn't a priority in my life, etc., etc., etc., regardless of the fact that we were together all the time, except during working hours for our respective jobs. It was apparent my needs were of no concern to Jon and his needs were the most important. ▶

Once Elijah hit the teenage years, he spent more and more time in his room alone, playing on his iPad and playing video games . . . anything to not be around Jon. My father often called and checked in on him to see how he was doing and to provide the fatherly guidance he wasn't receiving in the home. He started slacking in school, not completing assignments and turning in mediocre work. Doing the minimum necessary to get by regardless of how many conversations I had with him on the importance of school.

Jasmine and Max continued to be Jon's shadow, following him everywhere, fighting over who would get the most attention from Dad. They began to show signs of perfectionism and wanting to get things perfectly right. If it wasn't perfect, they failed and harshly came down on themselves. They, too, began to blame Elijah for things that went missing in the home without evidence of any wrongdoing on Elijah's part; even after I pointed out where they had misplaced things in their own respective rooms.

## THE FAMILY CIRCUS

By our twelfth year of the marriage, we were settled into our day-to-day lives. Elijah was fifteen. Jasmine and Max, ages eleven and six were cherished and adored by Jon. They were allowed to talk back, ignore Jon, and yell at him "no" when they didn't want to do something, whereas, Elijah was attacked vehemently. It took as little as looking away for a moment while Jon was talking to him to trigger

Jon's fury. His children on the other hand . . . could do no wrong and it was very apparent to everyone around us except Jon.

There continued to be a marked difference in his relationship with Elijah, compared to his relationship with his biological children. He also continued to tuck Jasmine and Max in bed every night at bedtime, singing "You are My Sunshine" while laying face-to-face in their beds with his arm around them, gently stroking their hair. ▶

Elijah began to experience a number of behavioral issues at school that required me to intervene. He was talking back to his teachers, being disruptive in class, fighting on the bus, and not getting his school work done. The constant turmoil between Elijah and Jon continued and escalated. It was as if I was watching a battle of wills between two children. I often told Jon he needed to be the adult in his conversations with Elijah, but that fell upon deaf ears. As time wore on, in an effort to escape the home, Elijah began to spend weekends with his friend Zack, which later led to him being away from home days at a time.

I didn't mind Elijah being away so much since I knew Zack's family had welcomed him with open arms and he was safe. He was definitely safer staying with Zack than he was in his own home where he was often subjected to constant ridicule and criticism at the hands of Jon.

I settled into my role in the relationship as the peacemaker. I cannot stand conflict. I didn't grow up in a home with conflict and will go out of my way to prevent it at any cost. Whereas, Jon told me he grew up at home watching numerous arguments between his parents. Based on that, I can only assume he saw this behavior as a way of life.

One Saturday evening, we were all sitting in the family room watching a TV show that was ending, when I decided to pull out my laptop to catch up on a few news articles.

Five minutes into reading, Jon looked over and said, "So, you're going to just sit there all night on Facebook?" He looked over in my direction full of disdain for what I was doing.

"I'm not on Facebook."

"Yeah right, you're always on Facebook. That's all you ever care about." He shifted his weight in his chair while looking at the TV.

"Jon, can we talk about this later?"

"As usual, it's all about you. We're supposed to be sitting here having family time and you're on your computer," he said, condescendingly.

I closed my laptop and sat there, staring at Jon while he focused on the TV. While lying in bed later that night, Jon chastised me for not sitting by him on the couch and holding his hand while we watched TV with the kids. That was a requirement in our relationship.

"Why didn't you sit by me on the couch tonight and hold my hand? As usual you focused on yourself and got on the computer. It's always about you. You're always getting on Facebook to chat with your friends."

"Jon, the show was almost over and I wanted to catch up on the news. I've been spending time with you and the kids all day."

"You're such a horrible wife and the worst mother. You never focus on us. When do I become a priority in your life over Facebook? When will my wife care about me?" he said, pausing for a moment to collect his thoughts, and then starting back up. "I saw you looking at your phone when we sat in the family room after dinner. Again, it's all about you and no one else. No one else matters in your life, but you; choosing your friends and Facebook over family."

As Jon continued to berate me over my actions, I began to tune him out, laying there not saying a word, waiting for the rant to end, wondering if I would get any sleep.

## NEVER ENOUGH

Over the years, I began to experience a number of medical issues that increased in occurrence as the years progressed. These issues made sex extremely painful. However, no matter how excruciating the pain was, I still had to sexually perform. The physical pain was more bearable than the mental pain from Jon's rage for not performing. Whenever Jon wanted to be intimate, I'd let him have his way with me, biting my lip with every tear until he finished, completely oblivious to my pain. I had my routine down . . . take a shower, grab an extra washcloth, place warm compresses on my tears, and slowly climb back into bed to get some sleep while Jon lay next to me snoring.

One night, I decided to tell Jon how I felt about our physical intimacy. I had been sexually assaulted when I was twelve years old and shared that information with Jon while we were dating, informing him how it impacted me into adulthood. He was very sympathetic back then and was hurt by what happened to me. I tapped Jon on the shoulder after I crawled back in the bed and told him I wanted to chat.

"Jon, I feel like you don't care about me or my feelings. Sometimes you're rough when we have sex and it reminds me of when I was raped."

Jon sat silently for a moment staring at the ceiling, rolled over and went to sleep without saying a word. I laid awake, reliving the day's conversations and the night's events until I eventually fell asleep hurt and confused, wondering where the man I dated and fell in love with had gone. I felt like I was only meant to serve Jon emotionally and physically and receive nothing in return . . . not even acknowledgment for my own feelings. I was overwhelmed and alone in my marital relationship.

## THE SHARED DREAM

When I was ten years old, I was assigned a project for school on what I wanted to be when I grew up. I drew a picture of myself standing in front of a building with my name etched on the top of the building. I wanted to own my own business and I had that dream into adulthood. I shared the dream with Jon when we were dating and he said he had the same dream of owning his own business. It was something I believed we both aspired for. So, I thought, *here's an opportunity for us to do something together, a dream we both shared. This will be great.*

Real estate was a great option for passive income to explore this notion. For a few years, we purchased a couple of rental properties and started a small software company. However, Jon never seemed interested in running either business nor did he exhibit the drive to make either of them succeed. Marketing, managing, and day to day operations always fell on my shoulders until it became too difficult for me to manage on my own, raise kids and hold a full-time job.

## THE FAILURE OF MY SUCCESS

In the spring, I decided to pursue a business I could manage on my own on a smaller scale. I did some online research and came across a direct sales jewelry company I was interested in. I contacted a nearby consultant and set up a time to meet. After learning about the company and its rewards, I talked it over with Jon and then decided to sign up. I started scheduling parties and talking to others about the business and their business model. Jon was supportive in the beginning and helped me prep for parties. He would help me put information packets together, help me pack my bags and load the car for my parties.

By my second month in business, I was doing really well. I was building a team and getting lots of referrals and new customers. I was on my way to becoming a leader and top seller. The most time I spent from home during the week for in person parties was four hours. I tried to split that time between one party during the work week and one on the weekend. Two hours of dedicated time for each party and I always made sure the kids had what they needed prior to me leaving for each party.

I also invited my daughter to attend on the weekends, but she chose to stay with her dad. The time commitment became a major issue for Jon no matter how much money I brought in. Late one evening while sitting in the family room, Jon was watching a TV show while I was building posts on Facebook for my jewelry sale items. I knew, from the way he occasionally looked over to see what I was doing and rolling his eyes, he was upset. He paused his show, shifted his weight in his chair and looked over at me.

"You're never home."

"What do you mean, Jon?" I inquired, still staring at my computer screen.

"You're always away doing that *business*. It's having an effect on the children." What he really meant was that I wasn't giving him my undivided attention all the time.

I stopped working on my posts and looked up at him. "I'm only gone four hours a week, and I invite the kids to attend parties with me. I make my best effort to include them in my activities."

"The kids complain to me all the time," he replied.

"So, what do you want me to do, Jon? Do you want me to quit, even though this business has brought significant income into the household?"

"Do what you want. I'm just saying, the kids are complaining," Jon snapped back while unpausing the TV.

"It's always about you as usual. It's never about anyone else. It's fine… the kids don't want to be around you anyway. As long as you're happy, that's all that matters," Jon said condescendingly while reclining his chair to continue watching TV.

I continued to build my posts for the evening trembling with every key stroke. Before letting Jon see the hurt on my face and reveal that he had gotten to me, I shut my laptop and went upstairs to take a shower. I stood in the shower for twenty minutes just letting the water roll down my body, staring at the shower floor watching the water go down the drain, thinking about my life. *Why does he constantly complain about everything I do? Can I not do one thing that makes me happy?* The next day I decided to no longer pursue growing the jewelry business to keep peace in the home. ▶

My success had become my failure; something I should have never ever attempted to do, according to Jon.

I was emotionally numb and more and more resentful of Jon every single day. I was constantly on guard contemplating every action, every spoken word, and facial expression before dealing with Jon to combat the sudden outbursts of anger, irrational demands and reasoning that always came my way.

## TRAPPED IN THE FOG

Work became my escape. I looked forward to work on Mondays and dreaded heading into the weekend on Fridays. My stomach tossed and turned and tied up in knots as I walked through the garage door and stepped foot into the home on Friday evenings. I never knew what type of weekend I was going to have. One that was fun and exciting, and everyone got along, or one that was filled with chaos, arguments and verbal attacks.

As much as I tried to provide a stable environment for my children, trying to balance out Jon's erratic behavior, they would often witness the chaos. Between Jon's constant criticism of Elijah and complaints about me, it was impossible to shield the younger two children. No matter how many times I'd ask Jon to not act out in front of the kids or to talk about something alone later, he never listened. Everything had to be argued at that moment in time. It was always about him and what he wanted or how he felt. Everything also had to be done a certain way. If I didn't hug or tell him I loved him exactly how he wanted me to tell him, it didn't count as showing affection. Therefore, he repeatedly told me I didn't love or care about him.

Over time, the kids learned to navigate their father's moods and adapt when necessary, often retreating to their rooms to avoid witnessing or being the center of conflict. Elijah often questioned "What's wrong with Dad now? He is always mad about something." I tried my hardest to provide some enjoyment to my kid's childhoods. We played family games, enjoyed different activities around town, took the occasional family vacation and did little things as a family as much as possible. However, the negative aspects of our family life far outweighed the positives as the days progressed.

To the outside world, we were a perfectly happy family and married couple. Little did anyone know that I was on an emotional roller coaster of highs and lows that I had absolutely no control over. Or, that I hid behind a smile to not show my true feelings or feel the embarrassment of having a failed marriage.

## THE BEGINNING OF THE END

Jon prided himself on being a man of love and loyalty. That's what his mother groomed him to be, therefore that's the persona he presented. Considering he consistently spoke on this trait to family and friends, I felt comfort in the fact he would never betray me, not realizing the magnitude of destruction that would come my way.

Jon now worked for a medical device company getting the job not long after Max's birth. He worked his way up to the management level and now had direct reports. His division was building a new device in Germany, which required Jon to take a number of trips overseas to ensure the device was being built to specifications and medical standards. It was during this time that our relationship took a significant turn for the worse.

I started to notice subtle changes in Jon's behavior and daily routine, but I didn't really think much about it at first. ▶ He was never a phone person and didn't maintain relationships with "friends", so it was odd that he began constantly texting in the evenings after work. He said he was in a group chat with his coworkers, so I thought nothing of it. He was also becoming a little more distant, detached and preoccupied with something I just couldn't put my finger on.

His overall appearance was beginning to change as well. He was taking more of an interest in his selection of clothes for work. Becoming more stylish with tapered European shirts from the local boutique and fitted slacks as opposed to the khaki pants with holes and color faded polo shirts he typically wore to work every day. He sent me a text one evening on his way home from work saying, *"Thinking about watching a movie tonight. Looking forward to spending some time with you. I love you." He's in a good mood.* I thought to myself, this should be a good night.

Jon came home, we ate dinner with the kids and got the younger two ready for bed. Then, we made some popcorn and watched a movie in our bedroom. He was so kind and gentle. It reminded me of when we were dating. Things were good until we hit the weekend and the bomb dropped.

It all started with a Saturday family trip of shopping. Elijah wanted to stop at the shoe store to look at shoes. Jon wanted to drop Elijah off and come back to get him once he and I finished shopping two stores down from the shoe store.

"Elijah, how long do you need in the store?"

"I don't know, maybe twenty minutes. It depends on if I find something and if I try it on. I don't know."

Jon, clearly getting upset, pipes up, "Why don't you know how long you need? You should know how long it will take you."

"Jon, he doesn't know. He can call us when he's ready," I replied.

Jon turned to me with his lips pulled back baring his teeth and yelled, "Stay out of this!" Then, seething and staring at Elijah through the rearview mirror, Jon started in on him again.

"Come on, Elijah, it's not rocket science! How long do YOU need?"

"Leave him alone, Jon. You're being ridiculous," I responded.

"Don't talk to me like that in front of the kids!" He snapped back.

I turned around to look at Elijah and told him to call me when he was ready. Jon dropped Elijah off and sped off to the next store almost running into an elderly couple trying to cross the street. He was angry for the rest of the night and had an attitude the rest of the weekend, alternating between belittling and screaming at me for showing Elijah "preferential" treatment. By Monday, he was apologetic and sent a text, *My apologies for a shitty couple of nights,* with a heart emoji.

The next weekend was approaching, and Jon was preparing to leave for another trip to Germany. He left for Germany for seven days, leaving me to be the sole caretaker of the kids. A week later, he arrived home late Saturday night and instead of being happy to see everyone, he was in a bad mood. Everything was an argument leading the kids to retreat to their rooms to escape. Jon and I sat in the family room for a little bit when he pulled out a bottle of Southern Comfort liqueur.

"What's that?" I asked. Jon never drank alcohol and told me he wasn't a drinker while dating. I was shocked to see him pull out a bottle of whiskey.

"Southern Comfort," he said, looking at the bottle in admiration. "Ed introduced me to it in Germany. He said it would help calm me down and help me sleep."

"Since when did you start drinking alcohol?" I asked, looking at Jon in bewilderment.

Jon ignored my question and continued to lean his head back, taking a drink from the bottle. After about an hour, we headed up to bed and laid there chatting about his trip for thirty minutes before he nodded off to sleep mid-sentence. I fell asleep as well and woke up to him fuming.

"I've been gone a week and you're just going to go to bed? As my WIFE, you should be excited to see me," Jon said sarcastically.

"You fell asleep. It's late and I'm exhausted," I replied, half asleep.

"I wasn't asleep. You're lying," Jon said in a dismissive and condescending tone.

"You were asleep. I didn't want to wake you because I know you're tired from traveling."

Jon, now angered by my perceived lack of concern for him, went into a rage. "I can't believe you're just going to ignore me after I get back home! I've been gone all week and you're just going to go to sleep?! What about me? You're always so mean to me!"

Jon yelled and condemned me until four o'clock on Sunday morning, leaving me confused, emotionally drained and sleep deprived.

*Over time, the narcissist manages to control every detail of the victim's life, from what they wear, eat, and do to their*

## THE OTHER SHOE DROPS

Late Sunday morning after we woke up, Jon acted as if nothing happened. He asked if we could go to the local park, just the two of us. An odd request, since we hadn't been to the park on a date since our initial meeting, but I obliged. It was a beautiful clear summer day. The perfect day to go to the park. I remember thinking to myself, *this is such a perfect day for a date. Maybe this is Jon's way of apologizing for his behavior.*

Once we arrived at the park, we found a picnic table to sit at and have a conversation. "I have something to tell you," Jon said. I got excited and smiled from ear to ear because I thought what came next was going to be a huge surprise.

"I want to separate," Jon said.

My face dropped.

A million feelings overcame my mind and body all at once. It was as if I had run into a brick wall at 100 mph. I suddenly had tunnel vision and Jon was the only person in my sight. The sounds of children playing in the background had become a distant fade.

Jon was emotionless and looked at me with a blank stare. He showed no concern for my feelings as he dropped this bomb on me. After I caught my composure and processed what he said, I responded, "What?"

"I want to separate. I'm not happy and I'm ready to move on. I've asked you to change a lot of things over the years and you never change. This is your fault." ▶

I sat there quietly and thought, *after I supported this asshole through school, paid off his debts and put up with all of his shit, he wants to leave ME?* I briefly sat there for a few minutes, not knowing exactly what to say.

"Are you willing to go to counseling?"

"No, I've made up my mind and I'm DONE. This is because of you. Again, I asked you for a lot of things over the years and you never changed. This is all your fault and there's nothing you can do or say to change it," Jon dismissively said.

As I sat there in utter shock by the entire conversation, I didn't know what else to say. I was completely caught off guard and unprepared for the conversation. "Okay," I replied.

As we got up from the picnic table, I noticed all the little children and their parents happily playing in the park. It was at that point that I realized my world, my life, and my family were in jeopardy. We walked back to Jon's car and drove home in silence the entire way. My mind was running a thousand miles a minute with all the things I did wrong or could have done differently in the marriage. *What just happened? What did I do wrong? Where did I go wrong and what could I have done differently?*

*Was it my fault?*

My mind was in overdrive. I began second guessing every comment and every action that occurred over our twelve years of marriage. I didn't want to date again. I would be a single mother with three kids and stretch marks. What man would want me and the responsibility of dealing with my children? Before Jon's trip to Germany, he sent me a text saying, *"Not sure about timing with kids tonight, but if you have any thoughts on dinner or a movie tonight, let me know. I'm perfectly happy staying in as well. Just looking forward to spending some quality time with you."* That text in no way implied he was ready to separate. I was confused. *Why ask for a separation now? What changed?*

## THE WRECKAGE THAT WOULD FOLLOW

There was no way I was going to get through work that Monday morning. I couldn't sleep, I couldn't eat, I could barely function, and Jon didn't want to talk about the situation and was non-supportive. I called my boss and informed her I would be working from home that day while I got myself together. The entire situation didn't make sense to me. Jon came out of the blue with the separation, didn't want to attend counseling, and didn't want to talk things out. Something just wasn't right.

By Monday afternoon, I finally persuaded Jon to see a marriage counselor as a last-ditch effort to save our marriage. We met at the counselor's office after Jon got off work. During our session, he was extremely disengaged and angry for being there. He immediately started attacking me and stating everything I did wrong in the entire marriage, with no mention of anything he did wrong. I countered with all of the changes and sacrifices I made for him along the way to satisfy him, giving up things I loved and enjoyed throughout the marriage. The more I spoke, the more my eyes filled up with tears.

"I gave up a successful network marketing business for you, Jon, and you know that."

"You did that for the kids, you didn't do that for me," Jon replied, staring at me, emotionless.

Before I knew it, I completely broke down. The counselor provided me with tissues while Jon sat there stone-faced the entire time.

"She's sitting here in tears. Does that not bother you?" the counselor asked.

"No, not really, I'm done with her," Jon said with the absence of feeling.

"Are you sure you don't want to try to salvage your marriage?"

Jon shook his head at the counselor and said, "No, I'm done."

"Ok, well, I think you need to seek a lawyer and begin the separation process," the counselor replied.

*What kind of counseling is this? I sought counseling to mend my marriage and the counselor is encouraging him to separate?* The experience was a waste of time and didn't change Jon's mind.

That night after meeting with the marriage counselor, Jon came on to me by caressing my shoulders while I lay in bed trying to sleep. The same man who said he was done with me and was no longer interested in me, came onto me. I was so confused by his hot and cold demeanor. I didn't know what his true feelings were one moment to the next. He was toying with my emotions. I asked him if he was interested in someone else and he immediately responded, "No."

The days and nights continued to be hard living with someone who had no regard for my feelings and couldn't wait to move out.

Shortly after this bomb drop at the park, my girlfriend, Tonya, sent me a text asking if Elijah could take a trip to Florida with her family. I asked Jon what his thoughts were as Elijah's father.

"That's your decision since I'll be gone."

"What do you mean, Jon? Just because you're gone doesn't make you any less of a father."

He didn't respond. I texted my girlfriend back and told her it wasn't a good time for Elijah to take a trip.

Later that day, we took Jasmine and Max to the park. Jon sat on his phone texting the entire time, ignoring everyone around him. Max had to constantly pull on Daddy's arm to ask him to play with him. After an hour, I told the kids it was time to leave. It wasn't the family outing I was expecting.

While lying in bed the next night after a mentally exhausting day, Jon lay there still texting on his phone before turning to me and saying, "I want to hurry up and separate because you're not *the one;* and I feel like I'm wasting my time being with you."

I sat up in bed, confused. Turning to him, I said, "I was *the one* when we were dating, and now all of the sudden after twelve years of marriage, I'm no longer your soulmate?"

"Yes, I believe we were brought together for a purpose and that purpose was met. You're my best friend and I'm attracted to you, but you can't make me happy."

I lay back down, turning my back to him. He placed his hand on my shoulder and whispered, "I'm starting to resent you for constantly trying to change my mind and win me back. I finally found my confidence and courage to move on and I want to do it now." I was mentally crushed, and my heart was broken. There was nothing else to say. As tears streamed down my face, I silently cried myself to sleep.

## THE MASK COMPLETELY REMOVED

The weekend was tough to get through with Jon being distant and cold, unless there was something he needed from me. Then he became loving and engaging. While getting ready for work Monday morning, putting on my makeup, Jon told me he had a dream, an epiphany. He walked over to me, gently grabbed my shoulders and whispered in my ear, "I dreamt of you and your new man having family dinners with me, my new woman, and the kids."

I pulled away and looked at him with a pained expression as my chest caved in. *Why would he say that to me?* It felt so cold and uncaring for my feelings and what I was going through. He could clearly see I was hurt by this entire situation. *Why further torture me?* I continued to put on my makeup, trying to disregard what Jon said, even though it was eating me up inside. I quickly pulled myself together and told the kids it was time to go and we headed off to school and work. I was a complete wreck at work, sitting at my desk trying to fight back tears. I felt like a failure. I packed up my things and told my manager I wasn't feeling well and needed to go home. The entire drive home, all I could think about was whether or not Jon was seeing another woman.

I arrived home around noon and became a detective, going through Jon's email looking for answers while he was at work. I found a few interesting things. I found a list of things Jon disliked about me, notes about what he considered his good qualities and a poem on how he tends to fall in love deeply. I also found another love poem that sounded like it could have been written for me, but I wasn't quite sure. I copied the poem in an email and sent it to my friend, Angela, to review.

I called her up to get her opinion on the poem. "Angela, check your email," I said as she answered the phone. "I found a poem in Jon's email. Can you read it and let me know your thoughts? It sounds like it could be for me, but then it doesn't." Angela opened up her email and started reading the poem. I sat quietly waiting for her thoughts, tapping my foot on the floor the entire time. "Do you think it's for me or someone else?" I inquired.

"Interesting," Angela said. The phone was silent as she continued reading. I anxiously sat waiting for what else she had to say. "I don't think it was written for you. It has weird references to a single child and possibly having another."

"I saw that too. I keep asking Jon if he's seeing someone else or interested in someone else and he repeatedly says no. I knew something didn't sound right about this sudden separation."

"Do you think he's cheating?"

"It sure does sound like it. What man all the sudden decides to leave his wife and kids with no one to go to? Especially someone like Jon who is so needy and wants unlimited attention."

"It does seem strange and I don't know of any man leaving his wife without a backup in place."

"Exactly," I replied. "I'm going to text him right now and ask again. Thanks for your help."

I hung up the phone and began texting Jon, asking him if he was interested in someone else or if he was seeing someone. He immediately responded, *"No, our separation is because of you and no one else."* I informed Jon I found a few emails in his account that were concerning.

Jon immediately called me after receiving my last text. "You hacked into my email account?" he inquired.

"I sure did. This sudden need to separate just doesn't make sense to me. All of a sudden after twelve years of marriage you want to pack up and leave. Things just don't add up. There has to be another reason like another woman in the picture."

"There is no other woman. I TOLD you the separation is because of you. I'm not seeing anyone else." ▶

I started rolling my eyes, listening to Jon explain what I found.

"What you found were notes, journals never shared with anyone; and the poem was about a woman I admire at work for how she speaks so positively about her husband ▶."

*Hmm, okay.* "Are you sure there is no one you're interested in, Jon? What about that woman you *admire* at work?" I asked. "Things just don't add up for me."

"No one," Jon replied. "I have to get back to work. We will talk more about this tonight after I get home."

Jon hung up the phone and I continued to think more about the poem and emails I found, running different scenarios through my head. We never had another discussion about the emails that night after Jon came home, even though he said, "We'll talk more." He acted as if nothing occurred, continuing to text on his phone all night. I busied myself with the children, ensuring they got their homework done and were fed for the night.

When we laid down to go to bed, Jon decided to snuggle with me while we slept. *Maybe he's changing his mind about the separation.* I was wrong, the next day he was back to being distant and disengaged.

## THE TRIP FROM HELL

In early fall, we started preparing for our family vacation. We had a planned family vacation to Jamaica and didn't want to tell the kids about the impending separation until after we returned. Therefore, Jon and I were obliged to act as if nothing changed in the household for the kid's sake. Although, clearly the kids could see and feel the tension. Since Jon acted distant and disengaged whenever I was around, I can't believe he thought he was fooling the kids into thinking nothing was wrong. In the meantime, Jon started planning to move out of the home.

He was looking at apartments every night, determining what items from the house he wanted to take, and started negotiating with me on child support and the splitting of assets. Negotiating basically meant he didn't plan to pay anything toward the kids. That was his form of negotiation. Although I hadn't been happy in my marriage for years, I still felt obligated to make the marriage work for the kid's sake and our family unit. ▶

I started sending Jon love notes, texting him throughout the day, and trying to spend more and more time with him to hopefully fall back in love like our dating days. Sometimes, I got to experience the softer side of Jon during this time and other times he was extremely cold and uncaring. It kept me confused and unclear on what his intentions were with the marriage. Was he going to stay in the marriage or continue to separate? I couldn't tell from one day to the next, but I continued to try to be the nurturing, caring wife he claimed he desired.

Jon informed his parents he was planning to move out. His parents didn't agree with his decision and told him he was making a huge mistake by leaving his family. One night, Jon's parents called and asked him to stop by their house to talk about his decision to move out. He drove to his parent's house that night to talk. When he arrived home, he burst through the front door with furrowed brows as he slammed his laptop bag on the couch and sat down. He was infuriated.

"How are your parents?" I asked.

"I'm sick of everyone telling me what to do! It's my decision, my life, and I want to do what I want without being judged!" Jon screamed in anger.

Max came running downstairs to say hello. He ran and jumped on Jon's lap, giving him a hug as Jon sat there infuriated by his conversation with his parents. "Hey buddy," Jon said, hugging him back. Jon continued to vent, and I just sat there listening. It wasn't worth engaging in the conversation and being attacked for no reason because he was upset with someone else. I let him vent until he decided to go upstairs to take a shower.

Jon's behavior became bizarre. He would calmly converse with me one minute and then yell at me for no reason. I couldn't tell who I was dealing with from one minute to the next. He was like a Dr. Jekyll and Mr. Hyde on a daily basis.

It was the week of our family vacation and I couldn't wait to leave. I thought this would be the time for Jon to see how happy the family was together, reconnect with me and not want to separate. After the trip he would change his mind about separating and we would start over trying to make the marriage work. If I really was the problem, I wanted to rectify it. I wanted to keep my family together and I was willing to do that by any means. As it turns out, I was completely wrong. It turned out to be a nightmare just like our honeymoon. ▶

Jon was hot and cold the entire time. He had his moments where I thought, *maybe he will change his mind and stay* and other times, he acted as if I didn't exist until it was time for bed and he wanted sex. Jon's parents and his brother's family traveled with us so he had outlets when he didn't want to be bothered with me. He was still texting nonstop throughout the trip, due to work issues, he would say. I cried and cried the entire trip. The mental stress was becoming too much to bear and I often found myself crying off and on throughout the days. Jon's mom offered some support, but at the end of the day she was going to respect her son's decision. She, too, told me what I needed to change to make Jon want to stay, since he had vented to her his frustrations to justify leaving.

While preparing breakfast our second morning in Jamaica, Jon's mom felt inclined to tell me what I should do to make Jon happy. "You know if you spent more time with him in the evenings holding his hand while you watched TV and paying more attention to him instead of working on other things, he would be happier," his mom said. I stepped back and looked at Jon's mom. I was at a loss for words.

"Are you serious? I have to sit next to him and hold his hand for him to feel secure in the marriage? I'm not allowed to read a book, a magazine, or shop online at night when Jon is around?" I asked.

"That's what he says he needs and if you want to keep your marriage you'll make those changes," she replied, scraping eggs into the serving dish for breakfast.

I was speechless. She was serious and saw nothing wrong with what she said. I forged my way through the vacation trying to make the best of it, but in reality, I didn't enjoy Jamaica at all and couldn't wait to return home. Jon used me for sex every night and showed very little interest in me during the day, taking advantage of my willingness to rebuild our marriage.

## THE DOWNWARD SPIRAL

After we returned from the Jamaica trip, Jon was ready to move out. In North Carolina, you have to be legally separated for a year before you can divorce. Jon started putting pressure on me to get the marital separation agreement paperwork together so he could move on. We weren't making any progress with negotiations, since he was not willing to negotiate on splitting assets or the care of the children.

While sitting at the kitchen table editing a draft of the agreement, Jon turned to me matter-of-factly and stated, "I'm not paying child support for Elijah. Your parents buy him clothes and send him things so there is no need for me to support him."

I placed my hands on the table and looked Jon square in the eyes. "Jon, you adopted Elijah. You are financially obligated to support him as his father."

Jon looked back down at the paperwork, shaking his head back and forth. "Well, I'm not paying. I can't afford to pay all this support and take care of myself. I have to pay for an apartment. I have to buy furniture and everything else to start over," Jon said.

I got up from the kitchen table and walked away in disgust.

According to the North Carolina child support calculator, he was financially obligated to pay a specific amount toward the children and he refused. How dare he feel that his comfort and well-being were more important than our children!?

Arguments over child support and assets continued to be a huge issue. Living in a home with someone who has zero respect for you is the hardest thing in the world to do. Jon became extremely distant, often going off to another room and texting with a huge smile on his face. He took his phone everywhere, ensuring I didn't have access to it; he made sure it was always by his side, even when he showered. He was taking no chances that I may go through it and discover his secret.

One time, I walked into the room while he was feverishly texting and laughing; he immediately put his phone away and became stone-faced. "Who are you texting?" I asked.

"They're telling jokes on the work group chat."

"Really, I want to laugh. What are they saying?"

Jon scrambled with his phone to quickly find a meme in his messages to show me.

"Hmmm, ok. That's what's so funny?"

I just shook my head. Clearly the meme wasn't what he was enthralled with, but I didn't say a word. I turned around and walked out of the room to check on the kids.

It was mid-September, exactly one month after Jon told me he wanted to separate. He went out with *friends* on a Saturday night around 8 p.m. and didn't come home until 1:30 a.m. I sat downstairs in the family room watching TV, waiting for him to arrive home. When he arrived, he quickly said hello and immediately ran upstairs to jump in the shower — no hugs, no kisses, nothing. I decided to investigate his odd behavior. I rummaged through the hamper and pulled out the clothes he wore that night. They smelled of women's perfume. I threw the clothes back in the hamper, walked back downstairs and waited for him to get out of the shower.

Jon finished showering and came downstairs to ask when I was coming to bed. I paused my movie to look up at him. "I noticed a weird scent on the clothes you wore tonight. They smelled of women's perfume."

"I don't know why they smell like that."

"Were you with another woman tonight?"

Shocked by my line of questioning, Jon began fidgeting on the stairs, shifting his weight onto two steps. "I hung out with the guys from work and that's it."

"Are you sure, Jon?" I questioned.

"Yes, I hung out with the guys."

I stared at him not blinking an eye. He was clearly uncomfortable by my line of questioning as he fumbled over his words, avoiding eye contact. I grabbed a blanket from the basket beside the couch and sat back down to continue watching TV in the family room. Jon stared at me a few moments and then returned upstairs and went to bed.

We were at a deadlock with the marital separation agreement and Jon was becoming impatient. He started resorting to bullying tactics to get me to accept his demands. He kept me up night on top of night, screaming and belittling me, trying to get me to adjust to his wants and sign the paperwork. Abruptly, he said, "So, when are you going to sign the paperwork?"

"I'm not signing the paperwork until we agree on child support and splitting the assets."

"I DON'T WANT TO BE WITH YOU! Why are you being such a bitch about this?" Jon yelled.

"Jon, name calling is unnecessary. If you don't want to be here you are free to leave. I'm not holding you here," I responded in an even-toned voice, trying to calm the situation.

"I don't understand why you won't just sign the paperwork. Typical, it's all about you and what you want. Everything has to be your way. You're a spoiled only child so used to getting your way," ▶Jon sniped back.

I stopped trying to reason with him and became silent, waiting for his rant to end; cringing every time he raised his voice. He finally stopped at 3 a.m. and I was able to get some sleep before getting up at 6 a.m. to go to work.

**Dissociation:** *a defense mechanism used by the brain to emotionally block the impact of pain in order to survive traumatic circumstances.*

The episodes of nightly rage were becoming unbearable. ▶I was sleep-deprived and weak from not eating. I could barely keep myself awake at work. Nor was I able to adequately function in my job. I asked Jon to move out while we worked on the agreement because it was apparent that he didn't want to be there, and I couldn't take much more of his nightly rage. I told him to move in with his parents for a little bit, while we settled things out — they lived a mile away and he could see the kids whenever he wanted.

"I'm not leaving. Who knows when you will let me see my kids again," Jon said, sarcastically.

I was sitting in a chair across from Jon in the family room. I stood up, walked over to Jon. "Jon, as their father, you are legally allowed to see your kids. I legally cannot keep them from you."

"You're such a crazy bitch, there's no telling what you would do just to hurt me," Jon lashed back at me▶.

I turned around in disgust, walked back to my chair and sat back down.

## REFLECTION

> Victims living in a household where there is narcissistic abuse are living in a torturous war zone, where all forms of power and control are used against them (intimidation; emotional, physical and mental abuse; isolation, economic abuse, sexual abuse, coercion, etc.). The threat of abuse is always present, and it usually gets more violent and frequent as time goes on. The controlling narcissistic environment puts the victim in a dependency situation, where they experience an extreme form of helplessness, which throws them into panic and chaos.
>
> The narcissist creates a perverse form of relationship wherein the victim has no idea what will happen next (alternating between acts of kindness or aggressive raging). This prolonged torturous situation is likely to trigger old negative scripts of the victim's childhood internal object relations (attachment, separation and individuation). To survive the internal conflict, the victim will have to call on all their internal resources and defense strategies in order to manage their most primitive anxieties of persecution and annihilation. In order to survive, the victim has to find ways of reducing their cognitive dissonance, the strategies they employ may include — justifying things by lying to themselves if need be, regressing into infantile patterns, and bonding with their narcissistic captor.

> Most defense mechanisms are fairly unconscious, so the victim is unaware of using them in the moment; all they are intent on is surviving the madness they find themselves in.
>
> —Christine Louis de Canonville, "The Place of Cognitive Dissonance in Narcissistic Victim Syndrome."

In regards to the children, Jon subconsciously began to assign roles within the narcissistic family tree after Jasmine's birth. Jasmine became the golden child and Elijah the scapegoat. Narcissists often emotionally reject a child (the scapegoat) that reminds them of their own insecurities and flaws. All the rules and roles in the family are designed to make the narcissist's life and daily interactions comfortable, taking the feelings of anxiety and pressure that seem normal off of him or her. During Jon's childhood, he was referred to as the golden child by his father and brother since he was his mother's favorite person and confidant.

Elijah was Jon's trash receptacle of blame and projection. A narcissistic parent will make a child feel guilty for the "needed" forms of abuse the child "forced" the parent to inflict on them. The narcissist uses guilt to remedy their displeasure and will also make the child feel guilty/responsible for whatever is wrong with the narcissist. They also see people who they perceive as having traits they desire, but do not possess as a threat to their fragile egos and lash out as well. As a result of scapegoating, the children often set their bars of achievement low to avoid failure and have problems setting and accomplishing their own goals. Significant emotional and psychological wounds are imposed upon the child into adulthood.

Narcissists thrive off of internal conflict in the family and stoke the flames among family members. In narcissistic families, children are pitted against each other and taught to be in competition with one another. There is a constant comparison among the children by the narcissist. As a result, siblings rarely grow up feeling emotionally connected to one another. By the time we were a family of five, this routine was well in place and Jon, in his attempts to create conflict and perpetuate his abuse, not on me but my children, would now surface in various ways.

*Chapter 4*

# THE NEW SHINY TOY...

The notion of dying on that hill is where Jon had firmly planted his flag of denial. Narcissists live and die by their own version of the truth and until the actual truth was revealed, he would not relent. The fact that he was so adamant about leaving without working on the relationship continued to prey on my mind day by early October day in and day out. It just didn't make any sense to me how he could discard his family so quickly after twelve years of marriage.

By this time, Elijah lived at Zack's house, coming home occasionally to grab clothes. He could tell something was going on between Jon and me from my continued sadness every day. He asked me if I was okay one day before he left to go to Zack's house; and I told him I was fine. I'm sure Jasmine and Max could feel the tension as well, but didn't know how to respond to it.

I decided to take off from work one day to further investigate what was going on with Jon. I downloaded all of our cell phone records from the past year and started reviewing them. I noticed one particular phone number continuously appeared all day long for the last few weeks. I called up my friend, Angela, for her assistance once again. Angela ran the number through a reverse phone number lookup site and found its owner. She called me back as soon as she had answers.

"The number belongs to Anthony Johnson," Angela said.

"Anthony Johnson?? I don't know Anthony Johnson. I wonder why Jon is calling and texting him so much?"

"Could it be an old friend?"

"Jon has never mentioned an Anthony Johnson and he doesn't have friends."

I sat silent on the phone for a few moments, trying to figure out who Anthony Johnson could be and then I remembered Jon mentioning he worked with a woman named Tasha Johnson. He asked me in April if we had any open positions at my job because Tasha was interested in changing careers. He wanted to know if I could assist her with getting a job.

"Jon works with *Tasha Johnson*," I replied. "She's his direct report and a part of the group that travels with Jon overseas."

"Do you know her husband's name? Could that possibly be her husband?" Angela asked.

"I don't, but I can find out."

I got off the phone with Angela and began searching property records online and found a property owned by Anthony and Tasha Johnson. I jumped up out of my chair and yelled, "AHA!" That's when it clicked. Jon was having an affair with Tasha, which explained the constant late-night texts on the work phone, taking the phone with him everywhere, even to the toilet, pulling away when I tried to give him hugs and kisses, and the OUT OF THE BLUE separation. That traitor!

## THE LIGHTBULB TURNS ON

From that point on, I started a full-on investigation. I searched everywhere, starting with our bedroom. I looked through his clothes, his drawers and under the bed, where I found a recently purchased penis pump. I started searching his computer files and came across a few love notes he had written Tasha, as well as his teenage porn collection. *Really, Jon? Teenage porn?* ▶

I hacked another one of his email accounts that I came across on the iPad and read every single email. My stomach turned in knots and I became nauseous as I read through the various emails. He wrote down the many qualities he loved about Tasha and titled it, *"The Things I Love about Tasha Johnson."* I found emails to her that talked about me and my inadequacies, bringing me to tears. *How dare he do this to me?!*

I followed up on every phone number on the phone bill, I hired a private investigator, and I began to watch and scrutinize Jon's every step. Around 11:30 p.m. one night, two texts popped up on Jon's work phone from Tasha. He wasn't home at the time; he was at a birthday celebration with coworkers. I tried my hardest to figure out his passcode to read the message without any luck. I actually ended up locking up the phone due to so many attempts.

When he returned at 1 a.m., I questioned him about the text messages. He came into the house and sat down on the couch across from me. "What a crazy night," Jon said with a huge smile. "The guys had me all over downtown. We did the beer trolley and hit a few restaurant bars to celebrate Shawn's birthday." He began to take his shoes off and walked to the closet to put his jacket away.

"Sounds like you had a good time," I replied as I reached for Jon's work phone, picking it up from the living room table, and handed it to him as he sat back down on the couch.

"You received two texts from Tasha at 11:30 p.m. Why would she text you so late on a Friday night?" I asked.

"I don't know," Jon said shrugging his shoulders, looking down at his phone.

"Don't you think it's odd?"

"She probably sent me a meme or something," he replied, placing the phone back on the table and going upstairs to take a shower — dismissing the conversation.

From the day we met, Jon was adamant he never had and never would cheat in a relationship ▶. I believed him and trusted that he would not hurt me in that way. It was disheartening to think he was having an affair. What was even worse would be the pathological lying that would follow from this point on.

## THE TRUTH REVEALED

Jon made another overseas trip the following week. The perfect opportunity to engage the private investigator. I had the private investigator place a GPS tracker on Jon's truck while it was parked at the airport. I set up surveillance times with the PI for when Jon returned, in hopes that he didn't disappoint. He's a creature of habit and I knew that about him. His first day back to work, the PI sat outside of Jon's job waiting for him to go to lunch.

Jon retrieved his truck from the back parking lot, drove to the front of the building and picked up Tasha. Tasha got into the passenger side of the truck and they drove to a nearby fast food restaurant to pick up something to eat. Once they had their food, they drove to a nearby park and moved to the back seat of the truck, remaining there for an hour and a half before emerging from the truck, fixing their clothing. They both walked to the park's restroom before getting back into the truck to return to work.

The PI caught this entire interaction on video tape every day for a week. They were like clockwork. Each day, I watched the GPS tracker from a webpage and tracked every move Jon made in his truck. I became obsessed, finding myself logging in during any break I had during the day; he became my sole focus and obsession to my detriment. Watching him further inflicted the pain of the betrayal. I still wasn't eating. I wasn't sleeping well, and I had chronic headaches. I was unable to adequately focus on work or my children.

Jon sent me a long email one Monday morning, detailing his need to possibly have to work nights the next few days. The email started off with the following:

> "Just like a few months ago when I had to come in at night to support some automation changes, I have to do that again this week, and maybe into next week some. The reason is because I am the only person ▶ on the project with both the access rights and the knowledge to do some of the automation changes needed for the equipment."

The email continued to explain why he may not be available at night and how awful he felt about not being able to be home to help with the children. It was an elaborate five-paragraph email.

While lying in bed that night, Jon received a text on his work phone at 11:30 p.m. "I have to go into work to fix the production machine. They are having difficulty getting it back online," he said.

I turned over in the bed and looked at him as he proceeded to get out of bed to get dressed. "Is there no one else on your team that can go in? It's midnight."

"It only takes my password to reset it and I'm not allowed to share it with anyone else. Remember the email I sent you today, explaining this may happen?" Jon replied while putting on his shoes. ▶ *Why would a manager have to do all of these things during odd hours when the facility is open twenty-four hours a day with an operations staff for these specific issues?*

"How long do you think you will be gone?"

"However long it takes to get the machine back online. I'll call you on my way home."

Jon walked out of the bedroom, walked out of the house and jumped into his truck. I watched him pull out of the driveway while I grabbed my phone to call the PI to have him followed. The investigator pulled up the tracker on Jon's truck and followed him to Tasha's house. Jon parked his truck across the street at a neighbor's house and walked to the back of the house.

I texted Jon two hours after he left to see when he was returning home. After thirty minutes he replied, *"It shouldn't be too much longer. We almost have the machine back online."* I laid in bed, awake the entire time, thinking about him at Tasha's house. My mind was going a thousand times a minute and I couldn't shut it off. He arrived home three and a half hours later. He got back into bed, put his arm around me and went to sleep. I laid in bed awake, disgusted, and hurt by his actions until it was time to get ready for work.

## ONE LAST ATTEMPT

My mind was going crazy trying to comprehend and make sense of what was going on with Jon and my marriage. I began to have conversations with Jon's mom about my cheating suspicions, thinking she may be of support since they were so close. I drove to her house one Saturday while Jon was playing with the kids outside our house one afternoon and sat in her kitchen to talk.

"I think Jon is having an affair," I said while his mother moved about the kitchen preparing cookies. She stopped in her tracks, looked up at me and said, "He would never do that. That's not Jon," while shaking her head back and forth in disagreement. "There were two married teachers at our school and the husband decided to have an affair. Jon asked me why he would do that to his wife. He was in tears and couldn't understand it."

"Well, things do not add up for me; besides, I've found suspicious things in his email that lead me to believe he's cheating," I replied. "It just doesn't make sense that after twelve years of marriage, he just wants to leave without seeking counseling."

"Who do you think he's having an affair with?"

"His direct report. Her name is Tasha. A woman he travels with to Germany."

"Ohhh... what color is she?"

*Why does this matter? (thinking)*

"She's black," I responded.

"Well, it's not like him at all to cheat. I just find it hard to believe he would do that."

Jon's mom dismissed my opinion just like that and continued making cookies, while telling me I was wrong. Her son would never do that. Not her precious child. I chatted with her for about ten more minutes before getting up to return home.

I decided to make one last ditch effort to win Jon back. He was sitting on the couch, searching for apartments when I sat down next to him and gently grabbed his hand. I looked into his eyes and said, "Jon, I really want to make this marriage work. I've lost eleven pounds due to the stress of all of this." Jon looked bewildered and caught off guard, but never said a word as he looked at my desperate demeanor. He proceeded to close his laptop and stood up, grabbing his keys off of the nearby table.

"Where are you going?"

"I need to step out for a minute," Jon replied. Then, he walked out the door, jumped into his truck, and drove off.

I pulled up my laptop in the kitchen and watched Jon's car sit at a nearby park as I prepared dinner for the night. I also pulled up the phone records to see who he was calling. He called Tasha. When he returned home, I asked where he had been.

"I met up with Shawn from work. He was having marital problems and needed to talk," Jon said.

"What's going on with Shawn?"

Jon started fumbling with his words, "Oh, just the same old issues."

"I hope everything works out for him."

"He's not worried about it; he already has a plan in place," Jon responded.

*Lies on top of lies.* ▶

Two days later while sitting in our living room, I sat down next to Jon on the couch and asked, "Did you give any thought to our conversation from the other day about us working on our marriage?"

Clearly uncomfortable, Jon stood up and moved to the loveseat to put some distance between us. "No, I'm not interested in staying with you. How many times do I have to tell you that!?"

"Well, what about my weight? Are you the least bit concerned about my health and well-being?"

"I know you're a strong woman and no matter what I say, you're going to do what you want to do," Jon snapped back.

"Do you even love me anymore, Jon?"

Jon jumped up and yelled, "WE'VE BEEN OVER THIS A MILLION TIMES! I'M TIRED OF ANSWERING QUESTIONS... I'll just write you a letter." ▶

I slid back in my chair and didn't say another word. I didn't recognize the man sitting across from me. ▶ So cold with dead, soulless eyes. He was a complete stranger. A monster. Not the loving, caring, charismatic man I married and longed to see return. I was confused and hurt by how someone could have zero empathy and feelings for someone they claimed to love for so many years.

## REACHING MY LIMIT

After a lot of contemplation, sleepless nights, consulting with friends and family and praying, I decided to contact a lawyer. I needed to figure out a way to have Jon legally removed from the home for my own mental sanity and physical health. I had collected the evidence needed from the private investigator to make a case to have Jon removed from the home through legal means. He refused to leave on his own, yet continued to berate and harass me every day. ▶ I just wanted him out of the house so I could sleep at night and have peace of mind.

Lorraine was an attorney recommended by the private investigator I had hired. The best family law lawyer in the area and she was a bulldog. I arrived at the law firm to meet her and her assistant one afternoon after work. She was a southern woman in her mid-sixties with long beautiful salt and pepper hair. She was dressed to the nines and wore four-inch heels.

Her assistant was a recent law school grad, dressed in a power pantsuit. During my consultation, they took turns interviewing me, having me tell my story from beginning to end. They were well-versed in infidelity cases and played to win. They were also known for taking the husbands for everything they had and making the wife financially secure. Both of them commented on how frail I looked and how the stress was taking a toll on my body; it was apparent, through my outward appearance, that I was experiencing emotional and mental turmoil — I was not sleeping, not eating and just plain tired. They asked what I wanted to do.

"How can I get my husband out of my house? He harasses and berates me every night and he won't move out. I can't sleep, I can't eat, and I'm struggling mentally to be a parent to my three kids."

"Divorce from Bed and Board," Lorraine said. "That will get him out of your house."

I sat and thought about what she said, writing her comments down in my notebook.

"Now what are you going to do about this other woman?" she questioned.

"What can I do?"

"You can sue her and your husband for Alienation of Affection."

"I can?" I asked, shocked and intrigued by this possibility while writing it down in my notebook.

"Yes, you can," she answered.

I sat quietly and thought about this for a minute. *How much is this really going to cost me? Divorce, Divorce from Bed and Board, Alienation of Affection (2x).*

"Ok, let me see what funds I can pull together and get back to you," I told her, gathering my things and taking the folder of prices from Lorraine's assistant as she handed it to me on my way out of the office.

"One more thing, Mrs. McAdams," Lorraine called out as I had one foot out of the door.

I turned around to see what she had to say, holding the door open to the lobby area.

"If you go through with this, your marriage will be over and your husband will be extremely upset with you. You have to decide if this is really what you want to do."

"Yes, I understand. Thank you," I responded as I continued to walk into the lobby.

Walking back to my car, my mind was all over the place and I had butterflies in my stomach. I sat in my car thinking, *should I go through with this or should I just let it go? I can't take anymore late-night attacks and Jon is not willing to stop. I just have to accept the fact that this marriage is over. Jon has made it clear he wants to move on.* I called my friend Angela on the drive home and told her about the conversation with the lawyer.

"What are you going to do?" she asked.

"I'm going to move forward with the lawsuits. I have to get Jon out of my house. I can't sleep, I can't eat and he harasses me every night, in bed, about signing the separation agreement, calling me a selfish bitch for not doing it. I can't take it anymore. It's unbearable and taking a toll on me mentally as well as physically."

"I can see that," Angela said. "You have to do what's best for you and the kids. I know it's hard for you right now."

I got off the phone with her and continued my drive home, thinking of all of the things I needed to do once I got there to prepare for battle. Once I got home, I pulled out my laptop and looked up my 401K loan availability. I had enough money available to initiate a loan to pay the lawyer. By week's end, the lawyer was fully retained and the fight began. The lawyer gave me very explicit instructions to document every single interaction with Jon and to not inform him I had spoken to a lawyer. I was not to discuss anything, including the separation agreement until the lawsuits were served.

## THE BATTLE BEGINS

I started reading various blogs and journals on how to survive a marital separation. I also had nightly calls with a girlfriend from college, Marie. She prayed over me every night. We prayed for mental strength to get me through the turmoil I was experiencing. We prayed for Jon to see the error of his ways and we prayed for the kids. I realized the full power of prayer when Jon called me one morning at work.

"Is everything ok?" Jon asked.

"Yeah, everything is fine."

"Ok, I've had a queasy feeling all morning and I typically don't feel that way unless something is wrong with you or the kids."

"I'm fine Jon. Thanks for the call."

I immediately called Marie and told her what occurred.

"That's God making him feel uneasy," she said. "God is sending him signals to straighten up and do right."

Jon did not straighten up or do right. In the middle of all of the separation drama, he had been experiencing stomach pain. He went to see an internal medicine doctor who ran a number of tests and informed him his gallbladder needed to be removed. Surgery was scheduled for the following week. I decided to work from home to care for Jon during that time, even though he was being a complete terror to me. Technically, I was still his wife.

The day of surgery, I kissed him on his forehead and told him I loved him before they wheeled him off. He never said a word in return and looked away, annoyed that I was even present. Surgery was over within two hours and he was released within four. We returned home where he immediately went to bed.

The next day, Jon woke up, came downstairs, and sat on the couch in the family room, watching TV while I worked on my laptop. Around 11 a.m. is when the nonstop texting began. Within ten minutes, Jon said, "I need to pick up Scott to meet for lunch. We're having lunch with a few other co-workers."

"Do you think it's wise to go out, Jon? You literally just had surgery yesterday."

"I'm fine. It's not like *you're* paying attention to me. You're over there on your computer," he said sarcastically.

"It's called working from home. Why burn a PTO day when I can still work while caring for you?"

"Well... I'm going out. I'll be back later."

By noon, Jon was dressed and walking out of the door ONE day after surgery. I looked up the GPS tracker and watched his truck travel from our house to the park where he would take Tasha every day for lunch. After two hours, I sent him a text, asking when he was coming home.

"Soon," he replied and then went radio silent for two more hours. He would return four hours after leaving, saying lunch went longer than expected. The guys got caught up in conversation. I looked at him in confounded and continued working on my laptop. *He really thinks I'm stupid. It's a workday. No one takes a four-hour lunch during a workday.*

Jasmine started playing volleyball during the summer and was a huge fan of a local college team. Since the games were free to attend, we tried to take her as often as possible to see a women's volleyball game. We agreed to take her to a game over the weekend and at Jon's request, we drove separate cars. When we arrived, we found a place to sit upstairs, middle court. I glanced over at Jon's phone; he was engrossed in texting with someone named "Nesquik" the entire game. He was texting so much that he didn't even know what was going on in the game. It was pointless for him to be there. He ignored me and ignored our daughter. He briefly looked up to inform us that he was leaving.

"Tonight is a going away dinner for one of my co-workers that took a job in Germany; they asked me to tag along," Jon said, fidgeting with his phone.

"Are you leaving now?"

"Yes, I shouldn't be gone long."

"Ok, let me know when you're on your way back home."

I reached over to give Jon a kiss goodbye on his way out. He quickly turned his head, kissed our daughter on the forehead and walked away. My daughter and I stayed until the game ended and went home. By ten p.m. that night, Jon was still out. I texted him to let him know Max was looking for him and wanted Jon to tuck him into bed. Jon wrote back, "He's fine, I'll tuck him in tomorrow night." Max was disappointed and continued to ask when Daddy would return home.

When Jon arrived home in the early morning hours of the next day, he took off his clothes, jumped into bed, and began caressing my back. I didn't say a word and didn't move. He eventually stopped and went to sleep. When I leaned over to give him a kiss the next morning, he turned away saying, "I'm not clean." ▶

I looked at him in shock. "Not clean?" I asked. I rolled over and went back to sleep as Jon got up to take a shower.

## THE FAMILY CRUMBLES

To my surprise, by that afternoon, Jon decided it was time to tell the kids he was moving out.

"Do you think that is wise right now, Jon? Don't you think you should wait until we are further along with the separation agreement?" I asked, walking over to the bathroom where he was clipping his nails.

"No, I know the kids want to see me happy. They will be fine with it."

"Well, I don't think it's wise to do that at this time."

"Well, I do," Jon responded, clipping his thumb nail. "I'm tired of wasting time. I'm ready to move on."

Jon finished clipping his nails while I pulled the kids together for a family meeting in the family room. Elijah was at Zack's house as usual; therefore, it was just Jasmine and Max. The kids sat on the couches, wondering what the impromptu family meeting was about as Jon walked down to the family room.

Standing in front of the kids, looking down on them as they looked up, waiting to hear what he had to say, Jon said, "I'm going to be moving in with Grandma and Papa soon," Jon said. "Mommy and Daddy have problems and *we* believe we can take care of them better apart than together."

"You're moving in with Grandma?" Max asked.

"Yes," Jon replied.

"Why?" Max asked again.

"I already explained why, buddy."

There was an awkward silence while the kids processed what Jon said, not knowing how to react. Jasmine looked down at the floor and Max stared at Jon, still confused by his words.

"Well, I guess I have to tell my teachers at school," Max said.

Jasmine took the news the hardest. She didn't ask any questions and she didn't like the news. She got up, went to her room and shut the door. She stayed in her room for the remainder of the day. We continued on with our day as if nothing happened.

On the way home from school shortly following this, Max told his teachers, "My mom and dad are separating. Mommy is always on her phone, on her laptop or watching TV." ▶The same language he heard his dad use, multiple times, while complaining about the little time I got to have to myself in the home.

As the days progressed while waiting on the lawsuits to be served, Jon became more and more upset with me for any and everything. The kids stopped speaking to him when they found out it was his decision to split up the family. Somehow that was my fault like everything else that went wrong in Jon's life. Also, for some strange reason, Jon felt as a part of the separation, that he would remove the kid's furniture from their rooms to furnish their rooms in his new place.

"Jon, you can't take the kids' beds with you. What will they sleep on while they are here?" I inquired.

"You can buy new beds. I need something for them to sleep on. I want them to want to come see me in my new place, so I need furniture."

I looked at him, shocked by his reasoning. "How is it fair for you to remove the beds from this home to furnish a home that you are choosing to move to? I shouldn't have to purchase new kid's beds because you want to move out."

Jon turned red, he turned around and looked at me with a flushed face and pursed lips. "You're such an asshole," he blurted out.

*Did he just say what I thought he said? An asshole.* I stood in silence, processing what Jon said and thinking of how to properly and calmly respond to diffuse the situation. I sat down on the couch to collect my thoughts before speaking. I looked down at the floor and said, "You just called your wife an asshole!" Befuddled, I said, "What is going on, Jon? Material things should not make you resort to name-calling. You're crossing the line here."

This just further enraged him as he stomped off in anger. Between the kids not speaking to him and me not allowing him to walk all over me by taking everything out of the home, he was losing it. He continued to berate, degrade and yell at me that night as we laid down in bed to go to sleep. He was upset about the kids not talking to him, me not allowing him to remove the kid's bedroom furniture, me not allowing him to cutoff financial support for Elijah), and me not signing the separation agreement in its current draft. I was, again... an asshole.

He finally stopped at 4 a.m.

## THE HIGH DRAMA AND THE MELTDOWN

*Narcissists have a unique ability to flip from rageful anger to utter despair and sadness to benefit and feed their ego. It's confusing and entirely disorienting. One minute everything is fine, and the next minute you're on the receiving end of fierce narcissistic rage. It is sometimes referred to as the "drama triangle," a form of control and manipulation.*

The next morning while Jon was in the bathroom getting ready for work, I said, "Please don't call me names. We can communicate as civilized adults without name calling." Jon instantly burst into tears. I stepped out of the room to let him get himself together before having to head off to work. He came downstairs, laid his head on Jasmine's shoulder as she was preparing her lunch and continued to cry, causing her to do the same. Our life was in shambles.

It had been two months since Jon informed me that he wanted to separate; he was becoming impatient with me. He was continuing to pressure me to sign a separation agreement, but not willing to negotiate on the terms. I also had to wait for the *Divorce from Bed and Board* papers to be served before I could sign anything. His rage was getting worse and worse by the day. He lost all respect for me and treated me as if I was some stranger he just met and got tired of seeing. I didn't recognize who he was. He was a true monster.

He exhibited a completely different personality; one I had not been exposed to until this time. One I wished I'd never seen because he terrified me. ▶

I was called *bitch* and *asshole* on a regular basis and endured endless nights of projection, blame-shifting, and name-calling, keeping me up all hours of the night. I was a *bitch* for not signing the separation papers. I was a *bitch* for wanting him to pay child support. I was an *asshole* for trying to keep the marriage together, and I was playing the victim to get what I wanted. Jon felt entitled to leave the marriage without giving me a dime to take care of the children, and since I wouldn't conform to his way of thinking, he made my life a living hell.

The stress was becoming unbearable to deal with. My weight was down twenty pounds by this time, and I looked like death. My eyes were sunken, my hair was dry, brittle and falling out by the day, and my skin color was ashen and pale. I was so tiny, my eleven-year-old daughter could fit into my jeans.

Then it finally happened . . . Jon was served the lawsuits as we sat at home watching TV one night as a family. The cat was finally out of the bag and I could breathe a sigh of relief. It was 6 p.m. when the doorbell rang.

"Who is that?" Jon asked, looking at me as he got up to answer the door. He opened the door to a man standing in uniform, the sheriff.

"Are you Jon McAdams?" the sheriff asked.

"Yes, sir," Jon replied with a smile.

"You've been served," replied the sheriff as he handed Jon an envelope.

Jon took the package from the sheriff and closed the door. He opened the envelope and began to read the stack of papers enclosed. Jon's smile on his face quickly turned to a look of shock and disbelief. Then his face changed to a look of innocence the more he read. He couldn't believe what he was reading.

The lawsuits detailed all of the video surveillance of his excursions to the park, his late-night trips to Tasha's house, and his date nights. Even the days he took paid time off from work to spend the day with Tasha were captured in the documentation; everything he thought he was getting away with. He walked upstairs to our bedroom and asked me to follow. I walked in and sat on the bed as Jon closed the door behind me. A softer, warmer side of Jon sat beside me, chin lowered to the floor — the same man who had cursed me out the night prior.

"What's this?" he asked in the sweetest voice, while holding up the papers he just received. A voice I hadn't heard in the last two months.

"It's self-explanatory."

"Couldn't we just talk about this instead of reverting to lawsuits?" Jon asked, looking like a caged animal trying to figure out how to escape.

## THE FLIP

I responded in a firm and even-toned voice. "I tried that, but you refused to talk or listen. You ignored all of my efforts to communicate with you peacefully and you've treated me horribly these last two months. This is what it has come down to."

"Is Tasha getting served, too? Please don't go after her; this is all my fault. She's a really nice person. I pursued her."

I acted like I didn't hear the question and didn't respond. Jon sat there silently contemplating what to say next as he looked down at the carpet. After a few minutes, he gathered his things and the paperwork he had received. "I'm going to my brother's," he said. "I'll be back later." Jon's brother was his listening ear whenever he was in a difficult situation and didn't know how to handle it.

He returned home a few hours later after the kids and I were in bed. He came into the bedroom, sat beside me on the bed, and said, "I want to work on the marriage."

"Ok," I replied.

"I didn't think I was cheating since I TOLD YOU I wanted to separate. ▶I called Tasha tonight and told her it was over. But you have to drop the lawsuits for me to try. I don't want this hanging over my head. Tasha started out as a deep friendship that led to romance. She is innocent in all of this and is a really good person. There is nothing wrong with what happened." *(In his mind as someone who felt like he was the victim of neglect, his actions were 100% justified. He will never hold himself accountable for anything.)*

"Are you serious? A good person? She participated in the affair, but she's innocent?"

"I'm willing to reconcile if you do not sue her. I don't want anyone else to get hurt. You will be considered a "bad" person if you sue her. No good will come from it. How I feel about you going forward will be based on whether or not you sue her."

I sat there in silence trying to make sense of what he was saying, perplexed by his defense of Tasha and their marital affair.

"We had an emotional affair," he said, before pausing for a moment to collect his thoughts and shifting the conversation to the children. "I'm really concerned you will get full custody of the kids and that will crush me."

"If you truly want to work on the marriage, I'll drop the suits. But you need to prove you are serious about reconciliation," I responded.

Jon kissed me on my forehead and laid down beside me with his arm around me.

## The Flop

Just when I thought things were finally going down the correct path, two days later, Jon presented me with a list of questions and things he needed from me for reconciliation. Number one being, drop the lawsuits.

"I really can't have these hanging over my head," Jon said, sitting down beside me on the family room couch. "I mean, what happens if I can't be what you *need* me to be or expect?" he inquired.

I knew at that point his heart wasn't truly set on reconciliation. He just wanted to get out of being sued. "I just need for you to be a decent human being and treat me with love and respect. I don't think that's too much to ask," I responded.

Jon sat there silently as he always did when he didn't know what to say next.

As the days progressed, I emotionally shut down and mentally let go, settling in with the fact the marriage was over. While cleaning the house one day, I asked Jon if he could walk to the bedroom with me to talk briefly. He followed me upstairs and sat on the bed while I stood by the door.

"Jon, I don't want a forced reconciliation and it's very clear to me you feel forced. I want you to *want to* be in this marriage. I think we need to continue down the path of court-ordered mediation and you need to move on with your life. In the meantime, please move out of the house, since it's not fair to me for you to share a house with me that you don't want to live in."

Jon darted his eyes away from mine, looking out of the bedroom window. "I'm not leaving. I don't know when you will let me see my kids again and I want to be able to tuck them into their beds at night."

I leaned back on the door, crossing my arms looking at Jon intently. "Do you truly want to be in this marriage, Jon? You have been a complete terror to me these last two months, pressuring me to sign a separation agreement that you absolutely refuse to negotiate on. I felt my only course of action to relieve the stress and emotional pain you were subjecting me to was through legal means."

Jon turned his head toward the window to avoid eye contact.

"No matter how nice I was to you, no matter how hard I tried, you cut me down every chance you got. You refused to consider or negotiate on anything."

"I know and I apologize," Jon replied, looking toward me remorsefully, and then sitting in silence for a few minutes, not saying a word.

I walked back downstairs to continue cleaning.

Tension in the home continued to rise. I spoke with Jon's mom on the way home from work the next day. She called and asked me to drop the lawsuit against Tasha.

"No good will come out of it. Jon was feeling unloved at the time and was seeking love from her."

I began rolling my eyes while listening to her. I thought my head was going to explode. *How dare she minimize his cheating as if he wasn't aware he was committing adultery? Unloved? This man sucked the life out of me with his demands for my time and attention for the last twelve years.*

"So that makes it right?" I responded with disgust.

I couldn't believe what she was saying to me. My blood was boiling. *How can anyone justify adultery?*

"He knows it wasn't right. He was just... confused."

"*Confused?*"

"Didn't you cheat after Jasmine was born?"

"Uhhhhh.... having one lunch with an old friend and having a full-on romantic relationship with a person, other than your spouse, while married are two different things."

I was done with her at that point and knew talking to her about the situation was useless. She was going to defend Jon to the bitter end no matter how wrong or morally corrupt he was. I told her I had to go in order to get her off the phone. I no longer had anything else to say to her after that conversation.

Later that night, Jon continued to pressure me to drop the lawsuits, yet refused to negotiate on child support and custody.

## THE WOUNDED EGO STRIKES BACK.

"When you love someone, you don't sue them," Jon said.

"So now you're going to pull the love card out? Please."

"I'm really considering reconciling the marriage, but it makes it hard with you suing Tasha. She did not do all the things portrayed in the lawsuit and it is wrong to pursue her," he said sarcastically.

I sat in silence, listening to Jon's justification of his infidelity and standing up for his mistress.

"I wanted to separate because I was ready to move on. Starting a deep friendship and relationship with Tasha is not illegal. Destroying her family and going after her job is wrong."

"Adultery is frowned upon by North Carolina judges; you both should have considered how you were destroying *your families* when you decided to engage in a relationship. Second of all, no one is going after her job."

It was obvious he was entering into desperation mode, using any and every tactic to get his way, but I refused to back down; my eyes were wide open now. I had built a protective wall around my heart to keep myself from enduring further pain.

Two days later, our daughter had a volleyball game after school. Jon met me at the game after work and entered the building visibly upset. He sat down next to me on the bleachers, reading an email on his phone. He angrily deleted the email and began texting throughout the game. I looked over and noticed he was replying to an email titled *re: marriage. Hmmm... I think he just got dumped by Tasha.* He was frantically wiping tears from his eyes, not paying attention to our daughter play.

"Are you ok?"

"I'm fine," Jon quickly responded and started watching the game.

After the game, I took the kids to grab dinner and then we headed home. When we walked into the house, the kids started on their nightly routines while I walked upstairs to the bedroom to find Jon. He was standing in the bedroom, staring at his phone blankly.

"Do you need to talk?"

Jon turned toward me, hugged me tightly, beginning to cry deeply before shoving me away with such force that I lost my balance. "I've tried and it doesn't work!"

Shocked and confused, I walked out of the bedroom to make sure the kids got their homework done and were preparing for bed. I tucked everyone in and prepared myself for bed and work the next day. As I walked back into the bedroom, I noticed Jon was already lying in bed, crying quietly. He laid in bed all night with his back turned to me, crying for hours. He woke up the next morning still crying off and on. We continued about our day attending Jasmine's volleyball tournament where Jon laid on a bench in turmoil the entire event. We started up a new discussion the following night before bed.

"What do you really want out of the split to avoid a courtroom battle?" Jon asked.

It became very apparent to me he was terrified of my lawyer and her track record in the courtroom. "I want to continue with the process and negotiate at court-ordered mediation."

"I'm afraid things will get ugly in the courtroom and I will have to bring up dirt on you," Jon replied.

*Bring it on. Bring IT ON. I had way too much evidence for him to win anything against me. Plus, we lived in the south. Judges do not look lightly upon adulterers. He would feel the full wrath of the law.*

"I'm concerned we will no longer be friends once we go to court. Going to court will ruin any chance at reconciliation we may have."

"Ok," I responded, not giving him an inkling of emotion to run with. "How about we go away for a weekend to see if we can work on our relationship?" I offered.

"No thanks, I feel forced into making a decision about reconciliation. I'm starting to have feelings for you again, but I'm not 100% connected yet," he quickly responded ▶.

Jon laid still for a while and then began kissing my neck and rubbing my legs.

"If you don't have a connection with me, don't waste my time, Jon."

Jon rolled over in anger and went to sleep. The next morning, he tried again and I turned him down. This time, he started crying.

"What's wrong?" I asked.

No response.

"I don't want to be used, Jon."

"You are using me," he said, getting up to leave the room.

I followed him and asked again, "What's wrong?"

"I tried talking and it doesn't matter. I know what game you're playing," he said combatively, shaking his head up and down.

I looked at him confused by his response. I had no clue what he was referring too. *What game?*

Jon stayed to himself the rest of the day, not saying a word, caught in his own world. By that evening, he decided to speak to me again and to chastise me for suing. "It's hard to reconcile with you when you're suing Tasha and she did nothing wrong. Starting a deep friendship and relationship with her was not illegal, but destroying her family and going after her for me is wrong."

Jon was livid with me for filing lawsuits against him and his mistress. He was now getting emotional. "If you have a heart, you will stop this! You still have time!" ▶

I sat there in silence listening as Jon teared up.

"You caused a lot of trouble for me at work and now things are ugly."

"Excuse me?" I said in bewilderment. "I caused trouble for *you* at work? It's my fault that *you* decided to have an affair with *your* direct report?"

Jon didn't say another word.

An hour later, however, he rolled over in bed, rubbing my shoulder, hinting that he wanted to have sex. "I need a release," he whispered in my ear. I stayed still and pretended I was asleep.

As the days progressed, Jon became overwhelmed from the list of items he needed to provide his lawyer with for the lawsuits. The financial information, the children's school records, months of paystubs, and a list of all marital assets. His lawyer told him upfront that my lawyer was a bulldog and she's never lost a case. His lawyer was definitely scared of my lawyer and Jon was anxious. You could see the desperation as he struggled to get his information in order pacing back and forth across the room.

I noticed Jon staring out of the front door of our home one day, staring blankly at the grass. "Are you ok?"

Jon broke down in tears. "I'm fine," he replied.

It was obvious he was not fine and was trying to cover it up. I couldn't keep up with his various states of mind, since he seemed to shuffle through them so abruptly. He was angry, remorseful, vindictive and sad all within a matter of minutes. It's hard to have sympathy for someone who has no regard for your own feelings yet wants you to have empathy for theirs. It was obvious Jon needed help and I was in no mood to be his therapist, as I had been throughout the course of the marriage.

"Have you considered talking to a therapist?"

"No, I hadn't," Jon responded. "But, it's actually not a bad idea. I'll schedule an appointment for next week."

Jon made an appointment for Wednesday of the following week, and following his first meeting with the therapist, he came home that evening in the mood to talk and I was ready to listen.

"How was therapy?" I asked as we laid down to go to bed.

"Good," he replied.

"Were you able to get a few things off your chest that were plaguing you?"

"I talked to the therapist about you suing Tasha," he replied.

"Okayyy..."

Jon then proceeded to tell me the series of events that occurred when Tasha resigned. Apparently, Tasha's husband was served her lawsuit papers by the sheriff since he was working from home. He immediately called Tasha at work, telling her to come home ASAP. That night, Tasha sent her resignation letter to Jon, effective immediately. Jon said HR called him to their office the next day and asked why Tasha abruptly quit. He told HR about their relationship and the fact that she was being sued by me. Since Jon was in such a good mood to talk, I proceeded to dig a little deeper and get a few of my burning questions answered.

"Sooo, what were you guys doing in the back of your truck every day?"

"Eating lunch and talking. We enjoyed the scenery of the park."

*Whatever. This guy really thinks I'm stupid.* I continued to probe further. "What did you do at her house the night you went over while her husband was out of town?" I asked.

"Watched TV," he said quickly with a straight face.

"You always complain about watching TV at home with me, but you went over there to watch TV?"

"I never get to watch what I want here."

"I ask you all the time what you want to watch on TV, Jon."

"Well, she was interested in watching my shows and didn't complain about them."

"What did I complain about?"

"You didn't like the show *Scorpion*," he replied.

I was completely confused at this point. He was uncomfortable by the conversation and grasping at straws.

"Did you ever ask me if I liked the show?" I asked.

Jon got in my face, nose to nose and yelled, "You're suing an innocent woman!"

I was done with the conversation, rolled over and went to sleep.

The next day, I received the following email from Jon:

"Having lawsuits in any form shows vengeance, not forgiveness and a willingness to move forward. You can call it protection, but I never threatened you in any way; in fact, I was more than willing to work with you amicably and was always looking out for your best interests as well, not just my own.

I'm undoubtedly trying very hard for us and am trying to schedule another therapy session today, but pressure builds daily, and honestly, so do the bad feelings that come with it. Clean slates are needed to truly move forward, but only you know if you can do that.

Furthermore, if our marriage is truly the prize you are after, then getting me back (all of me) should be enough and no lawsuits are needed at all. So, it's really your intentions that are standing in the way as well (money and revenge . . . or love). To me, that speaks to your character (new vs. old you) and has truly been concerning to me. I'm not trying to be ugly, but I am trying to be honest. Every time I get close to the point of fully recommitting to us, I am reminded of this side of your personality that scares me.

I'm trying my hardest to protect your feelings. I'm not telling you I'm 'all in' to trying again until I am sure, in my heart, that it is what I want, and I'm getting closer. I could fake it, but I refuse to do that and don't think it is fair to anyone." ▶

Based on Jon's inaccurate description of my actions while conveniently leaving out his own, he convinced his therapist that I was a bad person, looking to hurt him, and that I would not change if he resumed the marriage.

## IT'S NOT ME, IT'S YOU!

Jon's therapist suggested a couple's meeting after his second session, so we met with the therapist at the end of the week. The therapist interviewed us both, asking about our individual pain points with one another. I voiced my issues with the marriage, explaining how Jon never listened when I spoke, how he treated me poorly, how he liked to push my buttons until I got upset, and then followed me after I walked away to calm down. I also explained to the therapist it was cycles. He would be nice for maybe two weeks and mean and evil the next week.

Based on my pain points, the therapist had us do a listening exercise. I would say something and Jon had to repeat it. Jon would say something and I had to repeat it. I passed the test with flying colors for my portion. Jon failed horribly. I expressed to Jon, "You make me feel devalued when you ignore my repeated requests to stop the late-night arguments. You don't listen to me when I talk to you."

Jon's repeated version, "You don't like when I talk to you expressing my feelings and you think I'm mean." The therapist looked at Jon perplexed and said, "That's not what she said at all." The therapist suggested we go home and work on active listening. Great suggestion by the therapist, but nothing changed. Jon continued to be Jon. Self-absorbed and entitled.

I felt like I was living in a Lifetime movie and every day was a new drama. A week later, after a mentally exhausting day at work, I came home and laid on the couch for twenty minutes. Jon prepared the kid's lunches in the kitchen with attitude while I sat back and relaxed. After he finished, we played a few games of Yahtzee with the kids before they went upstairs to prepare for bed. Jon came over to the couch and sat down next to me to talk.

"Are you willing to work on our relationship? I have needs that I'm scared you can't meet," Jon said.

This was Jon's way of telling me he was frustrated. Dancing around his actual issue with me was common. I came home from work and sat on the couch as he prepared the kid's lunches for the next day; therefore, he was upset. I thought to myself, *I left work today, drove for an hour to our daughter's volleyball game, picked up our youngest child from aftercare, stopped and bought the kids dinner and came home. What's wrong with decompressing for twenty minutes on the couch?*

"I had to make the kid's lunches while you sat on the couch. Then, when we played Yahtzee, the kids sat near you instead of on the floor by me," Jon said.

"Ok, I'm confused by the issue here, Jon. No one said you had to make lunches at that moment and when the kids and I walked into the house, you were laid out on the couch." I sat up tall on the couch, shifting my body towards Jon's direction to look him in the eye before continuing. "Let's go through your day . . . you drove fifteen minutes to work and drove fifteen minutes home from work. Your day in no way compares to mine, so if I want to decompress on the couch when I get home for twenty minutes, I deserve to," I quipped as I got up from the couch, unwilling to hear his response.

I walked upstairs to take a shower, infuriated that he had the nerve to complain. I was done being his doormat. My "voice" had finally returned, and I had the courage to use it.

## REFLECTION

Narcissists are unable to love and be in a healthy romantic relationship. They are dishonest, deceptive, and morally corrupt while constantly accusing victims of those very same qualities. They provoke, bully and intimidate, often calling the victim names. Victims of narcissists suffer potential infidelity, manipulation, put-downs, gaslighting, blame-shifting and deception throughout their relationships taking a toll on their physical, mental, and emotional well-being.

Narcissists are pathological liars. They use lies to pump themselves up to gain admiration and validation and to maintain power in a relationship. Lying helps the narcissist maintain a self-image and avoid shame. Lies also enable their smear campaigns against their victims. A narcissistic lie is a necessity to preserve a self-image that must be defended at all times.

Narcissists are also sexually abusive, typically forcing victims into having sex without consent and coercing victims into uncomfortable sexual situations. If they do not get their way, they verbally abuse, emotionally abuse, and make threats.

When a victim expresses feelings of neglect or behavior that makes them feel uncomfortable, narcissists will label the victim as "crazy," "sensitive," or will give them the silent treatment, invalidating their feelings.

Victims of abuse experience brain fog, negative thoughts, and feel as if they are on an emotional roller coaster due to the body constantly running on cortisol. When victims are in emotional turmoil, intuition and reason are harder to access.

Victims also become *trauma bonded* to their partner — a strong emotional attachment between a victim and their abuser formed as a result of the cycle of intense emotional experiences. Similar to Stockholm Syndrome, it holds individuals emotionally captive to a manipulator who has subjected an individual to physical and/or emotional abuse. The bond is usually strengthened by intermittent reinforcement of periodic love-bombing, false promises or glimpses of kindness that a manipulator utilizes to keep the victim intertwined in the relationship.

Trauma within an abusive relationship creates an unhealthy addiction to abusers. The occasional sweet behavior after an incident of emotional abuse, apologies, pity ploys, and rare displays of love and reassurance during the devaluation phase, help reinforce our reward system, rather than deter it prior to another incident of abuse. This, combined with the release of the oxytocin hormone and dopamine neurotransmitter in the brain, alerting the brain to "pay attention" as well as recall pleasant memories is a biochemical bond of disaster.

*Chapter 5*

# THE NEW BEGINNING

> **Hoover:** *similar to a Hoover vacuum. Attempting to draw a victim back into an abusive relationship by any means necessary: begging, crying, guilt-tripping, blame-shifting, etc. During hoovering, the idealization, devalue, and discard phases recycle over a shorter time frame.*

By mid-October, after enduring two months of blame-shifting, denial, distortion of truth, passive-aggressiveness, name-calling, and put-downs, I finally found my inner strength to move forward with my life. I was at my fifth stage of grief — acceptance.

I accepted the fact that the marriage was over, so I sat down and composed a text to Jon on the state of our marriage and informed him I was continuing down the path of separation. It was easier to put my statement in writing as opposed to a face-to-face conversation due to his lack of active listening skills and validation of my feelings during prior conversations.

> *"If you have to be on the fence that much about working on a marriage together, then the commitment*

*is not there. I shouldn't have to convince you what a marriage commitment means. It shouldn't be about, 'I'm going to see how you act and decide if I want to be with you' type deal. Either you want to work on the marriage or you don't. It shouldn't be this difficult. My idea of marriage and your idea of marriage are two different things. I believe in what it spiritually means and you don't."*

Later that night, as we sat watching a college volleyball game with our daughter at the local college, Jon leaned over and said to me, "I was taken aback by your statement to continue with separation, but I understand you can't wait forever." ▶

I looked at him in shock and shook my head. That statement did not require a response. I turned back around and continued to watch the game.

The next day, Jon left to see his brother and talk about our current marital situation. He was not doing well with me telling him I was done with attempting to reconcile the marriage and needed someone to talk to. While lying in bed that night, Jon said, "I'm trying to respect your wishes and keep my distance. I'm going to start sleeping in the bonus room." ▶

I found this odd for him. All of my attempts to get him to sleep in another room for the last two months were vehemently rejected.

"I think it's best since we are no longer having sex. I shut off my feelings for you months ago," he stated while grabbing his pillow and walking down to the bonus room.

I didn't say a word. I laid in silence. He had a sexual need he was trying to fulfill and was attempting to guilt trip me into giving in to his needs.

He returned to the bedroom within an hour, seeming conflicted and confused. I was actually surprised by his reaction. I expected him to be less conflicted since I had made the choice for him. I thought his mind would be more at ease. He could go back to Tasha if that was his choice. They could begin to build their new life together once she made the decision to leave her husband and child.

In the days that followed, Jon poured on the guilt of breaking up the family and devastating the kids. I offered one more weekend trip to go away as a couple and Jon agreed to go. We left the following weekend for Myrtle Beach, SC.

## LAST DITCH EFFORT

The trip was awkward and uncomfortable. Jon barely spoke to me and it was obvious he was mentally struggling to visually show he wanted to be there. He was quiet and despondent the entire weekend.

When we arrived back home, I asked if he still wanted to work on the marriage and he was adamant that he did. I agreed to seek marital counseling while we waited for our court ordered mediation. However, instead of things getting better, they continued to get worse.

## THE VOLCANO ERUPTS

As a result of Jon's indiscretion at work, he was demoted to an individual contributor with no direct reports. His salary was cut and he lost his bonus for the year. By the time he got home from work after a seemingly rough day of change, he was upset. He barely said a word all night and was in a full-blown rage by bedtime ▶.

"It's your fault I got demoted and Tasha quit her job!" ▶ He yelled in my ear as I lay in bed. The smell of Old Spice soap filled the air around me as he leaned in for his attack. "It's all because of those stupid lawsuits you filed! You refuse to take any accountability in all of this!"

I laid there with my back turned to Jon, listening to his rage, staring at the wall across from me. My heart began to pound and my stomach twisted in knots anticipating the further attack. He was upset about work and instead of reflecting on and taking accountability for his own actions, he took his pain out on me.

"You destroyed any feelings I had for you when you chose to sue! The only time I feel anything for you is when we are having sex. I can't stand you!" Jon shouted, briefly pausing his tirade to fiddle with his phone.

I shifted my weight ever so slightly scared any huge movements would set him off again.

"You're being vindictive and trying to get every dime from me! There is no reason to have lawsuits! You went against all marriage articles and therapist recommendations on how to rebuild a marriage by filing lawsuits," Jon yelled.

I calmly attempted to speak and Jon cut me off. He continued to berate me, refusing to leave me alone. Then, suddenly his voice began to sound distant, as if he were speaking in a tunnel while my mind began to tune him out. I slowly sat up in bed, got up, and walked downstairs to let him calm down.

When I returned, Jon was lying on his back looking through the bedroom door. I walked over to my side of the bed and slowly got in pulling the sheet up over me. "I don't want to argue," he said in the sweetest voice before yelling at me again until he needed a break. I started to have a panic attack and had difficulty breathing.

He got out of the bed and briefly walked out of the room. I grabbed my phone from the nightstand and immediately started typing an email to my lawyer with hands shaking uncontrollable and tears rolling down my cheeks, asking if I had grounds to file a protective order. I also texted my girlfriend to give her a heads up that I may be in trouble. As I heard Jon's footsteps come toward the bedroom, I put the phone down and laid back down, pulling the covers over me and closing my eyes. He returned to the bedroom and stood over me while I laid in the bed.

I opened my eyes to find him looking down on me, jaw clenched, nostrils flared, with pupils dark and dilated. He began to berate me again before pausing to say, "You're a vindictive bitch." I cringed in fear backing away from him in the bed. He had the look of pure rage, and I was terrified. ▶ My heart began to pound as if it wanted out of my chest. I tried to think of what to do to calm the situation. My palms were wet with sweat and no matter how many breaths I took, I couldn't get enough air. I panicked. *Is he going to hurt me? I have to do something to make this stop!*

"Leave me alone, Jon, or I'm calling the police!" I blurted out as he leaned in closer to me. Jon pulled back, looking at me in shock like an innocent boy who got caught stealing from the cookie jar. His entire demeanor changed.

"You're going to call the police on me now?! Well, that's just GREAT!" he yelled, abruptly leaving the room and stomping down the hallway.

I continued to lie there for a few minutes, staring at the ceiling, and replaying what just happened in my head. I took a few deep breaths to calm myself down — silently stating, *inhale... exhale... inhale... exhale.* I slowly began to calm down, but still feared Jon's return.

He immediately called his brother and told him I threatened to call the police. "If there are any charges placed against me, don't worry I was just trying to have a *conversation with her,*" I heard him tell his brother. "Calling the police is one of her tactics to get what she wants," he said sarcastically.

I heard Jon's brother apologize through the phone, showing empathy for the person invoking the conflict. Jon then called his mother and told her the same thing. Of course, he didn't explain his role in the situation to his brother or his mother while blaming everything on me. ▶However, I didn't care at that point. I was just glad he left me alone.

> **Smear Campaign:** *a narcissist's weapon to steer the narrative into their favor, attacking a victim's character to family and friends in an attempt to isolate the victim from any possible support system. They hide behind their own abusive behavior projecting it onto the victim. The narcissist is all about image and how others perceive them. Exposing them as the toxic, emotionally and verbally abusive individuals they are is an attack on the personal image they present to the outside world. They will lie, cheat, file frivolous lawsuits with no evidence in an effort to protect their image. They will also work extra hard to flip the script and take on the role as the victim to gain empathy and support. This then feeds into their ego and without corroboration, the victim becomes the villain.*

Eventually, he crawled back into bed and went to sleep. I didn't sleep for the rest of the night, fearing the next attack and physical harm.

> **Cognitive Dissonance:** *when the mind tries to rationalize two different beliefs. Narcissists are masters at creating dissonance in their relationships. They often use manipulative tactics - intimidation, gaslighting, emotional, physical, financial, and sexual abuse, social isolation, sleep deprivation,*

> and more to maintain power and control over their victims. The threat of abuse is always present and usually becomes more frequent with time. Victims of narcissists doubt their gut reactions and continue to cling to their narcissistic partner. There are three ways to relieve cognitive dissonance: change your behavior, change your beliefs, or justify your beliefs and behavior. Victims often choose to change their behavior to please the narcissist and try to restore balance.

I got up the next morning sleep-deprived and mentally worn out. I got the kids ready for school and went to work as usual like nothing ever happened.

## PUSHING THE ROCK UP THE HILL

I called my lawyer as soon as I got to work to go over what happened and asked if I could file a protective order against Jon. I did not feel safe in the home.

"Has there been any physical violence? Any attempted physical violence? Our domestic violence restraining order (50B) is a tool to protect against physical violence, attempted physical violence, or placing someone in the fear of substantial bodily injury. This is done by filing a complaint in civil court. Unfortunately, I do not believe mere verbal attacks rise to the level to warrant obtaining a domestic violence protective order."

"No physical attacks have occurred. I am documenting all of the verbal attacks in my journal."

My shoulders dropped while I laid my face in my hand as the lawyer explained. I felt lost and defeated.

"Please try to get the verbal attacks recorded on a voice-activated recorder."

"Ok, I will try," I said, holding back tears.

*How do I pull out my phone and start recording in the middle of a verbal attack? As soon as I go for my phone, he's going to lash out at me about grabbing my phone.*

When I got home that evening, Jon acted as if nothing had happened. A typical response from him after he's gone into a rage. He never apologized for how he treated me the night before. We went to marriage counseling that evening and the counselor came down hard on Jon. We were no longer seeing the counselor Jon originally went to for individual therapy, since it was a conflict of interest. I found a woman who worked out of her home in a nearby town for us to see. At our first session, Jon admitted he still had feelings for Tasha, but that he wanted to work on rebuilding his marriage. *I think he forgot that actions speak louder than words.* It was amazing how he showed ZERO regret or remorse for his affair and felt comfortable justifying his actions. ▶

"I didn't have closure in the relationship with Tasha because it ended so abruptly. *She* ended it, not me," Jon said, looking in my direction. "I need to see her one more time for closure and she refuses to see me because *my wife* is suing her."

The marriage counselor looked at Jon, baffled. I sat there listening as tears rolled down my face.

"I suggest you write her a letter, Jon," the marriage counselor replied. "Your *wife*, the woman sitting next to you in tears right now, was well within her right to file lawsuits. She needs to look out for her and her children. Did you even consider what you were doing to your family? That relationship wasn't real. It was a fantasy. You two were living in a dream world of no responsibility."

Jon sat there biting his lip, infuriated by the counselor's comments. She was holding him accountable for his actions and he hated it.

"You have obviously lost sight of what's important," the counselor said. "I don't think you know what you want and you are playing with your wife's emotions. You need to figure out what you want and make a clear decision."

We left the counseling session with even more confusion and unsettlement in my mind based on Jon's undying love for Tasha. Later that evening, I sat down with him and expressed my feelings about a possible relationship if we were to have one.

"I need a spiritual relationship, Jon," I said. I'm done with these emotional roller coasters. I can't take the stress any longer."

"I'm confused by all of this *God* stuff because you've never been this way before," Jon replied.

"We wouldn't be where we are today if we had a spiritual relationship in the first place. For you to be the Christian person that you say you are, *you* should be concerned that you broke three commandments. You need to seek forgiveness for your sins," I replied.

"I already asked God for forgiveness," Jon mumbled.

"I'm mourning a death with the end of my relationship with Tasha and the difference between death and her is that she's still around," Jon's voice began to tremble and crack as he spoke.

"You need to seek the tools necessary to get over the relationship. Write poems, journal, mail her a letter."

"Those things won't help. I'm just so angry with you for interfering with the relationship and causing it to end abruptly without a natural death," Jon said in a scathing tone.

"Well, it seems that she came to her senses when she ended things with you," I snapped back. "If she really wanted to be with you, she would have stood up to her husband and kept her job since she was getting ready to be a single mom and needed the income."

"She was scared and Anthony threatened to hurt me, that is why she quit her job," Jon said.

"Anthony should have kicked your ass for coveting his wife," I quipped.

Jon didn't respond. He sat there in silence for a few minutes, looking off to the side, thinking of what to say next. "My mind wants to be with you, but I'm waiting for my heart to catch up. You just don't understand!" he yelled, as he got up and walked out of the room.

I watched Jon in amazement. What is he even talking about? He says he's going from having lots of feelings for someone to zero feelings and from zero feelings for someone to having to develop feelings. Why do I even bother? Jon doesn't deserve me or my love. I have so many feelings I want to share with him, yet I can't because he doesn't deserve me. I want my feelings to be shared, to be mutual with someone who only has me in their heart. Someone who only thinks of me. Isn't that what marriage is supposed to be? Why does he touch me and kiss me? Is it because he wants to, he needs to or he feels that is the right thing to do? I don't think he knows. He says it's because he wants to, yet he says I'm not in his heart. I feel used and taken for granted. Used to help him get over mourning his "friend."

I feel like I am the one doing all of the trying when he's the one that cheated. He says he's "trying" because he's going to therapy and he prays the serenity prayer every day. I write him love notes, pray for him daily, go to therapy with and without him to continuously work on me. It seems like I'm the only one trying. I shouldn't have to tell someone who cheated on me what they should be doing to reconcile. He should be kissing the ground I walk on, but instead, he acts like he's doing me a favor by staying with me and he's the prize.

## FALSE HOPE

Four months after Jon said he wanted to separate, he left for an overseas trip that required him to be gone for a month. The counselor suggested we both take that break to figure out what we both wanted. It was during that time that he finally got his head out of the clouds and actually seemed like he was trying to rebuild our marriage. I dropped the lawsuits in November and fully committed to rebuilding the marriage. I visited Jon overseas for one week and we spent our time sightseeing and enjoying fine dining. I actually had a really good time and it appeared as though things were falling back on track. ▶

After Jon returned from his month-long trip, I was excited to start over and put the drama behind us. We began discussing making a move into a new home for a fresh start. We were in a new year and it was a new year for new beginnings. However, it didn't appear that was going to be the case. Jon became moody and distant again, going through hot and cold phases with me.

One would think that as the person who committed adultery, he would do everything in his power to ensure I was happy. He did the exact opposite. He continued to demean, belittle and condescend as if I was the cheater. He also became extremely jealous and suspicious of everything I did, making the relationship even harder than it already was. I continued to try to keep peace in the home and figure out what I could have possibly done to set Jon off during his incessant mood swings.

By May, I expected my birthday weekend to be an exciting time to spend with Jon and the kids after the rough fall and winter we had as a family. Birthdays were a big deal in Jon's family, so I expected him to go all out to make up for his infidelity last year. As I left work one Friday, I looked forward to a fun-filled weekend. I thought Jon would go out of his way to make it extra special considering everything we had been through.

My birthday fell on a Sunday leaving Saturday the best day to have a date night. Jon didn't mention any plans for the weekend nor did he ask me what I wanted to do for my birthday. Maybe he had a surprise for me, I thought. He got up early Saturday morning and went to his brother's house to see if his brother needed help with yard work. He didn't wish me a happy birthday or acknowledge it was even my birthday. He later went to his parent's house to help them with their yard as well before returning home.

While he was gone, I gathered up the kids and decided to get a few things done around our house. It was a beautiful spring day, the temperature outside was mild and the sun was shining. Jon returned home around three in the afternoon. After waiting for him to return all day, I met him in the driveway.

"Do you think you can help me with the yard work?" I asked.

Jon turned in anger and raged at me. "What!? I just spent five hours doing yard work with my family!" he yelled. "I'm exhausted. I want to take a shower and sit down."

Completely shocked by his reaction, I calmly said, "Never mind," as I walked away, grabbed a rake, and began to rake leaves. He stomped into the house, slamming the front door behind him. It took the kids and me three hours to rake the yard while he sat inside. As I walked into the house, tired, with blistered hands and sweat-drenched clothes, I found Jon calmly sitting on the couch with his legs propped up, eating Oreos and watching TV.

"I'll never understand how you don't take pride in maintaining your own home, yet you will go out of your way to help your family with theirs," I said to Jon.

"There are people there to help me when I help my family," Jon replied, staring at the TV while popping an Oreo in his mouth.

"Really, Jon?" I snipped back. "The kids and I raked leaves for three hours while you sat here eating bon bons and watching TV. You never even attempted to come outside and help."

Jon continued to watch TV, ignoring everything I said. I walked upstairs furious, took a shower, and got ready to prepare dinner.

Happy birthday to me. I was hurt by his lack of concern to help his immediate family and disappointed he planned nothing for my birthday. I didn't speak to him for the rest of the night and he didn't attempt to speak to me either . . . not once did he tell me happy birthday.

## ALL HOPE IS LOST

A few days later, I found myself doubled over in intense pain. I had an awful urinary tract infection. I was bleeding every time I used the bathroom. I had been self-treating myself with DIY remedies for a few days that didn't seem to work. I asked Jon to take me to Urgent Care when I could no longer take the pain.

"Is it that bad?" Jon asked.

"Yes, Jon, I'm bleeding and running a fever. I need to see a doctor. If I could drive myself, I would."

"Fine," he snapped back as he begrudgingly put on his clothes and shoes.

The kids were more concerned about my well-being than Jon was. "Are you ok, Mommy?" Jasmine asked. I could see the concern on her face as I slowly walked to the car, cringing in pain with every step.

"I'll be ok, honey. I just need to get some medicine. Go back in the house. I'll be back soon."

Jon was so disgusted with me that night, he didn't help me to the car nor did he say a word to me the entire drive to or from the doctor. He sat in the waiting room with me with a scowl on his face the entire time. The only interaction I received from him were looks of disgust and spitefulness. The doctor prescribed an antibiotic that took the edge off of the pain but didn't clear the infection. A week later, the last day of medication, Jon rolled over in bed, wanting to be intimate.

"I can't, Jon. The meds are not working. I still don't feel right. I think I need to see the doctor again."

"WHAT! It's been a week. Of course... ANOTHER EXCUSE not to have sex! I should have known this was coming."

"It's not an excuse. I'm in ACTUAL pain," I replied.

"Whatever, there's always something wrong with you!"

Jon reached into his nightstand to pull out Tylenol PM. He popped two pills in his mouth and rolled over.

I went to the doctor the next day for a checkup. When they re-tested my urine, the infection was still present and required another round of antibiotics.

Things did not get any better between the two of us over the next couple of months. I began to wonder why I even chose to stay in the marriage. ▶

## NEW HOUSE, SAME PROBLEMS

Even though there were highs and lows in the marriage, I still tried to make it work and keep the family intact. Societal norms and family advice kept me in a constant flux of trying to achieve marital bliss. Jon and I began to discuss purchasing a new home to fully start over after his affair ▶. In that moment, there seemed to be a sliver of redemption on the horizon.

By that summer, we began planning to move. We had been in our current home for ten years and I was ready for a new place. A place without painful memories. There were too many bad memories in our current home that I desperately wanted to escape. I found a few homes I was interested in and shared with Jon. Jon's mom also took it upon herself to search for homes as well. She found a home adjacent to her neighborhood that she believed was the perfect home for us.

Once Jon found that out, he had no interest in the other homes I found. He only wanted to put an offer down on the one his mom found. Against my better judgment, we made an offer and it was immediately accepted ▶. We packed up our current home and were moved into the new place by August, right before school started back up for the children.

Our first week in the new home, just when I thought things would begin to get better, Jon started in on me again. Elijah left for the weekend to go to the beach with his girlfriend. He planned to return home late Saturday night. We waited and waited for Elijah to the point Jon got impatient. It was day five of my menstrual cycle. Although I was still bleeding, Jon couldn't wait any more days to have sex, and waiting on Elijah to get home was interrupting his plan.

"Why are you so short-tempered over waiting for Elijah to get safely home from a beach trip?"

"Don't act like an asshole... because I want to be with you!" Jon yelled with veins bulging in his neck.

Jon walked out of the house onto the back porch and came back into the bedroom even angrier. "You don't have to say something mean just because I want to be with you!" Jon yelled, slamming the closet door, and stomped into the kitchen to continue his rambling. "I wish someone wanted to be with me as much as I want to be with you."

Jon was so loud, Jasmine came downstairs and asked who fell down. Jon sat down on the couch while I returned to the bedroom to lie down. I was in no mood to argue with him again. Elijah returned home later that night while Jon sat on the family room couch watching TV.

## LIES UPON LIES

Shortly after the move, Jon's propensity for drinking began to creep back in. He started making bi-weekly trips to the liquor store after work to purchase a large bottle of vodka or two. One night after a few drinks, he passed out on the bed. I grabbed his work phone and began to scroll through his email messages to see if his relationship with Tasha actually ended. Based on his behavior, I had zero trust in him and his commitment to the marriage. I looked at his Facebook messages and found multiple women he had communicated with the prior year.

My stomach tied in knots and my body was on fire as I scrolled through multiple email messages related to Jon's affair. I found emails from him to Tasha, her parents, her friends, and her co-workers attempting to reconnect with her. The emails were sent from the week I dropped the lawsuits all the way until I went to visit him in Germany during his business trip. A FOUR WEEK time span. *He LIED to me!* The entire time he claimed he was done and moving on, he was repeatedly attempting to reconnect with her with messages telling Tasha he had finally gotten me to drop the lawsuits and now they could finally be together. Messages telling Tasha how he felt she was a great role model for Jasmine and he couldn't wait to introduce them. Messages degrading my character, commenting on my parenting skills, wishing he was with her instead of me scrolled past my eyes email after email.

I was infuriated. I threw the phone at Jon while he was passed out and it landed on his chest. He jumped up, looked around, wondering what was going on.

"You lied to me!" I yelled.

"What, what happened?" he asked dumbfounded.

"I found your emails attempting to get back with Tasha. Now it *all* makes sense. This explains why you were so distant for so long and so mean. You are a LIAR and I was a fool for ever taking you back."

"I haven't spoken to her in months and she never responded to any of my emails. No one responded. I thought I deleted everything from my phone," Jon replied.

"I don't believe you," I yelled back, as I grabbed my pillow and slept with Max that night.

I scheduled a session with our fourth marriage counselor to discuss the emails I found and how I was feeling about the situation ▶. We had switched counselors again since Jon didn't care for the previous lady. I think he didn't like her because she called him out on his behavior. Jon is used to getting his way by being charismatic and putting on a false persona when needed. That didn't fly with the previous counselor.

## THE SENSELESS SESSIONS

During our marital counseling session, Jon finally admitted he was having a sexual relationship with Tasha during the affair after months of denial.

"Jon, it doesn't make sense that you were so torn up over Tasha dumping you and you tried to get in touch with her over and over if you weren't sleeping together."

Jon looked down at the couch, swallowed, took a deep breath, and said, "We slept together one time right before it ended." ▶

My heart sank and my eyes swelled with tears. It was one thing to assume he was sleeping with her, but to hear him admit his sexual infidelity broke my heart in two. Once again, Jon pledged his everlasting devotion to me and making our marriage work. He said the emails were old and no one ever responded to his attempts to make contact. ▶

"I thought I deleted the emails from my phone," Jon said. "I'm sorry for the pain I've caused you." ▶

"Jon, not only did you cause pain, but you didn't *choose me*. I was your last resort. When you no longer had Tasha, you decided you wanted to work on the marriage. If she hadn't dumped *you, you* would still be with her."

Jon was speechless. He betrayed me one too many times and lied so many times that I couldn't figure out what was fact and what was fiction. He was also a master at saying things people wanted to hear and he had an audience with the therapist. He had to show his concerned loving side to her for her buy in and she got sucked right in.

"I'm just so tired of the cycles," I said. "Our entire relationship has been cycles of meanness from Jon followed by a loving Jon. It's never a "normal" relationship. I always feel like I'm walking on eggshells not to set him off. Then on top of that, the endless need he has for sex. No matter how he treats me, he feels I'm supposed to be at his beck and call. He pressures me into sex all the time."

The therapist sat there with a vacant look while Jon put on the face of innocence awaiting her response.

"Well, per the Bible, the wife should submit to her husband at all times. You should be more willing to meet his needs," the therapist said.

I looked at her in despair. She didn't seem to understand what I was going through and what this man was constantly subjecting me to day after day. *Was it just me? Am I the problem? She seems to think so, just like Jon. In the modern age of female independence, empowerment and having more control of our lives, she defaulted to a biblical direction that I "should be following" and made me a subjugate of my husband. My lying, cheating, abusive, diabolical husband.*

After our marital session, I was disgusted and I was hurt. I started to sink back into a mental low point. I found myself reliving the episodes of rage and betrayal in my head over and over like a movie, crying in the shower, crying while cooking dinner, crying when watching TV, crying during sex, and crying on my way to work as well as experiencing never-ending nightmares. I was in bad shape. I was slowly sinking back into the space I was in when I found out Jon was having an affair.

I began reading the book, *After the Affair: Healing the Pain and Rebuilding Trust When a Partner Has Been Unfaithful* by Janis A. Spring. I found strength in reading the stories of couples in similar situations while identifying with their thoughts and feelings.

## THE TOLL TAKEN

I had to be strong and pull myself out of the rut for the sake of my kids. I had a support system, family, and friends ready to help when needed. I just needed to get comfortable with opening up about what I was experiencing and feeling, removing the guilt of everything that was happening to me because of something I did or didn't do.

My body had been through so much from my lack of eating and compounded years of stress. During my annual physical, my doctor informed me I was suffering from chronic stress. I sat calmly in the examination room while she reviewed my test results.

"You appear to be extremely stressed based on your symptoms and test results," the doctor said. "Thinning hair, chronic headaches, acne, and digestive issues are all stress related. Your cortisol levels are through the roof. Your thyroid is out of whack and I believe the cause of your bloating is SIBO."

"SIBO?" I asked.

"Yes, Small Intestinal Bacterial Overgrowth (SIBO)," the doctor said. "SIBO causes malnutrition due to malabsorption of food. This condition can be caused by stress. You really need to remove the stress from your life. If you continue down this path, you will cause irreparable damage to your body."

I sat there and listened as the doctor read off all of my physical ailments and poor nutrition levels. I knew I needed to do something about my stress levels, but how can you heal yourself when you live with someone who constantly keeps you stressed. I gathered my clothes and got dressed while contemplating what I could do to help my body. For weeks, Jon pushed me to quickly get over the affair, adding to my stress levels.

"Why can't you just move on from it?" Jon said. "It's over. When will you get over it so we can go back to how we were. It was a mistake that I regret." ▶

"The pain still runs deep in my soul, Jon. I can't help the fact that the pain is still there. You didn't appreciate me prior to the affair, yet you want me to return to how I was, prior to your *mistake* that you continued to consciously make when people told you over and over it was wrong." I replied. "Not only did you have an affair, but you treated me less than human during the entire ordeal."

Jon grabbed my hand and apologized as if that would immediately erase the months of hate and condescending remarks he spewed at me.

Jon began to apologize every day, over and over, sending me apologetic texts and writing me handwritten notes; the most apologetic he had been since the entire fiasco started. He had never apologized until now, one year later.

He also became very jealous, controlling, and developed a regular drinking habit. Vodka and cranberry juice was his drink of choice. He would down six to eight sixteen-ounce glasses every night. Coming from an alcoholic family, this was not a smart choice for him. He was also a very mean, belligerent drunk. He would often run baths at night and sit in the tub for hours, all the while drinking a bottle of vodka. Once he came out, he was ready to argue, badger, and coerce me into sex, no matter how much I pleaded with him to stop.

> **Morbid Jealousy:** *a range of irrational thoughts and emotions, together with associated unacceptable or extreme behavior, in which the dominant theme is a preoccupation with a partner's*

> *sexual unfaithfulness based on unfounded evidence (Cobb, 1979). It is extremely dangerous and often leads to emotional and/or physical abuse. It's a dangerous component of an abusive relationship.*

Due to Jon's constant need for attention from me, I neglected myself for years in the marriage and gave up so much of myself and what *I* liked to do; another reason why I felt so betrayed by his infidelity. The neglect was affecting me mentally and physically. I looked at myself in the mirror one morning and didn't recognize the person staring back at me. That person looked like death...like she had been through a war zone; a disheveled woman gaunt in appearance with pale skin, and dry brittle hair. That once fun-loving, strong, intelligent, goal-seeking, glowing woman I was prior to marriage was gone. ▶

I missed her dearly and wanted her back. I made every effort to change that after the affair and took my doctor's advice to start taking care of me. I began planning trips to see my girlfriends for social interaction. I started getting my hair and nails done once a month to uplift my mood; and I started working out by taking exercise classes. I made myself a priority once again instead of someone who took advantage of me for their own gain and gave nothing in return.

Jon was not happy with any of my personal changes into the new me, since he could no longer stop me as he had in the past from seeing my friends and family and doing activities that I enjoyed. He continued to push me to get back to the old me and to act like I did pre-affair, as the woman who was easily controlled and manipulated by his tactics. He grew increasingly frustrated with me day by day, unable to continue to treat me as he once did.

That part of me was gone. I still loved Jon, but I was finding that I didn't "like" Jon. I didn't "like" the true Jon, not the persona he portrayed to the outside world. I didn't "like' the Jon who badgered, berated, and demeaned me...

## REFLECTION

I mentioned cycles to the therapist. This is key to what was actually occurring in the home and the therapist did not catch it. I was describing without even realizing it, the narcissistic abuse cycle. Narcissists repeatedly subject their victims to cycles of abuse with short periods of endearment to keep the victim in the relationship. I later learned marital therapists are trained to find fault in both parties instead of looking for signs of abuse.

The therapist Jon did not like tried to inform me Jon was a narcissist. ▶I dismissed her observation, not fully understanding the traits of a true narcissist. She told me he would never change, and that I had two options: leave the relationship or deal with it.

My husband was not the typical narcissist everyone thinks about; the person who thinks they are better than everyone else, the flashy person who always tries to one up other people. Little did I know that he was a special kind of narcissist. He was a covert narcissist.

> ▶A covert narcissist is someone who craves admiration and importance as well as lacks empathy toward others, but can act in a different way than an overt narcissist. When considering the behavior of narcissists, it might be hard to imagine how someone could be a narcissist and be inhibited in their approach and behavior. A covert narcissist may be outwardly self-effacing or withdrawn in their approach, but the end goals are the same. ▶

The charming, sweet and kind narcissist lures you in with their charm to later devalue and discard you when you're down. These are the most detrimental people you will ever encounter. They are detrimental to your mental and physical health. They consistently need your supply of love, admiration, attention, and sex to supplement their inadequacies.

When those supplies run low, they subject their significant other to fits of rage, temper tantrums, emotional, verbal and sometimes physical abuse until they find another supplier. They do not like to be alone with their own thoughts and feelings of emptiness, for they are incapable of coping with those feelings.

If you do find yourself involved with a covert narcissist and are contemplating ending the relationship, use caution. When the narcissist feels you pulling away from the relationship, episodes of spontaneous anger, jealousy, insecurity, mistrust, stalking and paranoia escalate, putting you in danger.

*Caretaker Personality:* People who become caretakers for a BPD/NPD (borderline personality disorder /narcissistic personality disorder), also seem to have a certain set of personality traits. These traits do not constitute a "personality disorder". In fact, they can be highly valued and useful to relationships and families, at work, and socially, especially when they are at moderate levels. They include a desire to do a good job, enjoyment in pleasing others, a desire to care for others, peacemaking, a gentle and mild temperament, and calm and reasonable behaviors.

These traits can be the hallmark of someone who is easy to get along with, caring of others, and a good worker, spouse, and parent. But when you use these behaviors as a means of counteracting the extreme behaviors of the BP/NP, they can morph into more toxic forms and become perfectionism, a need to please, overcompliance, extreme guilt, anxiety, overconcern, avoidance of conflict, fear of anger, low self-esteem, and passivity.

At that point, these traits become detrimental to the mental, emotional, and physical health of the person and become caretaker behaviors."

Fjelstad, Margalis. *Stop Caretaking the Borderline or Narcissist* (p. 16). Rowman & Littlefield Publishers. Kindle Edition.

## Chapter 6

# LOSS OF CONTROL

Not much changed in my relationship with Jon at the start of the next year. He still subjected me to late night rants, conversations on why I couldn't turn back into the "old" me, and how he longed to go back to how we were, pre-affair.

Yet, his treatment of me never changed. He continued to belittle, demean and coerce me into sex after his nightly alcohol binges. It was still all about Jon and his needs and never about me or what I needed from him in order to heal. My needs didn't matter, and he made that very clear every time he ignored my feelings when I expressed them.

As for the kids, Elijah was finishing up his junior year of high school and working part-time at a local coffee shop. Jasmine, now thirteen, was a phenom in volleyball and was invited to her first elite summer volleyball camp at the local university. Max was almost eight with an interest in baseball and flag football. He still idolized Jon and followed him everywhere.

My girlfriend, Tonya, came down for the weekend and stayed with us to celebrate our birthdays. Jon was invited to a bonfire by one of his co-workers. Since he was going to be out, Tonya and I decided to go out to dinner for a birthday celebration. We headed downtown to a New Orleans-style restaurant. When we sat down to review the menu, I received the first text from Jon, asking how long we would be out. I responded with, "I'm not sure. I'll text you when we are on our way home."

Tonya and I had put our orders in and started catching up when another text from Jon came through. "Has anyone hit on you or bought you drinks?"

"No," I replied, shaking my head and placing the phone back down on the table.

"Is that Jon?" Tonya asked.

"Of course it is," I replied.

Jon continued to text me while we waited for our food, checking on our whereabouts. Our food arrived forty-five minutes later. I was ready to take my first bite when I received another text from him, asking if we were still at the restaurant.

"Is that *Jon* again?" Tonya asked.

"Yes, he keeps asking if someone is buying me drinks or hitting on me and when we're coming home. I already told him I would text him on our way home, but he keeps texting me, asking when we are leaving."

"He's ridiculous," Tonya said. "You can't even be away from him in peace."

"Welcome to my life," I responded.

Tonya shook her head.

While we were eating, a live band set up at the front of the restaurant. We finished our dinner and decided to stay a little longer to listen to music and enjoy our time out while we could. We had the best time listening and decompressing. I couldn't remember the last time I had that much fun. It was good to get out; I desperately needed a mental break from Jon. We headed back home around midnight, and I texted Jon on our way back.

When we arrived at the house, I said good night to Tonya and walked into the bedroom, mentally preparing myself for the impending verbal attack while my stomach tossed and turned. The lights were out, and Jon was lying there watching TV. He sat up in the bed, infuriated, as I walked in.

"What took you so long!?"

I closed the door behind me to shield Tonya from his rant. "I told you we went to dinner. We were enjoying our time at the restaurant. You texted me nonstop to the point that Tonya asked why you were texting so much."

"Great! So now you made me look bad in front of your friend!" Jon snapped, slamming his arms down on the bed like a child throwing a temper tantrum.

"Excuse me? You made *yourself* look bad. I didn't force you to text me all of those times. I told you where I was and what I was doing."

Jon glared at me, enraged. I quickly grabbed my nightclothes from the nightstand and walked into the bathroom to take a shower. By the time I got out, Jon was passed out asleep. He'd been drinking. I could smell the alcohol on his breath as he was ranting. I slowly crawled into bed to go to sleep, trying my hardest not to wake him.

By the next morning, Jon was fine and put on the mask of the perfect husband and father, playing with the kids in the pool and asking if I needed assistance with anything. My girlfriend and her kids left late that afternoon. As soon as they got into their car, Jon began complaining about their stay, as he typically did whenever anyone came to visit me.

## LIFE ON THE HAMSTER WHEEL

While doing a few things around the house one summer day, Max asked Jon to play baseball with him. They grabbed their gear from the garage and headed to the backyard. I watched them for a little bit while I folded clothes in the house. They threw a couple of balls back and forth to each other, playing catch. Jon collected a few balls into a pile and got ready to pitch to Max, practicing to hit with the bat. Max grabbed his bat and got into position before suddenly being distracted, running off down the yard, chasing the dogs just as Jon got ready to throw a ball.

Jon immediately became enraged, throwing the ball down to the ground as hard as he could, causing it to bounce back up at him. He walked over to the bat lying on the ground, picked it up, and threw it across the yard as he walked toward the house, yelling, "Max, I'm not going to play with you if you're not going to stay here and play!" He angrily stomped into the house toward the bedroom, as Max ran into the house, crying,

"Daddy, I'm ready to play. Can you please come back outside?"

"No, I told you to leave the dogs alone. I'm not playing now," Jon replied.

"Pleasssse, come back outside Daddy! I promise I'll listen."

"No, Max. I'm done!" Jon yelled back, before lying down on the bed and staring at the ceiling, ignoring Max's cry in desperation for his attention.

"Come hang out with me for a little bit, Max. You can help me fold some clothes," I said.

Max walked over and began helping me to fold a few washcloths while sniffling until he was able to calm himself down. After thirty minutes, Jon got himself together and emerged from the bedroom. Max's face lit up like a light.

"Daddy!" Max said, running over to Jon to give him a hug.

"Are you ready to play now?" Jon asked, while hugging Max.

"Yes, I'm ready," Max said, looking up at him with admiration and a huge smile on his face.

They walked through the kitchen toward the backyard to play baseball until dinner time.

## ABANDON ALL HOPE

Later on, that same summer day, Jon sat down with me to talk about our anniversary plans. Our anniversary was coming up mid-June, signifying fourteen years of marriage — fourteen long and tumultuous years. Jon planned a weekend trip to Myrtle Beach.

While he was looking forward to the time away, I dreaded it. I didn't want to spend any time with him without the kids, and I didn't feel there was anything to celebrate. ▶ Our marriage was volatile and tumultuous. I felt emotionally neglected and ignored. I was tired of living a lie of marital bliss that didn't exist. However, I felt obligated to at least try to have a good time, since that's what you're "supposed to do when you are married."

We arrived in Myrtle Beach on a Friday evening after work, the day before our anniversary. I tried to enjoy myself and have a good time, but it just didn't work. I had too much on my mind and too much damage had been done. While sitting outside our room the next day, I propped my feet up on the balcony bars and asked Jon about Tasha. It seemed a fitting moment to do so, since we were allegedly here professing our rekindled "love" after more than a decade together.

"Do you still love her?"

"Who? Tasha?" Jon said, pausing to look across the lake outside of our room for a few moments. "Yes, I still love her. We had an emotional connection I couldn't resist. But it was like the therapist said. We were living in a pseudo world. No kids, no bills, no reality."

Jon continued to stare across the lake in a trance, as though he missed the relationship. I found it hard to believe they only had sex one time, since he was so enamored with her; the late-night trip to her house where he spent two hours with her, the various trips to the park where they were caught on video emerging from the back of his truck fixing their clothing.

"Since you love her, do you honestly expect me to believe you only had sex with her one time?"

Jon suddenly got fidgety and attempted to sidestep the question. He looked down at the ground and then looked across the lake. "It happened more than once. We were sleeping together on our trips to Germany, at the park, and the nights I went to her house while her husband was out of town."

"I knew it!" I yelled. "I knew you were lying about it. You can't even be honest about your past actions, but you want me to trust you again and forget everything that happened? Please. If I hadn't asked, you wouldn't have told me."

The color drained from my face as I looked across the lake. I was hurt, upset, and frustrated. *Lie after lie... he still can't be honest with me, yet he wants me to quickly "get over the affair" and go back to the old me.* I got up, walked back into the room to take a shower and tried to calm down as tears began to stream down my face. After my shower, I noticed Jon had gone to purchase a bottle of vodka and cranberry juice and was enjoying a few drinks while watching TV. I crawled into bed and went to sleep. Jon actually left me alone for once.

By the next morning, I had calmed down, but didn't have a lot to say. I was still thinking about what Jon said about Tasha the day before. We decided to go out for breakfast before heading back home to North Carolina. I searched for a nearby restaurant on my phone and asked him if he saw something in the room with the hotel's address on it to map the directions.

"Why don't you just use "current location" on your phone to do it?"

"I don't have location services turned on," I replied, as I continued looking for an address, searching through the documentation we received from the hotel while Jon glared at me.

"Why not?"

"Because I don't want to. It's my personal preference."

"That's a *BS excuse*. You're just trying to keep me from tracking you," Jon snapped at me while frantically zipping up his overnight bag.

"Whatever, Jon. That doesn't even make sense."

I got up, finished packing my bag, and walked out the door to go to the car. Jon fussed the entire ride to the restaurant and sat quietly during breakfast. He later apologized on the ride home to North Carolina. I sat in silence the entire trip, reading news articles on my phone.

We arrived home by mid-afternoon and spent the rest of the day preparing for work and school the next day.

By the end of June, I decided to pursue career growth opportunities at work and began researching roles. I accepted a challenging position on a new team within the company. My new *male* boss demanded a lot of me, pushing me to learn and do more. He worked well into the evening, sometimes calling me after hours for clarification or assistance with work-related projects, to Jon's dismay. One evening, around 7:30 p.m., my boss called with a question about a presentation I developed for him to present to our vice president the next day.

Jon glared at me as I hung up the phone. "Why is your boss calling you so late?"

"I created a slide deck for a huge presentation he has tomorrow. He needed clarification on a few of the slides," I answered, placing the phone on the nightstand and plugging it into the wall to charge.

"Why were you telling him what we were doing? Why were you laughing if it was a work call?"

"Are you serious? People make small talk. It's rude to just jump into business talk when you call someone."

"He shouldn't be calling you this late," Jon muttered.

"He apologized for the late call, and as I *told* you, he has a huge presentation tomorrow he needed clarity on."

"Yeah, right," Jon smirked. "He's more interested in getting into your *pants*. I could tell by the way you were laughing on the phone that he was flirting with you."

Jon grabbed his laptop from the nightstand and began working while I stared at him puzzled by his reaction. I didn't respond to his last comment. I walked to the kitchen to grab a snack, then went to watch a show on TV, while Jon stewed over my phone conversation. It would later be the source of another late-night circular conversation lasting until 3 a.m. on why my boss called, my laughing on the phone, and my boss trying to have sex with me. Five times he asked why my boss called and five times I answered with the same response. He just kept ignoring and invalidating my responses and pleas to get some sleep for work the next day. As I dozed off halfway through his rant, Jon yelled, "So you're just going to go to sleep now!?"

"Jon, you're not listening to a word I'm saying. It's late, and I'm exhausted."

"Fine!" Jon yelled as he rolled over to go to sleep.

The next day, as usual, Jon acted like nothing happened. ▶

Two of my close friends, Angela and Marie, regularly communicated with me during and after Jon's affair. They were my support system. They checked up on me every day to see how I was doing. I was so grateful, since I was still living on an emotional roller coaster. I really needed people to communicate with to validate my sanity. After our busted anniversary trip, Angela invited me to visit her in

New York for a weekend to get away and have some fun. Jon interrogated me daily on our plans leading up to the trip and insinuated I was going on the trip to get approached by other men. Regardless of what he thought, I needed a break from him and his insanity.

Two weeks before my trip, some of Jon's extended family drove down from Arkansas and stayed with his parents. We spent three days with them having cookouts at his parents' and his brother's house, socializing and swimming in our backyard pool. By the third day, the kids and I were spent and decided to spend some downtime in our house. As we were sitting outside by the pool with Jon's family, I said I was going in the house for a little bit. Elijah and Jasmine got up as well. Jon turned red, biting his lip and became enraged. As I made my way into the house from the back porch, Jon came in behind me, slamming the porch door behind him.

"What are you doing?" Jon fumed.

"I'm tired, Jon. We've spent three days socializing and entertaining. The kids and I need a break. I just need some time to myself to take a nap. It's not like you let me sleep at night."

I walked to the bedroom while he followed.

"You *always* need downtime. I *always* have to defend you to my parents and I *always* feel stuck in the middle. Your parents raised you to be a cold selfish bitch just like them." ▶

I stood there staring at him in shock.

"See, this is why I wanted to leave before! I didn't feel like you loved or appreciated me and I still don't!" Jon yelled.

"What does needing a break from your family have to do with you feeling loved? We are constantly with your family. We live in the same neighborhood as *your* family. We're always doing dinners and parties with them; they pop up over here whenever they feel like it without calling first. They take advantage of our pool and invite their friends to swim without asking."

I paused for a moment while Jon stared at the floor. I was upset, yet still wanted to maintain a sense of calm. "If it's that bad, Jon, you should leave the marriage. It's not like you made the decision to come back to the marriage. You stayed because you got dumped. You were all set to leave before and it's obvious you don't want to be with me now as your backup."

Jon stomped off, going back outside to the pool, angry, while I laid down to take a nap. He later returned at 10:30 p.m. after everyone left and acted like nothing happened, but continued to question me about my upcoming trip as if I had something to hide.

## THE BRIEF RESPITE

I hadn't spent any substantial time with Angela in fourteen years, or any other friend for that matter, and I missed everyone. I felt like my relationship with my friends had been on hold for all of those years to please a man who could care less about my feelings or well-being.

I was immensely excited when it was finally time for my weekend getaway. I kissed the kids goodbye, told them they could call or text me anytime, and drove to New York. Angela and I were invited by another friend to an all-black-attire party and had planned a day of pampering to get ready. We got our nails, hair and makeup done. We felt so beautiful. The night of the party was glamorous. A professional photo was taken of us looking like fashion models. I was able to get a digital copy for my phone as a keepsake. The next day, we spent the day shopping. While sitting down for lunch, we discussed our plans for the evening.

"I thought we'd check out a jazz lounge tonight for dinner," Angela said. "I've heard great things about it from my co-workers."

"That sounds great. I've never been to a jazz lounge before. It should be fun. I want to experience as much as I can while I'm here because I don't know when I'll be able to get away again."

I felt extremely relaxed and stress-free on my trip. I felt as if I could breathe again for the first time since my dinner with Tonya back in May. After enjoying dinner at the jazz lounge, we went back to Angela's condo later that night. We made hot herbal tea and sat on the balcony, reminiscing about the weekend and how much fun we had.

I left early Sunday morning to head back to North Carolina. I had so much fun, it was hard to leave knowing I had to deal with Jon once I got home. I returned feeling relaxed and happy after a much-needed trip; I felt like the old me again after years of conforming and being someone else. My girlfriend who invited Angela and me to the all-black event called me during my drive and commented on how calm and relaxed I was. I was a very different person from when she had lunch with me in Cary a few weeks prior while she was on a short business trip. As I drove into the driveway of my home, the kids ran out to greet me, giving me huge hugs, bringing a smile to my face and warming my heart.

"We missed you so much, Mommy," Max said.

"I missed you, too, honey," I replied, giving him a hug and kissing him on his forehead.

Jon, on the other hand, had more negative things to say.

"They never greet me like that. I guess I know where *I* stand," Jon grumbled, looking at me up and down ▶. "You drove home in *that*?"

"Yes, it's called a sundress," I sarcastically replied. "Is there a problem with it?"

"Looks inappropriate for a drive," he responded, looking at me up and down again.

"Well, it's very comfortable for an eight-hour drive." I responded.

There was nothing fancy, nor revealing about my dress. I refused to let him ruin my high from the weekend and chose to ignore his comments. As I walked into the bedroom to unpack my bag, he followed me. He got right in my ear and said,

"Why didn't you call me throughout the weekend to check on me and the kids?"

I turned to him and replied, "I called you every day I was gone, Jon, to see how you were doing. I also texted you the entire weekend I was there."

At that moment, Jasmine came into the bedroom, asking about our dinner plans. Jon backed off. I escaped the conversation for the moment, but I knew he wasn't done. I walked into the kitchen to start dinner and to text Angela to let her know I returned safely. I also told her what happened between Jon and me when I returned.

She texted back, "Your spirit has been crippled by him. It's hard to see that when you don't get space and time from him. You really need to think about what you want for yourself. You deserve happiness."

"I really need to get my finances together and explore my options. This relationship is not healthy. I realize that now." I wrote back.

Later that night, I posted the picture taken of my girlfriends and me on Facebook. As we lay in bed to go to sleep that night, Jon began his nightly argument.

"That picture of the three of you was gorgeous," Jon said ingeniously.

"Thanks."

He got quiet for a few minutes, staring up at the ceiling while lying on his back. "Why did you post that picture on Facebook?"

"Because I wanted to share a beautiful picture with my friends and family."

"You never post anything with me, but you're quick to post a picture of you and *your friends*. You don't even have me listed as your husband on your profile," ▶ Jon sneered.

"You hate Facebook and claim you never use it. Now, all of the sudden, Facebook is important to you after complaining about it for years?" I challenged.

I laid in bed listening to Jon rant for twenty minutes about Facebook, not saying a word, waiting for his rant to be over. He calmed down for a moment and asked, "So, what activities did you do in New York?"

I attempted to explain my weekend, forgetting I was talking to someone who was not genuinely interested in what I did. But, as usual, I gave him the benefit of the doubt. "The first night we went to an all-black-attire event..." Before I could finish explaining it, he abruptly cut me off.

"Why didn't you tell me you were going to a party!? You got all dressed up to impress other people, but you don't do that for ME!"

He sat up in the bed, angry, glaring down at me.

"Jon, you and I don't go to events that require me to formally dress up. I don't need to get formally dolled up to see a movie or go to TGI Fridays. We attended an event I'll never get to experience again."

As Jon sat there in silence, I continued to talk about my weekend. "We also shopped and went to a jazz lounge to have dinner and listen to live music."

"WHAT?! You went to a *nightclub!*?" Jon yelled.

"No, Jon. We went to a jazz lounge to eat dinner and listen to live music. There is a difference," I replied.

Enraged, Jon asked, "Did anyone hit on you?"

"I had a couple of men attempt to talk to me that I quickly informed I was married," I replied.

"*What?* I can't believe you went to a nightclub and talked to men!" Jon shouted, flailing his arms around in the bed. "You're such a bad mom for going on a weekend trip, leaving your family and you suck as a wife. What mother of three goes to a *nightclub!?*" Jon criticized while looking down on me, full of rage. ▶

At that point, I started getting frustrated with the conversation and wanted it to end. I attempted to re-explain my actions to no avail. "Again, I went to a jazz lounge for dinner and to listen to music. I turned down the men that attempted to hit on me while I was out. Unlike *you,* I *actually* value my vows," I said.

"YOU DO NOTHING to help my insecurities!" Jon yelled, slamming his hands on the bed. ▶

"Jon, it's not my job to help your insecurities. I'm not the one who had the sexual affair. You did," I replied.

I was done with the conversation. It was getting late and I was exhausted from my drive home. I don't even know why I tried. Jon was infuriated for the rest of the night and went into his usual ever-looping rant that had no meaning or value. By 3 a.m., I was falling asleep.

"So, you're just going to go to bed now!?" Jon snapped, shoving my shoulder back and forth, abruptly waking me up.

"Yes, Jon, it's 3 a.m. and I have to get up for work in three hours," I replied, rolling over on my side.

"Typical. It's always about YOU. You never want to clear the air about anything," Jon said.

"What are we clearing the air about? I didn't *do* anything wrong and I refuse to let you make me think I did," I replied.

Jon laid in an angry stupor for a few minutes before finally rolling over to pop two Tylenol PMs. He then pulled the covers off of me and laid down to go to sleep.

The next day, I found a note on my dresser from him, apologizing for the argument, *"My words did not convey my intentions,"* it said and ended with *"You deserve better."* ▶ I called Angela on my way to work to tell her what happened.

"How have you endured him for so long?" She inquired.

"Mom told me to hang in there with him so I've been trying. I've tried really hard to deal with it over the years, but I'm breaking now and can no longer take it. That's why I need to work my way out of the relationship. It is going to be a battle based on trying to divorce him two years ago."

"You've been through *so much* with the affair, how he treats you and the constant jealousy. It's amazing how patient you have been with him." Angela said.

"I surprise myself sometimes with how patient I've been. I really hate conflict and that's probably why I always try to diffuse his outbursts. Do you know how many times I've heard from him, "*you deserve better*"? Too many to count. He will never change."

"I don't think he will change either. Not after all of this time," Angela replied.

"I'm trying to wait until I get my bonus next March to tell him it's over. I need to do some research to see what my options are for the house. Then, I have to figure out finances. With Jasmine going into high school next year, that's another huge expense. I'll need to wait to see what her tuition will be and get my bonus money before I can make any moves. But I don't know if I can make it until then."

"You need to do something. This is getting to be too much and it's nonstop," said Angela.

"It's a cycle. He gets upset, rants about *his needs* and then he's fine for a few days. This has been my life for fourteen years. Ever since he cheated, my tolerance for the cycle has declined. I was tolerating his bad behavior, thinking things would get better if I just changed me when he committed the ultimate betrayal."

I spoke to Angela for ten more minutes before arriving at work to start my day. Our conversation validated what I was thinking and feeling. After so many years of gaslighting from Jon, it felt good to hear that I wasn't overreacting.

## THE LONG AND ENDLESSLY WINDING, TWISTED ROAD

By August, it seemed like life never got easier with Jon. I was constantly tired from a lack of sleep and mentally exhausted from the irrational rants I was subjected to night after night. He liked late-night "conversations" because that's the only time he claimed he could "air" his feelings. He kept me up until 5 a.m. one night before finally wearing himself out and going to sleep.

"Why can't you just go back to the honeymoon stage and JUST MAKE THE DECISION to be in that space with me! I don't understand why you can't just do that? MAKE THE DECISION!" ▶ Jon demanded.

"I'm not in that space and you don't give me time to think. You've betrayed me multiple times, Jon. I'm still dealing with that pain, betrayal and anguish."

"Can you at least make your phone available to me every day to check and ease my insecurities?" Jon inquired.

"No, I will not and I'm tired... it's 5 a.m.," I responded as I rolled over to go to sleep.

*I just have to hold on until Jasmine turns eighteen years old. But, can I really survive five more years in this relationship?* ▶

With my new work role, I occasionally worked from home on Fridays. Jon decided to take off work spontaneously one Friday. After school started, I began my work day as usual, while Jon got upset that I didn't show him attention during the day. According to him, he expected me to shower him with love, hold his hand, give him hugs, and sit close to him while I worked. I was baffled and caught off guard by this unrealistic expectation. Did he not understand *"work from home"?*

Later that evening, he calmed down and asked me to pick out movies to watch. I selected two movies. We grabbed a few snacks from the kitchen and then sat down to watch them together in our bedroom.

"Those movies were boring. I couldn't wait for them to be over." Jon grunted while getting up to walk into the bathroom.

"Well, how about you pick the movies next time?" I suggested.

"I didn't want to watch movies anyway," Jon mumbled, putting his nail clippers into the bathroom drawer.

"Then, why did you ask me to pick out movies? Never mind, you know what... this is really getting to be too much for me. You should move on and find someone that meets your needs. It's obvious I don't make you happy nor meet your needs."

Shocked by my reaction to his comments, Jon became calm and concerned. He sat down on the bed and grabbed my hand. "I really want to make things work, yet I feel like I'm in prison because you can't just switch yourself back to how you used to be with me before *my mistake.*"

I looked at Jon, not saying a word. Then, his tone shifted from calm and concerned to a tit for tat attitude.

"You're not so innocent yourself, you know? You had lunch with that guy years ago. We both cheated."

"Really? You're comparing one innocent lunch in a restaurant to an ongoing *sexual relationship* you initiated with your married direct report? Please," I said, rolling my eyes.

"Yes, I didn't know it was an innocent lunch. I did a DNA test on Jasmine after that to make sure she was my kid."

"You're ridiculous," I sneered.

I got up and sat in the family room to watch TV, while Jon took a bath, drinking vodka and cranberry juice. I began texting Marie.

"Sooooo, I have to check myself sometimes because I know every relationship is not like my parents. Do you tell Tony you love him multiple times a day and compliment him every day? Jon says he "needs" it and I'm just trying to figure out if that's normal and I'm the abnormal one. I don't have that need so I can't relate to his needs. My world does not blow up if he doesn't compliment me every hour of every day."

"The answer is NO. We don't go around saying that all day long and complimenting each other. We keep it natural and genuine," Marie responded.

"Ok, so once again, he's in his own little world. He swears his coworkers agree with him on EVERYTHING."

After an hour of TV, I laid down in bed while Jon drank in the bathtub. The next day, he left me a note on my dresser saying, *"I apologize for the late-night fights and I know you're tired of going through them."* Just when I thought he was turning over a new leaf, he texted me a meme later in the day that read, *"You're cute - too bad you're an asshole."*

By mid-September I was really losing my mind and Jon's jealousy was increasingly getting out of control. I received a text from him one Friday asking, "Did you work from home or somewhere else today?" I responded with, "I worked at Starbucks for a change of pace. Does it matter?" No response. When he returned home from work that evening, he was angry. He came into the bedroom where I was lying on the bed watching TV.

"I do everything to make you feel secure and you DO NOTHING to make me feel secure!" Jon said, throwing his work bag on the bed.

As to what this "everything" comprised, I was never certain nor would that ever be defined. However, from my perspective, that statement was the opposite of the truth. He simply flipped roles and claimed he was doing everything, when in fact he wasn't.

"It's not my job to make you feel secure. You feel insecure because YOU cheated."

I got up from the bed and stood by the bedroom window, shocked by his actions and concerned with what he would do next. My heart began to race as if it was coming out of my chest and my stomach did somersaults anticipating an attack.

"You are always so secretive. I know nothing about your life," Jon criticized. ▸

"What are you talking about? What secrets? Working at Starbucks? I didn't know I had to tell you where I chose to work from home during my work day," I challenged.

Jon's face relaxed and he began to calm down. "I'm just worried you will leave me and I'm nervous," Jon said in a monotone voice, lowering his head into his hands and looking down at the bed, silent for a few moments. I didn't say a word, anxiously waiting for the next outburst. He walked out of the room and upstairs to see what Jasmine and Max wanted to do for dinner before heading to the liquor store to buy his vodka for the evening. When he returned home, he explained what happened at work.

Jon had applied for three manager positions since his affair with Tasha. Apparently, he found out he got turned down for the third position he applied for, adding to the news of me not working "out of the home." He was having a bad day and he chose to take it out on me as usual; the target of all of his frustrations when Elijah wasn't around to criticize.

Jon settled down and prepared himself a drink before watching TV. I left to pick up Elijah from the local coffee shop at 10 p.m. that night, as Jon was preparing to get in the tub to have his normal pastime of vodka and cranberry juice while soaking. When we returned home, I walked back to the bedroom to find Jon passed out on his back, on top of the bed, with his shorts partially pulled down and his private parts exposed. I was appalled. The bedroom door was wide open with Jasmine and Max upstairs in their rooms. I had no idea if they had come downstairs while I was gone or not. Jon was completely oblivious to what was going on around him. I was disgusted and took a photo to show him the next day.

The next morning, I showed him his partially nude photo from his drunken stupor the night before.

"That's hilarious!" Jon chuckled, tossing his back in laughter.

I was not amused and questionably looked at Jon to determine if he was serious. "The kids were upstairs. What if they came downstairs to ask you something?"

"The kids were fine," Jon said, blowing me off.

I shook my head. He had no remorse and didn't believe anything was wrong with his actions. I thought his actions were inappropriate as a father. We continued on with our day, spending time by the pool with the kids. Later that night, Jon sent me a long text apologizing for his behavior over the years.

> *"I wanted to send you a true heartfelt apology... for everything that has happened between us over the years and how much I've hurt you. I still feel horrible every day and I want you to know I'm truly sorry. I love you."*

I didn't respond. I was shocked and confused as to why he decided to apologize out of the blue after all of these years. *Was he really sorry or did he just want me to return to how I was pre-affair... falling for the gaslighting, being easily manipulated and controlled?* I chose not to respond to the text.

One afternoon, I decided to have lunch with my friend Beth. Beth had divorced her alcoholic husband two years before and was assisting me with my alcoholic husband (*unfortunately, neither she nor I realized what we were truly dealing with at the time*). She was well aware of my current situation and wanted to meet and checkup on me. Jon was doing some work on his laptop when I left and the kids were in their rooms watching TV and playing video games. It was nice to talk to someone who could identify with what I was feeling and experiencing in the home.

As we sat down, waiting for our lunch to come out from the kitchen, I updated Beth on Jon's continued use of alcohol and late-night rants.

"You need to come with me to Al-Anon meetings," Beth said, grabbing her glass of water. "They provide you with coping skills to help you get through living with an alcoholic."

"When and where are they?"

"They are Wednesday nights at 7 p.m. in Raleigh. Waiting for Jon to ever be logical or to think rationally is never going to happen, so you need to stop expecting it. People who turn to alcohol as their coping mechanism, and feel great relief from it have deep-rooted issues that stem from childhood. THAT'S what I learned in Al-Anon meetings."

The waitress brought our food out; I began opening up my napkin to grab my utensils while attentively listening. "Wow, really?" I looked at Beth, intrigued, wanting to hear more while taking a sip of my tea.

"Listen, I'm here for you whenever you need me. Call me anytime. If he hasn't admitted he has a problem, it will never get better. If you do decide to leave, you can always begin to stash a few things at my house in the meantime, like household essentials. Start building a stockpile and start saving your money."

"You're right, I just need to accept the fact he will never change," I said, feeling defeated, looking down at my plate. Thanks for all of your support. I really appreciate it."

We finished our lunch; I gave Beth a hug and drove home, seriously thinking about what Beth said. By the time I got home, Jon was in the kitchen making cheesy garlic bread. I made the mistake of questioning one of the ingredients he was using, since it was my recipe. He immediately got upset.

"YOU'RE ALWAYS CRITICIZING ME! You didn't pay attention to me all day, but made time to chat it up with *your* friend," Jon said, slamming a knife on the kitchen counter. He slammed it down so hard, I felt the wind from the impact, startling me and causing me to jump back from the counter.

Max ran out of his room to see if everyone was ok.

"And I STILL can't believe you went to a nightclub in New York with your other *friend*. You're a woman in your forties still clubbin'," Jon yelled.

Baffled and scared by his outburst, I looked at my husband. *Where was this coming from?* Max was confused as well, staring at Jon with an an open mouth and raised brows. It was uncalled for and rude. He stomped his way to the bedroom, calmed down, and then returned to the kitchen fifteen minutes later. His entire demeanor had changed. It was as if he had become someone else. He asked what he could do to help me around the house, to which I replied, "Nothing."

Later that night, he apologized for his behavior earlier in the day while we lay in bed. "I apologize for earlier. You always have fun when you hang out with your friends and it doesn't seem like you have fun with me. You're always so stressed at home."

*Hmmmm . . . I wonder why??*

"I always think you're out flirting with other men."

"I'm with you the majority of the week except for work. We go out every weekend on dinner dates. Don't you have fun when we go out?" I asked Jon.

"Yes, I do."

"Then *what's* the issue?" I inquired.

"I know how you are when you go out because your *friends* told me."

"Who? Who told you and what did they tell you? My friends don't even talk to you."

Jon didn't say another word. He waited a few minutes and then rolled over to take two Tylenol PMs and went to sleep. He didn't say a word because he was lying. My friends did not like him or how he treated me. They would never have a private conversation with him without telling me. ▶

It was fall and the leaves had begun to change to an orange-brown color. October was a great month for Elijah and Jasmine. Elijah found out he was accepted to East Carolina University, his first-choice school. It was such a load off of my mind to know he got accepted into college, considering high school was a struggle to get him to do what he was supposed to do. Jasmine tried out for club volleyball and made the top national team for her age group. She was very surprised and excited to make the team.

Also, in October, my alma mater, NC State University, was gearing up for Homecoming and my girlfriends wanted to know if I was going to any of the festivities. I hadn't been to a homecoming since I met Jon; I really did want to catch up with some old friends. I talked it over with Jon and he was ok with it at the time, but then had an issue with it once he found out my girlfriend bought me a ticket to the Black Alumni Gala.

"Is the party at a club? Is it an open bar? How will it be set up?" Jon inquired.

"The gala is at the Sheraton downtown. No alcohol."

He began to pace the bedroom floor, increasingly becoming perturbed by my decision to attend the Gala. "*Why* do you continuously go to "meat markets" to attract men? Dress to impress to get men? My friends don't take me to "meat markets.""

"I'm not continuously doing anything. I can barely have lunch with a friend once a month without you complaining."

Jon released a sigh conveying annoyance by my response.

"What friends, Jon? You don't hang out with anyone and expect me to do the same. Homecoming is NOT a *meat market*. It's HOMECOMING. A time for old classmates to get together and catch up," I said before pausing for a moment to collect my thoughts and decide how far I wanted to take the conversation. I looked down at the floor contemplating my next move. "This marriage is not working," I said softly.

"Now you want to give up and not try to make it work!" Jon yelled.

I looked at Jon in surprise. "I've tried and tried again. Nothing changes and nothing gets better. Let's not even get into the Tasha situation. You were still chasing Tasha behind my back when you claimed you wanted to work on the marriage. You lied, but expect me to trust you and you treated me horribly during that time and haven't treated me much better since. You treat me like a doormat to be walked on whenever you feel like it. I'm not the same person anymore."

Jon left the bedroom, grabbed his keys from the rack in the kitchen and left for three hours. While he was gone, I called Angela.

"Jon just left. He got upset over me planning to go to the Black Alumni Gala."

"What? Is he upset that you're going to a gala or the fact that it's an event for African American Alumni?" Angela asked.

"Probably all of the above. He called it a 'meat market.'"

"What did you say?" Angela inquired.

"I told him the marriage isn't working. He said, 'you don't want to try anymore?' I told him I've been trying and he still treats me like crap. He got upset and left." I paused for a moment and then told Angela about the brochure I received from Beth. "In other news . . . I was reading the Al-Anon brochure my girlfriend gave me. It talks about living with an alcoholic and the description of the alcoholic in the story sounds just like Jon. I thought I was reading MY STORY."

"YESSSS. He has a problem and won't admit it," Angela said.

"He will never admit it. He says drinking 'relaxes' him," I replied.

"There's a difference between *relaxing* and *dependency*. He definitely has a dependency."

"Agreed... I have to leave. I am unable to relax in my own home because he's so volatile, and I don't feel safe. He watches my every move. Every time I'm texting, he's looking at me, and my phone, if I'm near him. I keep my phone on silent so he won't complain about how many texts I receive. Every time I'm on the computer, he's looking to see what I'm working on and complains about me being on the computer. He reviews all of the cell phone bills, looking up the numbers, and on top of all that, he constantly calls me out for not showing him any attention, no matter how much time we spend together. Ohhh, and then there's the alcohol to top everything off, leading to insane late-night rants that are blaming me for everything wrong in his life."

"It's NOT healthy. You have to do something." Angela said.

"I'm getting my finances in order. I'm still paying off the lawyer from the last go round, so I need to get my finances in order to afford another lawyer. Also, Jasmine just made a national volleyball team, so that's another expense. It's never ending... what I have learned over time is that Jon is a people pleaser. He conforms to however he believes people want to see him. Therefore, our marriage was based on a fictional person that never existed. He was not being his true self when we were dating and over time, he was unable to sustain that lie. It really came to a head with the affair. Once I saw him for who he really was, I found that I did not like that person. While we were dating, I pushed him away for a long time. He continued to convince me of how great he was and how understanding he was. The "perfect" soulmate. ALL LIES."

"Girl, please get out and get out soon. Your kids are seeing this and it's not good for them," said Angela.

"I'm trying my hardest. I'm constantly trying to figure out a plan to move. He literally wants me to forget all and act like NOTHING ever happened, including how he treated me through all that mess with Tasha. He says I should make the *decision* to forget and stop letting it hold me back from him. Excuse me?! Forget all the name calling and torture you put me through for months?"

While standing in the dining room, I heard Jon's truck pull into the driveway. "Gotta go. I hear his truck in the driveway."

I hung up the phone and went into the bedroom. When Jon came in, he wanted to talk again.

"You don't want to talk?"

"About what?" I sneered.

"I'm sick to my stomach because you want to leave."

"This is not working, Jon. Our relationship is not normal. You're always accusing me of cheating, watching everything I do, and you're constantly jealous. That's not a normal relationship." I said shaking my head.

"I didn't want to come home because you don't care about me. You treat me bad and don't want me." Jon solemnly said.

I looked at Jon, wondering if he even listened to what I said. Then he abruptly switched.

"FINE. You can leave, but I'm not gonna help you leave. In fact, I'll leave. It's *obvious* you can't get over my *one* mistake and there's nothing I can do to change that!"

I didn't say a word. Jon got up, grabbed his boxers from the dresser drawer and went into the bathroom. Five minutes later, I heard the water running in the bathtub. He was getting ready for his nightly drinking ritual. I got ready for bed and went to sleep.

The next day, Jon didn't mention what occurred the day prior or a thing about moving out. He apologized and said he understood my frustrations. I decided to work from home that day, since I didn't have any meetings that required me to be on campus.

Jon came home around 3 p.m. from work. I was surprised, but couldn't ask why since I was in the middle of a conference call. He came in, grabbed some boxers from the drawer and went into the bathroom. A few minutes later, I heard the water running in the tub. Jon stayed in the tub until 5:30 p.m. I found it odd that he decided to do his drinking so early. This was new behavior. Once he got out, he had clearly been drinking.

"Were you drinking?" I inquired.

"No," he quickly responded, looking away to avoid eye contact.

Later that night while watching TV, Jon suddenly turned it off and looked over at me. Grabbing my hand, he said, "I want to apologize for lying earlier. I had been drinking in the tub. I don't want to lie to you and have secrets between us. I was afraid you were going to judge me."

I didn't say a word. *If that's the case, why lie about something so small?* His words did not match his actions, making him look disingenuous.

By the end of 2016, I looked forward to the year of 2017. I hoped the year would bring more joy than pain. I just wanted normalcy. *Was that too much to ask for?*

## REFLECTION

The last thing a narcissist wants to be is self-aware—they have zero desire to evolve and learn from their mistakes. Therefore, nothing is ever their fault. How they treat others or what happens to them is never their fault. By Jon having an affair and everyone knowing about it, he couldn't swindle his way out of the fact that he did something wrong, even though he tried his hardest to justify his actions. By me being hurt and unable to move on from his actions, it made him feel uncomfortable, facing the fact that he did something wrong; something he didn't want to face or feel.

Jon was also losing the ability to manipulate and control me as well as lock out family and friends, causing him to spin out of control and drown himself in alcohol. Control is a centerpiece of the narcissist's power. When disrupted, it can become perilous for the victims. After fourteen years of suffering emotional abuse and trauma from Jon, I stood my ground. Not realizing the true person I was dealing with would finally be revealed, putting everything into proper perspective. I was not simply dealing with an alcoholic, verbally abusive, promiscuous spouse. I was dealing with a highly skilled psychological manipulator; a predator who thrived on control and manipulation for his own personal desires.

I was stuck in a decade-long endless cycle, which was often dismissed by professionals as not being legitimate. It was clearly apparent by now there was so much more to this than I could have ever imagined.

*Chapter 7*

# EVERY DAY IS
# EXACTLY THE SAME

We had been in our new home for two years and my relationship with Jon continued to be turbulent. This new home was supposed to be a fresh start, a new beginning in a place that didn't have the echoes of the past. But, as each day went by, I was increasingly feeling disdain for Jon; he didn't help matters by how he treated me day in and day out.

A work bonus I was so desperately waiting for went towards volleyball and school tuition, delaying my plans to move out. I needed to be able to afford a new place and still pay my share of school tuition and volleyball expenses. It was beginning, again, to look like I would have to wait until Jasmine was eighteen years old before I could escape . . . a major disappointment for me.

The new year started out just as bad as the previous year ended and work continued to be a welcome escape from my home life. My body adapted to the sleep deprivation allowing me to function during the day on little to no sleep, since Jon continued to harass me at night for frivolous arguments and sex.

Jon had difficulty sleeping from the day I met him due to "things he heard in his head." He was always taking some type of over-the-counter sleep aid, if he couldn't coerce me into having sex with him to clear his mind, or to argue with me all night until he fell asleep. I laid down in bed one night and turned on my side with my back to him. I had a busy day at work planned for the next day. I desperately needed rest. Jon began caressing my back, but I didn't respond. He stopped, stared at the ceiling, laying there for a few minutes, sighing before saying,

"I *need* sex to stop the negative thoughts running through my head. SEX is the only thing that shuts them off." ▶

"Sounds like you need to seek a therapist and medication for that issue since it seems to be ongoing. Pressuring and harassing me to have sex with you after you talk down to me all day is not working. Plus, it's late and I really need to get some rest for tomorrow," I responded.

Jon immediately got angry and began tossing and turning in the bed, pulling the covers off of me. "You should be horny every night and ready to have sex!" Jon yelled in my ear, causing me to cringe.

"Why would I feel like that when you argue with me all the time? Why would I be attracted to someone who doesn't appreciate me and degrades me every chance they get?" I inquired. "You're the only person I know who thinks I'm the worst person ever."

"So, we are back to the old ways now!? Just shut up; you're just an asshole! You're just intentionally withholding!" Jon muttered.

I saw red and my blood started boiling. After suppressing my emotions for so many years, I snapped. As I laid on my left side with my back to him, I swung my right arm behind me, hitting him in the chest while yelling, "STOP!"

At that moment, he became the victim. I immediately became ashamed of what I had done. I had lost control and that was not my character. Jon had pushed me to my breaking point. *I can't believe I let him get to me after all of these years.*

"So, you're HITTING me now? I can't believe you just hit me," Jon said. "I'm just trying to love you and you're being mean to me." ▶

"I apologize for hitting you. I was wrong for doing that," I said, getting out of bed, grabbing my pillow, and walking upstairs to sleep in Max's bed for the night.

> **Reactive Abuse**: When a person has been abused emotionally or physically over time, the brain is impaired by the stress of the trauma. The connection between the "rational" aspects of the brain and the emotive aspects is broken. After periods of prolonged abuse, feelings that have been invalidated, denied, and ignored will build up, causing the victim to explode with little or no warning. Victims can only withhold feelings for so long. Being out of control scares the victim and is embarrassing. It can trigger self-criticism, self-loathing, and self-attack through possible suicide attempts. Everyone wants to be validated, cherished, and nurtured. However, after forgoing these feelings for so long, the victim doesn't realize how much those components are needed until they are exhausted, ill, overwhelmed, or completely beyond their ability to cope. The abuser, on the other hand, will use the victim's reaction to show how irrational the victim is during the abuser's smear campaign.

The next day, I was still embarrassed by my behavior from the night before. I sat Jon down for a talk in our bedroom to discuss our future. "Jon, I'd like to ask that you move out of the home for a little bit in order for us to re-evaluate our marriage. I'm still dealing with the aftermath of the affair, and I don't like the person I've become in the meantime. I think we need some time apart."

Jon looked down at the bed, thinking for a moment, caught off guard by my request. "Well, how long do you need?" Jon asked.

"I'm not putting a time table on this. However long it takes. I can't think with you in the house constantly nagging. If you are not willing to stay at your parents' house for a little while, then I'll move out."

Jon's face lit up in surprise as he looked at me. "Ok, ok, I'll talk to Mom and Dad and see if it's ok if I stay with them for a little bit."

That night Jon stayed at their house overnight and returned in the morning so to not alert the kids. He did this for a week before returning home permanently. It was the most peaceful sleep I had in the home in years. I could relax without being in fear or constantly nagged at night. The night he refused to leave to spend the night at his parents' house, he sat down with me to discuss his feelings.

"I don't want to stay with my parents any longer. Remember, the therapist said we need to be together to work out our issues, not apart. Can't you just think and clear your head with me here?" ▶

I suddenly became frustrated and stood near the window in the bedroom; my safe place when I was unsure of Jon's reactions. "No, I can't. You don't give me time to think. You're always over my shoulder and accusing me of cheating and when you're not doing that, you're just downright mean."

Jon ignored my reasons for not wanting him there, completely invalidating my feelings. "I'm not leaving," Jon replied with a smug look on his face. "I don't like being away from home. I'll get help and I promise I'll do better." ▶

Another promise. By that time, we were on the one-millionth promise from Jon to change his behavior. Jon always promised to change, but change was never permanent. We always ended up right back where we started within days of his so-called "change".

**Future Faking:** *In the hands of a skilled manipulator, future faking preys on your dreams and goals in order to fabricate a* *possible future so that they can string you along in the now. These promises are destined to be broken, and can be seen as a form of overpromising and under-delivering.)*

Everything wrong continued to be my fault and the late-night rants and name-calling continued. Our conversation continued for thirty more minutes until I gave up trying to rationalize and reason with him.

"Fine, I'll start looking for places to stay," I replied. I grabbed my nightclothes and went into the bathroom to take a shower, while Jon sat there staring at the carpet, thinking about what I said. When I emerged from the bathroom, he went in behind me and began running a bath. I began texting Angela to tell her what occurred.

*"Girl...I am DONE. It's too much...I'm just so tired of living like this with Jon and his behavior. I asked him to move out and he refused. He stayed at his parents' house for a week, but only went down at night. He constantly wants to "talk". In one of our conversations, I told him he's put our entire family through drama for fifteen years because he refused to seek help. All that nonsense he put Elijah through...he did this and just needs to accept the consequences. He wanted to stay in the house in another room as an alternative. I said "NO. Tried that last time and you were absolutely horrible to me. I need peace of mind." He says he was in a different place last time and made a mistake that he continues to apologize for. I said "Yep and those memories still remain, regardless of the numerous apologies. I said the compounding effect of your behavior has brought us to where we are today. I am mentally tired and done with all of this craziness. I actually want to enjoy the rest of my life without drama."*

I finished texting with Angela and watched TV for a little bit before falling asleep. Jon stayed in the tub until the early morning hours as usual, drinking vodka. He got out at 3 a.m., came into the bedroom and asked if I was asleep. I didn't say a word.

The next day, Jon made two appointments with a therapist for the beginning and end of the week. For the rest of the week, he subjected me to his "talks" at night to get me to change my mind about leaving. I called Marie a week later on my drive home from work to catch her up on what was going on.

"How's it going? Marie asked.

"Lots of talks. It's so uncomfortable in the home. He's been seeing a new therapist since last week. The therapist gave him some tools to work on how he sees things. He won't leave me alone to think about things. He always wants to "talk" and force me into changing my decision."

"Tell him you are not available to talk and need time for quiet. Explain this is why you want a divorce; there is no mental space for you in your home. Your mind cannot rest and this weighs on you physically. And, you see that he will never respect your request to SHUT UP!" Marie said.

"I have and it makes no difference. He's still trying to convince me to stay and I'm still saying "NO." I told him it would not be beneficial to his healing in my current state of mind. He said he realizes how I felt when he told me he wanted to leave three years ago," I replied.

"You know he's going to nag you."

"Yeah, I know. The therapist told him he has to consciously work on controlling his behavior."

"When he asks you to stay, just tell him, "This is what I am talking about and why I want to leave! You don't value how I feel and what keeps me sane so I can support our family. You only think about what will work for you and the rest of us have to be hostage to your happiness!"

"Yep, that's true! He's thinking about what he wants and what's beneficial for him," I responded.

"Always!"

"I told him it was unfortunate that we had to get to this point for him to actually take things seriously and seek help. Now, all of a sudden, he wants to open up about Tasha and how much he regrets how bad he treated me during that time. He claims he thinks about it every day. If he thought about that every day, then he wouldn't continue to try to control me all of the time with his jealousy and constantly talking down to me."

"It's easy to say that now. He sure didn't act like he felt bad when you found out. Well, he has the rest of his life to keep thinking about it, WITHOUT YOU," Marie quipped.

"Yep, he didn't act like it at all."

"I can tell it's weighing on you, keep your mind on the peace you have waited on," Marie said.

"I sure will. I'm almost home so I'll chat with you later."

After I got home, I walked into the kitchen and noticed that I had received texts from Jon's mom, trying to convince me to stay with Jon. He obviously brought her into the situation to be his ally.

From his mom:

*"Happy Anniversary, honey! Fifteen years and a beautiful family is worth saving now, just as it was a few years ago. We love you and surely hope if there's anything you need to talk to either of us about, you'll stop down like you did last time. We just love you both so much and can't bear to see the hurt."*

My response:

"Yes, there has been a lot of hurt. I should have never taken Jon back three years ago when he had the affair. I'm sure he didn't tell you he continued to try to speak to and see the woman after he claimed he wanted to reconcile. I told Jon for years to get help and he refused. You have no idea what my kids and I have lived through with him. I am not happy; I have horrible memories of the last fifteen years and I just want a break and stress-free life."

Jon's mom:

"He was wrong, I know at the time. But I also remember how upset you were that you might be splitting up. You came to me a lot and said how much you didn't want it to be over. And I wish you would have come to me because I would have really made him understand how much he was being so wrong. I think the OCD [Obsessive Compulsive Disorder] runs a little in all of our family and I'm really sorry he talked so wrongly to you. ▶ But I don't know what he's done to the kids. Can you clear it up for me? That's just so unlike him to hurt Max or Jasmine. I had hoped he was getting along better lately with Elijah. Are you talking about some years in the past? I know he blames himself so much and is trying so hard to better himself for you. He is getting medication and therapy and is just miserable at the thought of your family splitting up and him being without you.

I am not apologizing for him; I just know he's trying so hard. It's not too late if he genuinely changes for you, is it? Please don't take offense, I sure am not meaning any. I just didn't know he was hurting the kids and just want to know what he's doing, so I can help him understand to stop. I love all of you and want to help both of you if he's wrong. You deserve that. Please let me know how I can help...my heart is breaking for all of you."

My response:

*"The instance I'm referring to about the woman was after she quit her job. Jon was sending her, her family, and friends emails all the way up until he left for Germany that December. His problem is more than OCD. I know he's trying and I really am glad he's finally getting help. He's raged numerous times at Max, and Jasmine has witnessed him going out of bounds with Elijah multiple times when they were both young. She used to call me at work and ask me to come home. He typically feels bad after, but he continued to behave that way. There are only so many "I'm sorry" you can give a person until they just get numb. He's getting help now and that's great, but he could have saved everyone distress if he had done that a lot sooner."*

Jon's mom:

*"I agree with you wholeheartedly and wish he'd gotten help so much earlier. Maybe you scared him into it, whatever it took. But I'm a firm believer in not saying "too little too late". It's a lot, and I don't believe it's too late. He's determined and really wants to change his behavior. He's never told me he's wrong before. As far as the kids being scared before, I understand that he was wrong there too, but I think it was far in the past and they hopefully aren't afraid of him now. Know that both of you have hurt each other in various ways. You are quieter and deal with things differently than someone coming from a noisy, boisterous family. But sometimes both can hurt either by ignoring someone or being too loud. I'm not saying one is ok and one isn't, I'm just saying that you both have hurt each other in different ways and we just sincerely want you to be happy. Marriage is for better or for worse and takes a whole lot of "bending" to work.*

*Sometimes you're about at your breaking point, but need to take a step in the right direction if it's offered. Try to forget*

> *what's happened in the past and grab the happiness that can come; bring baby steps, but in the right direction. I need a lot more attention sometimes. I get hurt if someone won't speak to me or ignores me. Jon has some of that, too. You're good people who just need to go back to the drawing board. People can change. Can you forget the past; don't let it cloud your future, and trust that it will be a permanent change? We love you and believe you can."* ▶

Jon's mom stopped texting after that and so did I. She was more concerned about herself and the family breaking up than what the kids and I were enduring in the home. I put my things on the dining room table and began preparing dinner before planning Elijah and Jasmine's graduation party. It was one week before the party and I needed to plan and prepare.

## THE FLYING MONKEY

My parents, family, and friends drove down from Delaware for the graduation party to celebrate Elijah's graduation from high school and Jasmine's graduation from middle school. We celebrated with a backyard cookout. Jon was still reeling from our most recent conversation about me leaving, so he moped around most of the day at the party barely communicating with people who spoke to him. His mom kept chasing him around asking him if he was okay and what she could do to ease his pain. Her behavior was so obvious that my friends began asking me if she always acted like that.

Toward the end of the party, Marie got ready to leave and mentioned she was having problems with her truck. Jon offered to walk her out. I assumed he was going to help her with her issue and thought nothing of it. I gave her a hug goodbye and went back to the party. As soon as Marie got home, she called me. She wanted to tell me what was said during her conversation with Jon. Apparently, instead of helping her with her truck, Jon wanted to ask her a question and it stay private between the two of them.

When Marie said she couldn't promise that she wouldn't tell me what was discussed, he declined to ask her his question. ▶ He never once offered to help her with her truck and walked back into the party when he didn't receive the response he was seeking.

"I think he was going to ask me if you were seeing someone else." Marie stated.

"I wouldn't be surprised, he asked me last night not to make the mistake he did and try to see someone else to fulfill a need."

"Yeah, I could tell by the way he was setting up the question that he was going to ask me if you have someone else. I offered to let him ask me, but he declined. He got scared... he didn't even say bye," Marie said. "I looked up and he was gone."

"He's back to saying 'We've both made mistakes during the marriage' yet, he was the one who made the major one, was horrible to me during that time, and continued to treat me badly thereafter," I replied. "But I'm just supposed to forget it all and have sympathy. I told him I cleaned the slate when he said that he wanted to reconcile — and later found out he was still chasing her. I told him that he started at point zero again. Then, he continued to be a horrible person to me, so he has no leg to stand on."

"He can't give you a break or air to breathe."

"Not at all, which has always been an issue, so 'How am I supposed to believe you've changed?' He always claims he will change, but never does!"

I paused for a moment and then decided to get back to the party. "Well, let me get back to the party. We will chat later."

Later that night, Jon and I talked and he, once again, tried to convince me to stay and keep the family together to not disrupt the kid's lives. He wrote me a letter professing his love:

> "Please just love me again. Be free, start over, and just enjoy our love. All I want is to make you feel loved. I'm so sad and just want us to love each other beyond measure. Please love me again." ▶

I read the letter and put it in my dresser drawer with the rest of the, *"I'm sorry I'll do better,"* collection. I still didn't trust that he would ever change after receiving numerous promises over the years to treat me better and nothing ever came to fruition. This was a letter-writing tactic he began several years earlier and always employed as an attempt at "reconciliation" or apology as it was his stab at being sincere and remorseful.

## DESPERATE TIMES CALL FOR DESPERATE MEASURES

Jon's new therapist was an African American male. He went through four sessions before inviting me to one of them, per his therapist's request. We met at the therapist's office after work; Jon sat down on the couch while I sat in the chair across from him.

"Thank you for coming, Mrs. McAdams. I've been working with your husband for four sessions now and we thought it was time to bring you in. Jon realizes he has a problem and we've been proactively working on rectifying it."

I looked over at the therapist, not saying a word, wondering how Jon working on his issues was going to be any different than the thousand times he's claimed to work on them before.

"Do you think you can give him another chance, Mrs. McAdams? He said he is fully committed to making the marriage work? The therapist said. "The affair was a mistake and he regrets it."

I sat there expressionless looking at the therapist, not saying a word. *I see Jon has fooled you into thinking he's this great person just like he did the prior therapists.* ▶ I collected my thoughts for a moment prior to speaking. I looked down at my shoes and back up at the therapist. "I'm really just tired and done. It's so much more than the affair. It's how he treated me prior to, during, and after the affair. I'm so DONE with the cycles," I said, tearing up and slightly shaking. Then, my heart started to pound, my palms became sweaty, and my stomach began to toss and turn as I got increasingly uncomfortable with the conversation.

"No one understands how badly he's treated me. Everyone just wants me to quickly forget and move on from it, but nothing ever changes," I sternly told the therapist.

"I understand and so does he. He's really trying hard and just wants you to give him another chance. Do you think you can move on from the affair?"

Feeling defeated, once again, I decided to answer his question after realizing he was more on Jon's side than interested in determining the root cause of our marital discord.

"I'm not promising anything," I sniffled while trying to control myself from having a meltdown.

At that moment, Jon broke down crying, professing his love for me. ▶I just stared at him thinking, *where did that come from,* while the therapist consoled him, playing into Jon's hands.

By the time he calmed down, the session ended. We discussed the three of us getting back together at a later date to see how things were going prior to leaving.

We met with Jon's therapist a couple more times before I gave in and agreed to give Jon one more chance, based on the therapist's promise that he would continue to work with Jon and help with his behavior.

Three months later, nothing had changed in the marriage. Jon stopped seeing the therapist and his paranoia and jealousy got worse. School started back up for the kids. Elijah went off to ECU, Jasmine began high school and getting ready for another travel volleyball season, and Max was now in the fourth grade.

## THE EVERYDAY NIGHTMARE

Jon began collecting "so-called" evidence and asking leading questions to try to catch me in lies. His "so-called" evidence was never based on facts, but assumptions. He reviewed my phone records daily to see who was texting and calling my phone, and he listened to all of my phone conversations and commented on them when I hung up. I got so sick of it that I began to call people when I wasn't home or around him.

He also continued making comments on the number of texts I received in a day, annoyed if my texting conversation lasted longer than five seconds. I was living a nightmare, but I was trying to push through to keep the family intact and satisfy everyone except myself; sacrificing my own self-worth and happiness to keep a family unit.

One Saturday, I was invited to a cookout by a co-worker. I invited Jon to tag along, although I knew Jon's social awkwardness would be an issue. It was easier to just invite him to social gatherings I was invited to than to endure his accusations of cheating. It was a beautiful clear and sunny day when we arrived at the party. I was excited to get out and socialize with people other than Jon and his family.

I introduced Jon to all of my co-workers and we met their

significant others; we played games, ate great food, and had casual conversation. I mainly had the conversations while Jon sat there uncomfortably glaring at everyone off to the side. After three hours, we left the party. I could tell by Jon's quiet demeanor and the intense look on his face, he had an issue with something that occurred at the party.

As we got into the car to drive home, Jon began to question me about a particular co-worker. *Great, here we go again...*

"I noticed you looking at Tim all night," Jon said.

"What *are you* talking about, Jon?"

"He was staring at you too, checking you out. Just let me know if you want him and I'll let you move on."

"What are you even talking about Jon? I'm so confused right now," I replied.

"You know you want Tim. You were talking to him all afternoon, laughing and joking around," he said.

"Jon, I spoke to everyone just like I do during the day at work. You are so delusional," I said, shaking my head.

"I'll understand if you want to be with him. He's a good-looking guy. Just let me know so I can move on," Jon muttered.

I knew it was useless to even continue the conversation; therefore, I stopped engaging. We sat in silence for the rest of the ride home while Jon stewed in his own ignorance. Later that night while lying in bed, Tim became the focus of Jon's nightly rant, rehashing everything said in the car and more — a rant that lasted two hours with me barely saying a word. By the next day, he was fine and dropped the discussion.

## EVERYONE AND ANYONE IS A THREAT

As a part of getting my body back on track to heal from the stress I was enduring, I started regularly going to exercise classes. I attend two Total Resistance Exercise (TRX) classes during the week and a high intensity interval training (HIIT) class on Saturdays.

Sometimes, Jasmine would tag along with me on Saturdays and we'd grab smoothies after at the coffee shop on the way home. It was a great escape for me and helped with my mental stability. My mental break from living in insanity. However, one night, Jon asked to tag along to a TRX class. I knew the night was not going to go well after he asked to go. Not only was he going to ruin my relaxation time, but he was going to create some scenario in his head that was void of reality. I couldn't tell him I didn't want him to go because that would be perceived as me cheating instead of attending class. Therefore, I gave in and agreed to him tagging along.

We drove to the town Wellness center and walked into the class. There were seven people there and we all scrambled to find the perfect spot. Jon, of course, chose to stand behind me so he could watch everyone around me. The class was taught by a young, fit African American male in his mid-thirties with dark curly hair, a friend of Jon's brother. As we were going through the various exercises, I noticed the intense look on Jon's face in the mirror and how he kept staring at the instructor. I knew then that I was going to hear about it once the class was over. Instead of focusing on the proper form for performing the exercises, Jon focused on the instructor.

When class ended, Jon glared at the instructor as I put the weights I used during class away. As we began walking to the car, Jon started slinging his irrational thoughts at me.

"I saw the instructor looking at you the entire class. He kept hitting on you with his jokes; I didn't find them funny," Jon said.

"Paul is happily married with children, Jon. You sound ridiculous. I knew bringing you to this class was going to be a mistake. You always think someone is cheating because of your own guilty conscience," I stated.

"He wants you. I know men and how they think." ▶

I shook my head in disgust. It was useless trying to rationalize with Jon. He sat silent for the rest of the ride home. Once we arrived, he got his bottle of vodka ready for the evening while I showered. He spent three hours in the bathtub drinking into the night and came out ready to argue about the exercise instructor and demand sex. Our nightly routine ...

## MY LIVING NIGHTMARE

I typically called my cousin, John, on my drive home from work once or twice a week to catch up and see how he was doing. In one particular conversation, he mentioned my husband Jon called him.

"Jon called *you*? What did he say?" I asked.

Jon was not close to my cousin and in fact, had negative things to say about him all the time, so why would he call him? It was odd and uncanny.

"The person on the phone asked to speak to Michael. I told them they had the wrong number. Then, they asked who I was so I gave my full name and title. After that, they hung up," John said.

"Really," I responded, completely shocked by the series of events and trying to determine if my cousin was playing or if he was serious.

"When I looked at my caller ID, it popped up as Jon's work number," he said.

"How did you know it was his work number?"

"It was a 919 area code and the receptionist answered the phone with his company name when I called back."

"What!? He has really lost his mind. He's resorted to calling back numbers on the phone bill now?!"

I was livid. The fact that Jon called my cousin meant he was trolling the phone bill and calling back numbers to see who they belonged to. As much as I wanted to question Jon about his behavior, I never said a word. I kept the information to myself to store for later.

I arrived home around 6 p.m. after picking up Jasmine from school and started preparing to go out on my scheduled date with Jon. In an effort to keep somewhat of a connection in my marriage, Jon and I went on dates every Friday night to the local TGI Fridays.

Although my disdain for Jon grew every day we were together, I still felt obligated to try to make the marriage work. Making the marriage work was the direction his mother, my mother and Jon kept telling me was best for the children.

Jon loved TGI Fridays since the waitress gave him extra Vodka and Cranberry drinks free of charge. When you down ten plus drinks per setting, that begins to add up cost-wise. The night started out calm; we talked about our workdays and what was going on at our respective jobs with periods of silence after the small talk was out of the way. After Jon's seventh drink, he tensed up in frustration and his demeanor began to change. We sat and watched the basketball game playing above the bar for about ten minutes while Jon downed two more drinks.

"So where did you go last month that required you to take the toll road," Jon asked.

"The toll road, what *are you* talking about? I don't keep track of every place I've gone in the last month."

"The toll bill showed you were on the toll road near your boss' house. Did you go see him?" Jon inquired.

I was confused. Jon was stalking my boss due to his irrational thinking. "Are you serious, Jon? How many times do I have to tell you I'm not seeing my boss? I can't believe you looked up his address!" I scoffed.

"You're so secretive. I don't know what you do in your life. You barely texted or called me throughout the week during the workday, yet you went out to dinner and drinks with your co-workers," Jon replied, smirking.

"Yes, we had a vendor in town this week and it is customary for us to do a dinner during their visit. We've gone over this a million times. I'm still confused by why that's an issue."

I grabbed my tea to take a sip, frustrated by the conversation. The waitress stopped by to refill my glass and asked Jon if he wanted another Vodka and Cranberry to which he replied "yes."

"As far as going out with co-workers after work, that is something my boss established for team building. We are a new team and need to get to know each other outside of the day-to-day grind. Again, something I've gone over with you a million times. Other than that, I go to work, pick up kids, and come home. What more do you want from me to prove I'm not cheating? I can't even get my hair done once a month without you complaining about watching your own kids, who don't even need you to entertain them, yet you complain you are chained to the house, entertaining kids when I choose to get my hair done," I replied.

I might as well have been talking to a wall. Jon was not listening to a word I was saying. He kept drinking his Vodka and Cranberry looking at basketball while I spoke.

"Your friends know more about you than I do," Jon mumbled.

"My friends?" I questioned. "I barely see my friends because it makes *you* uncomfortable. Just because I'm maintaining my friendships shouldn't be a threat to you."

By this time, Jon was on his eleventh drink. His face was red and flushed. His eyes were glossy and he looked at me with an empty stare. "You're such an asshole," Jon condemned. "Your mom is an asshole and you're a replica of her." ▶

Jon was clearly intoxicated and I had reached my mental limit.

"Really, Jon? I'm leaving. You can find your own ride home," I snapped.

I grabbed the truck keys, walked to the truck, and drove back home, leaving Jon at the restaurant. Jon arrived home an hour later, took off his clothes, and went to bed. He woke up the next morning as if nothing happened and never apologized for his behavior the night before. I told Jon he had a drinking problem. He denied it and told me if I just paid more attention to him, he would be fine. *How much attention and validation does a grown man need to feel good about himself? Why is it my job to make him feel good about himself? I'm not his mother.*

## YOU'RE TOXIC

I called my divorce lawyer the next week and set up an appointment. When I met with the lawyer, she laid out my options similar to our discussion three years prior. She informed me that Jon would get worse before he got better and so far, I was seeing that. She also informed me that if Jon didn't leave the house on his own, I could file a protective order against him. I could use the emotional abuse clause with evidence gathered from his treatment of me in 2014 during his infidelity.

I found that interesting because in 2014 when I asked to get a protective order, she said I couldn't. I left the lawyer's office contemplating what to do next. I called Marie and updated her.

"Hey, I just left the lawyer's office. Jon called me an asshole this weekend and my mom one, too, while drunk at TGI Fridays."

"What! He wouldn't appreciate you calling his parents' names!"

"Not at all."

"Yes, he clearly has issues! Does he think this is normal?" Marie inquired.

"And he has yet to apologize. He thinks he's normal and I have issues."

"And you are supposed to forget about this and be lovey-dovey?"

"Yep," I replied.

"What did the lawyer say?"

"She told me I could file a protective order to get him out of the house if he wouldn't leave on his own, but I don't know if I want to be that drastic. I'd like to try to have a calm conversation about it."

"You know you have the upper hand with his past infidelity, right?" Marie said.

"I think my statute of limitations is over, but I guess it's still history."

"Yes, it still happened and he never sought a regular counseling program for healing the marriage nor to address the issues that he claims drove him to infidelity; therefore, his behavior is oppressive and makes you incompatible. He has no interest in improving the husband-and-wife part as long as he has to change," Marie stated.

"Yep, because he's perfect and I'm not. I think I would have to move out, as opposed to him. I know he will refuse, too," I replied.

"As a result of the infidelity, he was introduced to alcohol. He suffers from undiagnosed behavioral issues. The aftermath of the infidelity has been painful; he complicated things by adding alcohol abuse and he has NO accountability. I don't see why you feel you don't have grounds for divorce... the aftermath alone is toxic to your well-being and he thinks your mom is an asshole? Takes one to know one."

"It's very toxic. I stay stressed." I responded.

"And you've lost weight. It's not healthy."

"I need to find a place to rent; that's been hard to find someplace I can afford with at least three bedrooms and still pay my other bills."

"I know your heart is in the right place, but I don't want this to take years off your life."

"It's already taken years off, I'm sure."

"Think it through," Marie said.

The truth was, I had thought it through again and again and still found myself stuck in a relationship I couldn't escape. I felt financially strapped with Jon seeing all of the money that came in and out of our joint bank account. There was no real way for me to safely stash funds; he enjoyed spending my paychecks, claiming all of his money went towards gas while driving Max to and from school. Every night for a week, I reviewed my finances, trying to find a way out looking for loopholes, and going through the motions at home until I could get a solid plan in place.

I found myself at a crossroads after trying to figure out things on my own for a month. I decided to work at Marie's house one Friday, to get her insight and have her look over my finances. I sat down at her kitchen table and pulled up my laptop. "I need a solid plan before I say anything to Jon."

"You already know what he's going to want... joint custody so he doesn't have to pay child support."

"Right... and Jasmine should be able to choose if she wants to go back and forth. Jasmine is not as close to him as she used to be."

Marie pulled out her laptop and began typing. "Ok, I have some ideas on how you go about it."

"What ideas do you have?" I asked, looking over at her.

"Are you planning to start over from scratch? With furniture and personal items? If needed?"

"I think I'm going to have to, depending on how we divide things up."

"Stepping away easily would work best."

I nodded my head in agreement.

"If you have a friend you can live with or do a month-to-month furnished place initially; that would give this time to digest with him."

"I need space for the kids to stay."

"Maybe their home stays where it is, initially. Unless you are ready to buy them furniture. You know Jon will get in the way of making another home for them."

"Oh, for sure," I said.

"It would be best if he moved in with his parents."

"Yes, but we tried that and that didn't work."

"And I know you don't want to stay there. How about buying a foreclosed house?"

"I'd like to rent for a year and then buy. Pay some things off. I was looking at townhouses."

"Any thoughts on how to tell Jon? This will help us determine the living arrangement."

"I will tell him this is not working and we are not making each other happy, so it's best to go our separate ways."

"Do you need to go back alone to one of the counselors who met Jon, to see what the best approach is and plan for his personality type? You know he's unstable."

"I have to think about that one. Usually, he would be upset I brought stuff up there and not at home."

"You couldn't bring it up at home! He was too busy whining to listen," Marie stated.

"That's true," I said, shaking my head in agreement.

"Go by yourself to the counselor. Jon seems to be the type you have to bulldoze. He's not going to be reasonable."

"Nope, not at all."

"You have to ambush him with the news and be in control from the beginning so he has no wiggle room. You have to stand your ground."

"Right, which is why I was thinking of moving out. Otherwise, he will refuse, and just make the entire process difficult."

"Unless you have something to hold over his head, that forces him out."

"I have nothing."

"Maybe it's making a deal with him upfront... he's mentally abusive."

"Big time."

"You have a string of text messages to show that."

"I sure do. It still should be in an email to the lawyer as well."

"Record his drunken rants."

"I also still have my diary from last time," I replied.

"Good. Keep track of all of your evidence for later."

"I still have the issue of being able to move out now. I just don't see it in the finances and will have to wait until my next bonus, once again. At least with the next bonus, we will pay down another joint bill; something I don't have to worry about splitting with him once I leave."

Maria and I chatted for another hour before I packed up to head home. My next bonus wasn't until March of the following year, five months away. I had to find the strength within myself to get through the next few months with as little conflict as possible. At least now I had a plan and a vision to get out; pay down as much debt as possible to get to my end goal.

*Focus on the end goal,* I kept telling myself.

## REFLECTION

Jon's mother continued to be an enabler of Jon's bad behavior. As a skilled psychological manipulator in her own right, she attempted to gaslight me into thinking her son's behavior was forgivable and he deserved another chance, no matter how bad he treated me. The narcissistic mother idealizes her son and puts him up on a pedestal. By the time he is a teen, she resents her son for not pleasing her as he used to, which in turn, creates resentment in him. His defense mechanism is to keep building up his ego as a facade that covers deep insecurity and angst.

Just as Jon had pulled me into his dispute with his "best friend" over pulling back his invitation for him to be the best man at the wedding, he had his mother text me to convince me to stay in the marriage. He got an ally to work for him - Otherwise known as a "flying monkey" in the narcissist's playbook. The narcissist may use their flying monkeys as monkey in the middle, carrying information from party to party. The flying monkey may use gaslighting tactics, open aggression, and guilt-tripping in order to make another person feel bad and weak, whilst shoring up the narcissist. And they're often involved in pleading the case of the narcissist.

Furthermore, an abused brain is an impaired brain. My impaired brain kept me from leaving my abuser, feeling as if I was trapped in my situation. My cognitive dissonance led me to minimize the severity of the trauma I was experiencing as a coping mechanism. I still couldn't rationalize in my brain that the person I married was a pathological abuser. For years, I blamed myself for Jon's behavior and did everything in my power to please him. It was becoming more and more apparent that the problem wasn't me. It was Jon.

*Chapter 8*

# THE WALLS COME TUMBLING DOWN

I was mentally and physically deteriorating in my marriage at the start of the new year. My days and nights continued to be long and stressful, trying to prepare for my escape from Jon. It seemed like it was going to take forever to get into a financial position to leave. I was becoming increasingly discouraged day by day. I asked my Mom about giving me Dad's car and selling mine to have one less debt to pay. Dad was already considering buying a new one, so it was great timing. Unfortunately, she said he wasn't ready to give up his car, putting me back at square one.

Jon continued to drink heavily at night in the bathtub and berate me all night long after he got out. I tried recording him like the lawyer suggested, but it was just too hard to get the phone setup without him figuring out what I was doing and too risky for me in his drunken stupor. Jon had never been physical with me, but his sudden escalation to alcohol abuse, after claiming for years he never drank, indicated he was capable of anything.

I was beginning to fear closing my eyes at night. I really did not feel safe in my own home and worried about the safety of my children.

Marie called me on my way home from work to see how the new year was treating me. It was the day after an explosive weekend with Jon. "Happy New Year!"

"I'm done with Jon. The weekend was awful. Another drunken-filled weekend of bashing me. He cornered me in the bedroom this morning to ask where my head was. Of course, he apologized and was embarrassed by his behavior over the weekend."

"What, not again..."

"Yep, I told him I was done. He asked about counseling and kept wanting to talk through stuff, but I'm done. He left the house in the middle of the night; I'm assuming to go to his brother's house."

"Did you ask him to leave?

"Nope, he left on his own."

"Yeah, he has to go through his emotional roller coaster."

"As long as he lets me get some sleep tonight, I'm fine with him processing."

"Of course, he's sorry for everything he's ever done... I hear violins," Marie said sarcastically.

"He said he thought things were going well. Yeah, in his mind. How can things be going well when you consistently call me a bad mother and wife and nonstop complain about a trip I took to visit my girlfriend two years ago?"

"It's always a whirlwind."

"Always... never stops. That's what I told him."

"He seemed shocked?" Marie asked.

"Of course! How dare I want to leave him. He's so great," I said, rolling my eyes. "I made one vital error when I reviewed my finances to move out... I forgot to add in my car payment. Ugh. I can see now why they say "it's cheaper to keep her." I can't afford a decent place to live nor be able to travel to see Jasmine play volleyball. I have got to get out from underneath this debt!"

"Don't fret. If you only look at the face value of math, yes, but the value of sanity is priceless. You might have to refinance your car and lower the payments or sell it and get a cheaper one. You could dive into your retirement a little and borrow from yourself."

"I looked at retirement and they only let you take out one loan at a time. I took one out to cover the lawyer when Jon had his affair. I'll have to figure something out."

Later, I arrived at Jasmine's school to pick her up and head home to an apologetic Jon. He asked if we could talk in the bedroom. When I sat down on the bed, Jon began to beg me not to leave and apologized for everything wrong in the marriage. I looked at him without saying a word. *How many times was he going to apologize for bad behavior and not change?* His apologies at this point sounded like broken records and his words bounced off of me like ping pong balls hitting a ping pong table.

Jon did straighten up after our discussion and briefly gave up alcohol. We were doing great, and I no longer felt stressed. I actually thought we were finally on the road to a "normal" relationship. My measure of "normal" at this point was him being helpful and supportive without belittling or demeaning me when I didn't oblige to his wants. I began to relax, let down my guard, and reconsider leaving the marriage. However, good times were always temporary with Jon and in the back of my mind, I was waiting for the other shoe to drop.

It finally did right after Valentine's Day.

## THE LOVE BOMB EXPLODES

I was scheduled to go on a work trip to a national conference in Las Vegas, NV. I talked it over with Jon when I was first informed a month prior, and he was fine with me going. Now, he had a problem with it.

"Is your boss going on your *work* trip?"

"Yes, he's going."

Jon turned red and started to become angry with his brows furrowed. "Are you on the same flight?"

"Yes."

Jon began biting his lip and glaring at the wall. "I don't think you should go," he snapped.

"What? It's a work trip. Are you serious?"

"Yes, I'm not comfortable with you going. It's Sin City. Anything can happen. Someone is going to slip something in one of your drinks and assault you."

I looked at Jon confused. *Is he serious? Someone is going to slip something in my drink?* "I'll be with co-workers, Jon."

"Well, I'm not comfortable, so you shouldn't go. I don't think it's a good time for you to travel. You should be home with your spouse and children instead of Sin City."

I stared at Jon, perplexed, wondering if he was going to change his mind. When I realized he was not, I became frustrated with his selfish attitude and lack of concern for my need to travel for work.

"Fine! I'll inform my boss on Monday." *He traveled off and on for a year, sleeping with his co-worker and now he wants to hinder my career by telling me I can't go on a work trip.*

I was furious. If I went on the trip against his wishes, he would make my life a living nightmare, constantly nagging me about leaving him and the kids to sleep with my boss. My life would be worse than it already was. I would never sleep or have peace in the home. I barely spoke to Jon the rest of the evening.

The next day, Marie called me on my way home from work. "Hey! Just checking in on you."

"It's rough, but I'm hanging in. I'm keeping an eye on my finances."

"I know last week was tough."

"This weekend was the hardest since I cancelled a work trip because of him and his mouth.

"WHAT?! This has gone too far!"

"Yes, I was supposed to go to Vegas for a conference. He kept talking about how we never had a discussion when we did."

"Why do you have to ask him if you can work?!," Marie yelled.

"He said I was going to Sin City and should be with my spouse. He said I was going to have a date rape drug slipped into my drink."

"Oh Lord."

"I know! Girl…"

"I don't see how you do it! He's messing with your job performance now! That's not good! Was the ticket purchased?"

"Yep."

"OMG. So, what did you tell your boss?"

"I couldn't go because my husband wasn't comfortable."

"What?! NO!" Marie yelled.

"I didn't know what else to say."

"And how about the ticket? Is Jon going to pay for that? This is career limiting. We need to do damage control."

"Of course not! He has no funds."

"I would have told them there was an unexpected family urgency."

"That's a good one… I didn't even think about that."

"It was! My husband is off his meds!"

I burst into laughter.

"I know that was so humiliating!! I am so sorry you are living through this. Does your mom know?"

"Yep, my mom was upset. She said he is ridiculous."

"I am upset too… he traveled for a year and you put up with it! While he had sex! This is so WRONG! We need to meet up asap! How can we get you off of this roller coaster? YOU DON'T DESERVE THIS!"

"I'm hoping we get money back on taxes to pay some stuff off. I just need to get ahead financially and GET OUT."

"You studied too hard for your degree and you have worked too hard for your career and extra hard as a female and double time as a black female to have him degrade you, humiliate you, and oppress you! He's destroying you... if you have to be broke and free, it's worth it! You are strong enough to rebuild you. He's so inconsiderate, selfish and insecure. It's time to start praying again. It's war time . . . spiritual war... and this time we can't let go of God until he moves. Ughhh! I don't like him!"

"Yep, my crazy life... I guess I'm just used to it." I said.

"I want the real you back!"

"Me too. I miss the old me. Alright, I'm pulling up in the driveway... gotta go."

In a turn of events, Jon was required to go to Germany for work to help on a critical project. He tried everything to get out of it, but his director still required him to go. His presence was crucial to the success of the project. Since he *had* to leave for a business trip, he backed off of keeping me from going on mine.

With the continued drinking on top of Jon's overall daily moodiness and tyrannical rants, I continued to walk on eggshells to avoid setting him off. He continued to ignore my words and hear what he wanted to hear. He misinterpreted everything and then accused and blamed me for everything. If I said, "That's ignorant," he would retort back, "Don't call me ignorant!" I couldn't say or do anything right.

By the spring, things started to get really hectic. My dad had to have heart surgery. I flew up to Delaware and stayed a few days to make sure he was healing properly. A few weeks later, Jasmine and I drove to Atlanta for a mother/daughter photo shoot. I was turning forty-five years old and wanted to commemorate it with photos. We had a great time in Atlanta — just the two of us. It gave us a chance to bond; something Jon tried his best to keep us from doing. She and I had grown closer since she started high school. I think she realized how much she missed out over the years on getting to know me without the influence of her father.

## THE END IS NEAR

Not long after our trip, Jasmine began to show signs of depression. She was too hard on herself. She thought she was terrible at volleyball, even though she was being heavily recruited by colleges. She also thought she was doing terribly in school, even though she was on the honor roll. She wanted to be perfect at everything she did. She cried on the volleyball court during a game and didn't talk to anyone for four days. She was juggling school and travel volleyball commitments; therefore, I thought she was having difficulty with stress. We took her to see her pediatrician who believed she was experiencing anxiety.

I texted Angela to update her on what was going on.

"Hey, Jasmine has anxiety. She said school was stressing her out. Now, I'm worried that breaking up the family will increase her anxiety issues. I really just want her to go ahead and commit to a college now so I know she's good."

"Hopefully she will feel better once school is out and she doesn't have so much going on."

"I hope so. She's sleeping better with the help of melatonin. We're also looking at going to a Yoga or Pilates class. It would be good for us both. Jon is still Jon, of course. Last weekend he flipped out. Brought up old stuff like my girl trips; he complained about me not posting about him on Facebook, he complained about me taking time to get my hair and nails done. He complained about me not spending enough time with him. All signs of a person whose mind is not right..."

"You only get your hair and nails done once a month, right?" Angela inquired.

"Yep. He complains about having to "entertain" the grown children while I'm gone. To which my reply is always, that's a choice to entertain. They're not babies. Jasmine is fine doing her own thing. Max is fine, too. Jon chooses to be their only source of entertainment 24/7. Then complains he never has a break. I was accused of being a bad mom because I don't believe in that philosophy. I'm the weird one and my parents. We are cold-hearted people with no feelings."

"Girl, I don't see how you've taken it this long!

"I'm used to it after all of these years. I'm still desperately trying to find a way out... Gotta go... here's Jon."

I immediately put my phone back in my purse before Jon had the chance to complain about me texting.

In early summer, the same weekend as our anniversary, my parents had a celebration for their 50th wedding anniversary. We drove to Delaware to be a part of the festivities. A few of my cousins decided to get together to have a cousin reunion, since we were all in town for the gala. Prior to the reunion, Jon and I went out to dinner at an Italian restaurant to celebrate our anniversary. I was less than thrilled to celebrate another anniversary.

Jon, of course, chastised me for not having the proper excitement level. I didn't feel there was anything to celebrate. *What were we celebrating... years of misery?* We got through dinner having minimal conversation and then headed off to the cousin reunion. I was excited to see everyone since I hadn't seen them all in so long — so much had happened in their lives since we last got together, including my own. We gathered at one of my cousin's restaurants to have appetizers and chit chat. Jon sat there for two hours never saying a word. My cousins occasionally looked over at him to see if he was going to engage in the conversation and then gave up. We continued to talk amongst ourselves, ignoring Jon as he glared at the end of the table. If they weren't family, Jon would have accused someone of trying to hit on me afterwards.

We celebrated my parents' anniversary the day after the cousin's reunion. The gala was a huge event with friends and family from all over the country. As usual, Jon sat there antisocial and socially awkward while I conversated with family and friends. I enjoyed being able to see and conversate with people I had not seen in years. It was a welcome change from my typical day to day with Jon. I felt alive and happy.

The next day, we woke up early to head back home. Jon and I began our drive back to North Carolina in silence with him seething, since I had chosen to nap during the drive instead of entertaining him with conversation — my assigned role during the trip.

"So, you're just going to sit over there and sleep the entire trip?"

"Yes, I am. I'm exhausted," I replied, leaning my head against the window and going back to sleep while Jon stewed and writhed in anger.

Later that summer, we made another trip to Delaware for a family reunion. It was nice to meet family I'd never met before and spend time with my cousins, while Jon spent the entire time playing on the swings with Max and the other children. He didn't even attempt to socialize with my family or get to know family members we had never met.

I found this interesting since he repeatedly chastised me for not socializing with his family on a regular basis. Not only did his family live in our neighborhood, but his mom required us to do family dinners every week at her house. She also felt she had the right to pop up at our house multiple times a week, unannounced to my dismay, as well as my children.

During Elijah's junior year of high school, vaping was the new thing among high school students and Elijah had picked up the habit. Jon found vaping paraphernalia in Elijah's room on two occasions in the past and went ballistic. Smoking in any shape or form was not allowed in the house and Elijah was aware of the rule. Jon had a tendency to snoop around in Elijah's room and through his bank accounts, but never did the same with Jasmine.

In early September, a hurricane was forecasted to roll through the coastline and cause so much damage that the colleges sent students home to their families mid-week, including Elijah.

As we sat on the couch watching the TV updates on the hurricane, Jon decided to snoop through Elijah's bank account. "He's wasting his money on games again! I can't believe he spends so much money on games and fast food."

"Why does it matter what he spends *his* money on? It's *his* money and why are you monitoring his bank account?"

Jon began feverishly typing on his phone enraged. "Stop putting me down!" he yelled, glaring at me with the death stare.

"What?" I said, confused.

"You're putting me down and making me feel dumb!"

"How? By questioning your interest in trolling Elijah's bank account?"

Jon got up and stormed off into the kitchen, stomping his feet so loudly a picture fell off the wall. He eventually calmed down, but started up with Elijah later that night when, a couple of hours later, Elijah came downstairs and asked Jon if he could have the Xbox console in his room. The Xbox had been sitting in the family room while Elijah was away at school.

Jon looked up at Elijah and said, "Yes, if you can assure me, you did not bring home any e-cigarettes," Jon said.

"I have nothing. You can search my bags."

Jon walked up the stairs to Elijah's room to perform his search and found e-cigarette paraphernalia in Elijah's backpack. Enraged, he came downstairs and shouted, "Why do you attempt to lie to me?" shaking around the paraphernalia he just found.

Elijah walked over to Jon to inspect the backpack. I walked over as well.

"What, I didn't even know it was in there?!" Elijah replied. I haven't used that backpack in weeks. Why would I let you search my bag if I knew I had something in there? That doesn't even make sense."

"Don't lie! You knew it was in there and tried to get away with it!" Jon yelled.

"I had no idea it was in there," Elijah responded, perplexed by Jon's reaction.

Jon began to berate Elijah in front of Max and me while Elijah tried to defend himself.

"Shut up and don't say another word!" Jon yelled in Elijah's face.

"You need to stop. You told him to stop talking, but you keep yelling at him. That's enough, Jon," I said.

Jon turned in my direction, pupils fully dilated with brows furrowed and leapt at me in anger. I was terrified, but determined to stand up for my son.

"You stay out of this," he snarled back, standing so close to me our noses almost touched.

A jolt of fear and anxiety flooded my body. Jon was well over two hundred and fifty pounds; a giant compared to my thin-framed one hundred and twenty-five-pound body. I looked over at Max who stood nearby in terror, watching the entire interaction.

"I don't understand why you're so angry," Elijah said.

Jon, nostrils flaring, quickly stomped over to Elijah and began forcefully shoving him toward the kitchen door, knocking Elijah off balance with every two handed shove squarely to the chest.

"GET OUT!" Jon roared as he shoved Elijah into the kitchen island, causing Elijah to yell out in pain.

Elijah's fell back onto the island with bulging eyes. He collected his composure and Jon shoved him five more times toward the kitchen door with such force that Elijah never fully regained his balance and fell to the floor.

"GET OUT OF MY HOUSE!" "GET OUT OF MY HOUSE!" "GET OUT OF MY HOUSE!" Jon repeatedly yelled at the top of his lungs. ▶

By this time, Max had run upstairs to get Jasmine. Jasmine emerged from her bedroom to see what was going on. She and Max watched the entire incident from the second-floor balcony, terrified and in shock.

"What's going on?" Jasmine asked.

Elijah's eyes darted from side to side as his lips trembled. He couldn't believe what was going on and neither could I. I was paralyzed with fear. I didn't know what to do or how to handle the situation. Jon had escalated to physical abuse and I feared I was the next target. Elijah kept his composure. He got out of Jon's clutches when Jasmine called out, pulling Jon back into reality. He then quickly ran upstairs to pack a bag.

As an adrenaline rush overcame my body, I got in Jon's face, "You crossed the line, Jon!" I fumed, shaking the entire time. "You had no right to put hands on my son like that!"

"You stay out of this!" Jon screamed in my face as saliva hit my eyelids.

"STOP IT or I'm calling the police!" I screamed in fear.

Elijah packed his bag and walked downstairs to leave the house.

"Where are you going?" Jasmine questioned.

"To Zack's house."

As soon as Elijah walked out of the door, Jon's denial began while everyone else was still trying to process what occurred. I was shaking, trying to calm myself down to de-escalate the situation.

"I didn't do anything wrong and I'm not apologizing. He can stay over there forever as far as I'm concerned. He's not allowed back into this house until he apologizes to me like a man," Jon quipped.

"Do you really think you are innocent? You shoved him multiple times and into the kitchen island. YOU WERE WRONG."

"I didn't shove him multiple times." Jon declared.

"YES, you did!"

Jon paused and stared off across the room. "So, I guess you're leaving me now?" Jon said sarcastically.

I didn't answer.

"Well... I wasn't trying to hurt him," Jon said in a low neutral tone.

I didn't say a word. I grabbed my laptop off of the couch and began feverishly searching for apartments. It was time to go! Now he was getting physical. Jon got up and walked upstairs to Jasmine's room to attempt to talk to her. She refused to listen to him and turned away, giving him the cold shoulder.

I, too, had nothing to say to Jon for the rest of the night. The incident was a turning point for me. It opened my eyes to the fact it was seriously time to move on. He was now physically acting out his frustration, endangering the children. My kids and I were not safe in the home. Our home had become physically violent and it would only escalate from there with the amount of drinking he was doing every night.

I texted Angela to let her know what was going on.

"You're not going to believe this... Jon shoved Elijah multiple times, trying to get him to leave."

"What?"

"Yes, I'm so upset!"

"Where's Elijah now?" Angela asked.

"He left the house to go stay with Zack. The safest place for him right now."

"You have got to leave him and save yourself and your kids! This is nuts!"

"I agree. I got on the computer tonight to see what's available. The money to move has been the issue, but I've got to get out!"

"I have to ask you this: Does Jon abuse you emotionally, physically, or verbally?" Angela asked.

"When we were going through all that cheating stuff, he was very emotionally and verbally abusive. Now, I feel it's more manipulation to get what he wants."

"You are in a prison! Do you really think it is better to stay? The kids have to live in this, too. You have NO freedom. He tries to keep you in an invisible cage, a prison. And he put his hands on your son!"

"I feel trapped not having the money to move out."

"If I can pay off the car and two to three more things. I will be in a better position to move."

"You really need to pay off your car to move? Sell it and get something cheaper."

"Also, I need to find a place for me and the kids that's decent with at least three bedrooms. Everything near the kid's schools is pricey. I need to have good cash flow for volleyball trips and tuition."

"It's time. The timing will never be perfect or ideal. But it is NECESSARY. It is time."

"True, my Aunt Olivia told me the same thing before she died. I was just trying to do right by the kids and get more things paid down. But it's not worth the hassle anymore."

"Not worth your peace of mind, safety, overall well-being, I could go on, but you understand the point. Tell me how I can help."

"Definitely not worth my peace of mind and freedom. I'm going to ask for your opinion on a few places as I find them." I texted.

"I gotta tell you... it hurts me and has been hurting me to watch you go through this for years now. You deserve so much more, and sometimes I don't know if you really believe that. YOU DESERVE BETTER! Your family (that includes me) loves you and would do anything for you."

"I know... my kids are in danger now. I'm getting out."

## BREAKING THE ENDLESS LOOP

The day after Jon kicked Elijah out of the house, he stayed home from work. He believed Elijah would retaliate against Max for the weekend's events. Why Jon believed Elijah would hurt his little brother baffled me. Max expressed being scared someone was going to die during the heated altercation the night before. Jon assured him no one was going to die and everything was okay.

*Was it really okay?* It appeared to be "ok" to Jon, but no one else. The younger children witnessed physical conflict between two people they loved dearly. It was traumatizing for them both as well as it was for Elijah. Elijah returned home mid-afternoon, after staying at his friend's house for the night. Jon asked to speak with him so they sat down in the living room to chat.

"I apologize for last night," Jon said. "I'm concerned about your health."

"Ok," Elijah replied, staring off to the side, avoiding eye contact.

Elijah had come to that realization that apologies meant nothing from Jon. ▶ His behavior never changed. Elijah knew actions speak louder than words.

Jon wrapped up his conversation with Elijah; then Elijah went to his room for the rest of the night — his place of refuge.

Jon chose to stop interacting with Elijah after the blowup. It was probably for the best, considering how heated he got for no reason. "I'm not driving Elijah back and forth to school anymore," Jon said as we sat watching TV.

"Ok, so I'm the only parent that's going to be responsible for him?"

"I'm done with him," Jon snapped. "He's your responsibility from now on."

As usual, Jon felt his way was the right way and refused to budge. He wrote Elijah a two-page letter that evening, explaining his concern about the smoking and how he was wrong for shoving. However, after the huge blowup with Elijah, it was apparent Jon's instability was escalating. I needed to leave to provide a stable home for my kids. Once I had everything in order, I planned to tell him I was moving out. I was having a difficult time finding something large enough for all of us to stay that was affordable. My girlfriend offered to rent me her house, but it wasn't available until late November. I wanted to move in October. I needed other options.

The hurricane rolled in by the weekend, so we were housebound due to high winds and rain. I watched a couple of mini series' over the weekend while Jon did some work for his part-time job The kids mainly stayed in their rooms, watching TV all weekend. Late Sunday night, the kids were upstairs in their rooms asleep. I laid down to sleep as well, since the next day was a work day. Jon retreated to the bathtub to drink. After drinking vodka in the tub for three hours, Jon emerged at 2:30 a.m., amped up and ready to argue.

"Are you asleep?" Jon asked, shoving on my shoulder.

"Yes, Jon, it's 2:30 a.m.," I replied.

"Why didn't you talk to me all weekend?"

"What are you talking about? We talked over the weekend."

"You spent all weekend watching *movies* and didn't talk to me," he responded.

"I did talk to you, numerous times. What did you specifically want to talk about?"

"It doesn't matter," Jon said, shaking his head.

"Obviously, there was something you wanted to talk about and you didn't get a chance to bring it up."

"It doesn't matter," Jon said sarcastically.

"Yes, apparently it does because you are bringing it up at 2:30 a.m.," I said. *"What did you want to talk about, Jon?"*

"It doesn't matter!"

Again, typical Jon. He wanted to have sex; I didn't offer and therefore, he started an argument about something frivolous.

"You never show me any attention. Why can't you sit by me and hold my hand while we're watching TV at night?" Jon asked. "Why don't you write posts about me on Facebook and list me as your husband on your profile?" he asked, staring at the ceiling while lying in bed.

I laid there silently, not moving.

"You need to unfriend all of your male friends on Facebook to avoid temptation," Jon continued.

I was in and out of sleep, listening to Jon rant. Then the conversation turned to me going on girl's trips without him, unnecessarily getting my hair and nails done once a month, and not spending enough time with him, even though we were together 99% of the time.

"We are together all the time, Jon," I said. "I'm with you more than I'm with anyone else. You are never satisfied with anything that I do for you and repeatedly ask for more and more without giving anything in return."

After the endless loop of conversation that had no end in sight, continued past 4 a.m., I couldn't take it any longer. I hit my breaking point.

"I'm moving out!" I blurted.

"HUH," Jon mumbled.

"Yes, I can't take this anymore. I need peace of mind. You *never* change," I said.

"All those other women I turned down to be with you," Jon said condescendingly.

"Well, now you can tell them you're available," I replied.

"So, you're going to leave after one argument?" Jon asked.

"*Are you serious*! You argue with me ALL THE TIME over stupid stuff." I replied.

"You're a selfish *bitch* and you don't care about your family! You're going to destroy the kids!" Jon said.

"Yes, Jon. I'm selfish and whatever else you want to call me. It still doesn't change the fact that I'm leaving," I calmly replied.

Jon's entire attitude changed. He was immediately calm and concerned, realizing that his tactic of calling me names, calling me a bad mom and a bad wife were no longer affecting me as they had in the past, so he changed his tactic. ▶

"Are you *really* going to throw away our marriage over one argument?" Jon pleaded.

"No, I'm leaving over YEARS of late-night arguments over nothing . . . the name-calling and you making me feel like I'm not worthy of anything or anyone. You never change, no matter how many times you say you will, and I just can't take it any longer. I'm taking back MY LIFE. I don't like who I am when I am with you."

Jon backed off and let me sleep while he laid in bed silent. He didn't know how to respond. The next day, he threw away all of the alcohol he had stashed in the bedroom closet.

## LOSS OF CONTROL

I narrowed down my apartment selection and scheduled three viewings. I also began looking at townhomes to rent or purchase. My girlfriend, Beth, began walking me through the steps I needed to take to leave. I also began working on the separation agreement to protect myself from a possible abandonment claim from Jon.

By the next week, I found a townhouse to purchase in a nearby neighborhood, changed beneficiaries on my life insurance, found a mortgage company, and started working on the draft separation agreement. The home wasn't far from our current one, so Jon was comfortable with it — as if he had any say in where I was moving. However, I was trying to purchase a model home and the builder didn't know when he would be ready to sell. I had to course-correct and continue to look at apartments. I settled on a luxury apartment complex downtown, twenty minutes away from the house. Within two weeks, I had a draft separation agreement together and found a place to stay. The earliest I could move in was the beginning of November. Two months away.

Two months I would have to endure Jon and his condescending attitude. I dreaded the thought of it.

I asked Jon to review the draft separation agreement one evening after work. He put it off for two hours and then finally agreed to go over it together, sighing the entire time. He balked at a few things and then told me he was taking it to work to review again and provide edits. In other words, he needed to run it past his co-workers to get their opinions before he could provide me with his thoughts. Later that night, we laid down for bed and Jon began caressing my back and kissing my neck.

"We're not having sex, if that's what you're after."

"Why not?" Jon sat up abruptly in the bed.

"We're *separating*. We are no longer a couple. It's not fair to you to get your hopes up on repairing a relationship that is dead."

Jon rolled over onto his back in anger. "Are you having an affair?"

"No, I'm not," I responded.

"Then why can't we have sex? Plenty of couples have sex while they are separating."

I sat still and didn't say a word, enraging Jon even more.

"I don't understand. You're not being nice and you're soooo happy to leave me. You're not sympathetic to my pain at all! I can't even have a drink to help my pain!" Jon screamed.

"Jon, I'm not seeing anyone and I don't think it's fair to have sex with you when I'm leaving you."

"Can we do counseling again? I don't understand why you don't want to work on the marriage!"

"I've tried and it doesn't work. I'm tired and need a break. I haven't fully gotten over the affair and I just need time to myself to think." I calmly responded.

"Fine!" Jon yelled, grabbing his pillow and going into the living room to sleep on the couch. By 3 a.m., he came back into the bedroom and got in the bed to sleep.

The next day, Jasmine had a volleyball game after school. Jon picked me up at the house after work and we drove together to the game. As soon as I got in the car, Jon started complaining about a clause in the separation agreement.

"Why do I have to buy you out of the house?"

"Because you are choosing to stay in the house. Since my name is on the house, you owe me half of the equity that we've accumulated thus far."

"You're the one choosing to leave. You should just take your loss and move on. It's your decision to leave, not mine."

"Jon, that's how it works when you share a house. Google it."

Jon continued to rant the entire ride to the game. I was an awful person and everything was my fault. I sat in the car, stoic, staring straight ahead. By the time we got to the location of the game, I had no desire to sit by him. I sat on a separate bleacher with friends while Jon sat with his parents. He sat down and texted his co-worker to confirm my statements on buying me out of the house. Once his co-worker confirmed I was correct, he came over and apologized. I continued watching the game, ignoring Jon's efforts. When I didn't respond to his apology, he became very sincere and said "Hey, I'm sorry, you were right," while pushing my shoulder.

I knew I was right. I didn't need his confirmation. We finished watching the game and drove home to get the kids ready for school the next day. After everyone was down for the night, we continued to discuss the separation agreement.

"This is hard for me because I won't get to see my kids every day and may have to sell my dream car and dream house," Jon said.

"Yes, everyone is going to experience change, but we will all get through it. That's the third new vehicle you've had that you claimed was your dream car. I'm sure you will be able to get another one later if you need to sell."

Jon pursed his lips and continued reading the document. "Here are a few of my edits. I'd rather not put in the agreement how to do visitation. I think we should let the kids decide." ▶

"I'm fine with letting Jasmine decide, but Max should rotate week to week."

*Jon didn't want to commit to a visitation schedule because he believed the kids would choose to stay with him full-time.*

"Why am I paying you part of my retirement?"

"Well, let's see . . . I supported you through college when you were jobless, paid off all of your debt, and reduced my retirement contribution to have more cash to spend on the household for the entire marriage. Your current retirement account is three times the worth of mine."

"No one put a gun to your head and asked you to help me back then," Jon said condescendingly. ▶

"Are you trying to have a productive conversation or throw jabs?" I inquired.

Jon got quiet and then agreed to the retirement clause.

"So, when do you move into the townhouse?"

"I decided to move downtown instead. The townhouse isn't going on the market any time soon."

Jon jumped up in shock. "WHAT?! Twenty minutes away! I didn't agree to that," Jon screamed.

I looked up at Jon as he went into a fury. "It's not up to you, Jon. We are separating. I can move wherever I want."

"Of course, it's ALL about you as always," Jon mumbled.

Jon threw the separation papers down on the bed and stomped out of the room to the kitchen to grab a glass. He had stopped by the liquor store on his way home from work to purchase a bottle of vodka, so I guess he was no longer giving up alcohol. He came back into the room and poured himself a glass before getting into the bathtub while I got ready for bed.

The next day, Jon used more manipulation tactics to try to convince me to stay. He drove Max to school every day while I drove Jasmine to high school on my way to work. Then, after dropping Max off at school, he called me at work to tell me that Max had separation anxiety when he dropped him off.

"What do you mean, Jon? What happened?"

"He didn't want to leave me and started crying. I think he senses you are leaving."

"I think Max is traumatized from watching you physically assault his brother during a very heated altercation."

"Possibly, but it could also be because you are leaving."

"Monitor him the rest of the week and see how he does," I replied.

Max didn't have separation anxiety. That was Jon's way of trying to guilt me into staying. Later that evening, he came home with an attitude and asked to talk to me in the bedroom.

"My co-workers think you are having an affair and that is why you are leaving."

"Ok, not true and I've told you that multiple times," I replied, staring at him, confused by his questioning.

"You're just being conniving," Jon mumbled.

I didn't react or respond while he paused for a few minutes, looking down at the carpet. "Do you think you can help me figure out how to pay down some debt and afford to pay my bills?"

"Talk to a financial advisor," I uttered.

Jon got up and walked out to the living room and sat on the couch, infuriated. I continued to go on with my evening, not paying him any mind. He finally calmed down later that evening.

## BREAKING THE NEWS

We finally decided to tell the kids I was leaving after we settled on the terms of the separation agreement. We gathered everyone into the family room for a family meeting. I sat on one side of the sectional couch while Jon sat on the other. Jasmine and Elijah sat near me while Max sat near Jon. Jon sat there, not saying a word; therefore, I began the announcement.

"Mom and Dad are separating, guys. I'm moving into a tiny two-bedroom apartment downtown," I said.

"Max, you will visit Mom every other week and Jasmine, you can decide where and when you want to spend your time. Elijah is moving with me full-time."

Jasmine smiled and Elijah didn't say a word. Max asked where I was moving to downtown and if they had a pool.

"Yes, buddy. They have a pool and an entertainment area where you can play corn hole."

"Elijah, you and I can play games with each other from separate houses," Max excitedly said.

"I just want you guys to know it's not your fault and we love you. It's OUR fault," Jon said.

The kids looked at Jon who, all of the sudden, burst into tears. He was the only person in the room crying about the situation and no one offered to console him. Everyone else was fine, as I predicted they would be. The kids weren't blind or deaf. They witnessed the turmoil in the home for years.

Prior to the discussion, Jon tried his hardest to convince me that the kids would be devastated. I asked the kids if they had any more questions and they said no. Jasmine said she had to go to Grandma's house to pick up a jacket she left behind. Jon offered to ride with her. They returned within fifteen minutes; Jon still wiping away tears that later turned to anger.

While they were gone, Elijah asked me why Jon was keeping the house when no one was going to stay there. I told him that was his choice and he was entitled to keep it if he wanted. I personally didn't care about the house. I never liked it and never wanted to move into the same neighborhood as his family. I wanted a clean slate to start over without watchful eyes.

## FINALIZING PLANS

After Jon and I agreed on the separation agreement, I had a lawyer formalize the document for filing. I didn't want to miss any possible loopholes in negotiating with Jon.

I received a call from the apartment complex that week informing me that I either had to move in two weeks earlier than planned or wait until the end of November, when the next apartment became available. I opted to move in two weeks earlier. The decision meant I had to pay for two places at the same time; the apartment and the house. Even though Jon was going to receive three paychecks in the month of November, he still wanted me to pay half of the mortgage payment. So, I paid half the mortgage for the month of October and November, in addition to rent for my apartment all within the same month.

I was still looking for a shred of decency in Jon to offer to pay all of the November mortgage since I wouldn't be living there. However, instead, he asked when he would receive my half of the payment, disappointing me again with his lack of empathy.

Five days before my official move out date, I received the legalized separation agreement from the lawyer; I emailed it to Jon for final review. Later that evening, while wreaking of alcohol, Jon informed me that he had a few comments.

"I just wanted to let you know my 401k value has gone down since we first spoke about your share. I don't think it's fair to pay the amount we agreed to."

"I don't think it's fair that my 401k has suffered over the years to help pay bills, especially for all your brand-new vehicles, when your 401k has flourished. We agreed upon a percentage. The amount to be disbursed will be determined on the day of disbursement."

Jon sat silent for a few moments. "I need to consult with a lawyer."

"That's fine. Have your lawyer communicate directly with the lawyer I've retained to write up the agreement."

Jon pursed his lips in anger and walked out of the room. He, like clockwork, apologized for his behavior later that night, blaming frustration for his behavior.

As the days progressed, I became increasingly fearful of my safety in the home at night as I laid down to sleep. Jon already demonstrated he was violent and his mood swings from day to day, along with his profuse drinking, made me even more fearful of sleeping beside him at night. I was terrified and couldn't wait to move out; he was still argumentative and upset I was leaving. Everything set him off, it seemed, and I continued to walk on a tightrope day in and day out. I felt like a prisoner.

I continued to pack boxes, having conversations with Jon on what we would split. To avoid frivolous arguments, I gave up a few things I really wanted, like some of the family portraits on the wall. Jon refused to part with the specific photos I wanted and became angry with me for wanting to take them.

Two days before my move out date, we finalized the separation agreement and met at the bank to have it notarized. Hallelujah! One of the happiest days of my life! On my way home, I called Angela to share the good news.

"Just left from signing the separation agreement. Yay! Can you believe on the way there, Jon was still trying to add clauses about him being able to date during separation and not be sued? We already had a clause in there that said each person was allowed to date during the year of separation. He can't WAIT to find a replacement for me."

"Are you kidding me? Well, I congratulate you for taking the necessary steps for self-preservation and care for your children," Angela said.

"Thanks. That relationship was detrimental to us all. Jasmine is living with me full-time once I get the townhouse."

"Oh snap! Does Jon know?

"Not yet, but he will next year. She told Elijah that on one of our tours of the townhouse."

"Is she going to tell him it's what she wants? It will have to come from her in order for him to hear it."

"She will when it's closer to move time. He agreed to let her choose where she wants to stay and when. I really don't want him pressuring her. It's not fair to her."

"Talk to her and reinforce that she doesn't have to be guilted by her father."

"That's my plan."

"So how do you feel right now?"

"Great things are coming my way. I can feel it in my heart and soul. I needed to drop the dead weight; the weight that was holding me back from living my best life."

"I am proud of you. Proud of you for putting yourself first!"

"Thank you for all of your help during my most difficult times. I don't know what I would have done without you, especially during Jon's affair."

I hung up the phone with Angela and drove home to continue to pack, dreading the next two nights with Jon, but reveling in the fact that I only had two more nights with him and then I was free.

Moving day finally arrived. In the sincerest voice, Jon sat down next to me on the bed, grabbed my hand, and asked if I needed help financially with moving.

"Do you need any money to help with the move?

"I'm fine. I saved up some money and Elijah is helping out with money Aunt Olivia left him."

As soon as I said Elijah was helping me, Jon dropped my hand and his tone and demeanor changed. His face turned red and he got angry. "Oh, so you're using Elijah's money!?"

Just when I thought he had a heart and was being helpful and sincere, he removed the mask of sincerity.

## REFLECTION

Once I had decided that I was completely done with the marital relationship, I devised a plan to leave the family home. I knew my husband wasn't going to leave. It wasn't worth my sanity or time to fight over it; therefore, I made the decision to find a new place to live. Leaving a narcissist is dangerous.

Once you inform them you are leaving the relationship, they will maneuver in and out of masks in an effort to get you to stay, so they can continue to manipulate and abuse you. You always have to be on guard due to their unpredictability. I had to be extremely strategic in my escape to limit as much verbal abuse as possible prior to my leaving. I told my husband I needed time away to overcome his affair. I wasn't over it and I just needed time to myself. This was a viable reason for him since I had asked him to leave in the past for this very same reason. If I told him the real reason I wanted to leave and that I wasn't coming back, my escape would have been contentious.

Since my husband had already engaged in violent physical contact with my son, I lived on eggshells until I was able to move out of the home. He continued to taunt and verbally and emotionally abuse me as I made preparations to leave the marital residence. Thankfully, my armor was strong and I practiced the "grey rock" technique of no emotion to my abuser's dismay.

The "grey rock" method involves communicating without emotion when interacting with abusive or manipulative people. The name refers to how those using this approach become unresponsive, similar to a rock. The aim is to cause the abusive person to lose interest and stop their antagonistic behavior, to protect a person's emotional well-being. While it is not a surefire strategy with people like Jon, it can be a useful strategy, especially in situations like the ones I had been in leading up to moving out.

*Chapter 9*

# THE FOG LIFTS

It took one full month for me to come to a settlement of property and child custody with Jon in the form of a separation agreement. In the state of North Carolina, you have to be separated for one year prior to divorce, and I couldn't wait for that year to be up. I signed a lease on a small two-bedroom apartment downtown for six months to get myself together before purchasing a new home. I had a realtor lined up to research properties for me in the area. I packed up my things, hired movers, and moved out of the marital home one-and-a-half months after Jon's altercation with Elijah.

The moment I stepped foot into my tiny two-bedroom apartment, I shut the door as tears rolled down my face. I stood in silence, enjoying the peacefulness of freedom. It was the most freeing and uplifting experience of my life. *It was as if two hundred pounds had been lifted from my shoulders and I could breathe again.*

The first night in my apartment was the most peaceful sleep I had in years. For the first time in years, I felt safe. I could lay my head down without someone waking me up in the middle of the night to argue or demand sex; I no longer had to sleep with one eye open, fearing for my safety. I woke up fully rested and at peace the next morning, to birds chirping outside of my window. I was finally FREE from years of torment, pain, and mental anguish.

Two weeks later, Elijah arrived on a school break. While sitting in the kitchen, reflecting on the events that occurred over the last month, Elijah sat down next to me. "Mom, you are so much happier now."

"That's because I am, son," I replied, smiling.

It took me a couple of weeks to settle into my new routine. I didn't know what to do with my time. I wasn't used to my time being my own, so I found myself looking for places to go and things to do. I was starting over and I felt lost. *It was as if I had been in a sixteen-year coma, and I woke up to a brand new world.*

Even though my body had aged, mentally, I felt as though I was the same age as when I entered the marriage. I couldn't just call up a friend and say, "Hey let's go hang out for the day." Their lives had changed as well over the years. They had new responsibilities and families.

I knew I had been through a traumatic experience that required healing. But I couldn't quite put my hands on the definition of my experience and how to heal from it. I just knew my mind and body needed to heal. I scheduled a physical with my doctor and signed up for personal training to start exercising again. I also joined a couple of local self-help groups for support.

It was during this time that I came across a Facebook post detailing a woman's experience with her narcissistic husband. Reading her story felt like I was reading my own; the details of her experience and the correlation to my own was uncanny. One of the first marriage counselors Jon and I had spoken to during his affair told me she felt Jon was a narcissist. I didn't believe her at the time and thought her assessment was wrong. It was like a blinding light had just been switched on.

## HOW WRONG I WAS

She told me that he would not change because he was incapable of changing — it's a personality disorder. I could either accept the fact that he would never change and deal with it, or I could choose to leave the relationship. Against my better judgment, I chose to stay at the time, teaching my kids that it was okay to let people treat you the way he treated us. I thought narcissists were grandiose people who were in love with themselves; that wasn't Jon. Fast forward four years later, everything she said made sense.

Hindsight is indeed 20/20.

I began educating myself on Narcissistic Personality Disorder and reading about other people's experiences and stories. It was eerie reading how all of the stories were similar but different. The true difference being, these were different people, all exhibiting the same traits and following the same patterns of behavior. I finally had an explanation for what I experienced throughout my marriage and now it was time to heal from the physical and psychological damage.

When I left Jon to start my new life, I knew Elijah would leave with me. After the years of neglect and mistreatment he had suffered, there was no doubt in my mind he would tag along. He even sent him a text when he moved, informing Jon he appreciated him for raising him, but he was severing their relationship. I did not, however, expect my daughter to live with me full-time and limit her time with her father so quickly.

Jasmine started out living with Jon until it became too difficult for her to be there without Elijah and me for support. For many years, she was a daddy's girl — his pride and joy. The golden child. Jon isolated her from me, her older brother, my family, and outside friends. He chose to be her mother and her father, pushing me out of the way when I wanted to do things with and for my daughter. Now, she was more independent, a teenager, exhibiting her own thoughts and feelings.

Jon's emotional incest with Jasmine from birth developed into an unhealthy relationship, in which he treated her as a partner/best friend as opposed to a child. Jasmine told me he sought sympathy and encouragement from her, often crying on her shoulder when he was sad, putting undue pressure on her and the constant feeling of uneasiness. He also continued to lay with her at night for his "night time routine" with her before bed, often falling asleep in her bed until she was fifteen years old.

The week of my move, Jon scheduled a therapy appointment for Max, citing separation anxiety. ▶ Max met with the therapist after school later in the week who concluded that he was not exhibiting any signs of separation anxiety or signs of having a hard time with his parent's separation since he got to see both parents equally. Max told Jon and me that he was fine and no longer wanted to see the therapist. Jasmine, on the other hand, was having a rough time. Jon sent me the following text:

"Jasmine has been sad and I don't know what to do."

"Why is she sad?" I replied.

"Her entire world changed," Jon texted back.

"I'll talk to her about it at dinner this week."

I met with Jon, Jasmine, and Max for dinner and gave them each journals to write down their feelings and put on paper what was on their minds. I also informed Jasmine that I understood it was a tough time and she could come to see me anytime. She was not on a weekly schedule and could stay with me whenever she wanted. Two days later, I Facetimed with her.

"How are you doing?" I asked.

"I'm fine. I decided not to try out for travel volleyball this year. I didn't enjoy it last year, so I'm not going to play."

"Ok, it's your decision. Just make sure you inform your coaches."

"I will," Jasmine replied.

Jasmine and Max stayed with me for the first week of exchange in November. Jon called me to see how the kids were doing during my week.

"I'm taking a couple of days off," Jon said.

"For what?"

"My whole world has turned upside down and my boss knows that. On top of everything else, my boss from my part-time job yelled at me today about the work I'm doing for him," he stated, as he began to cry. ▶

"I think you should express your feelings to your part-time boss," I replied.

"I have. It doesn't matter."

Just as quickly as Jon had started crying on the phone, the tears immediately dried up, and he was fine. ▶ "Anyway, it's not your problem."

There was a long pause on the phone.

"Well, I need to go. I'll talk to you later," I replied. I didn't want to stay on the phone with him any longer than I needed to.

When I informed Jon I was moving out of the home, I didn't tell him my intention of never returning. I needed to get away from him as safely and as smoothly as possible, even though he still made my life a living hell until moving day. Thinking my move was short-lived and I would eventually return to him, Jon decided to become the perfect husband; willing to lend a hand when I needed one, checking in to see if I needed anything and even assisted with moving in the new TVs I purchased for my apartment.

Jasmine decided to stay an extra week with me while Max went back to Jon at the end of my custodial time. When we arrived at Jon's house to drop Max off, I noticed the bench seating I requested he build in the kitchen, for three years, was completed.

"So, you finally decided to get the bench seating done. What sparked this?"

"Oh, I've been thinking about doing it for three weeks. I decided to go ahead and get it done. Doesn't it look nice?"

"Yes, it does. I only requested it for three years. I'm just shocked that all of a sudden you decided to do it."

Jon didn't say a word. I asked Jasmine if she needed to grab anything while we were there and then headed back home to the apartment.

> **Hoover:** *Jon was attempting to lure me back into the relationship by being sweet and kind and doing every little thing around the house I asked for, after years of blowing me off with a million excuses as to why he couldn't get things done. He couldn't get things done because they were not beneficial to him or his ego.*

For Thanksgiving, Elijah and I headed to Delaware to visit my family. Jasmine and Max stayed with Jon to have Thanksgiving with his family. After Thanksgiving, Jasmine returned to the apartment as soon as I arrived back in town. She decided she didn't want to rotate from home to home with her younger brother every week, and chose to stay with me full-time.

This infuriated Jon. Per our separation agreement, she had the right to choose where she wanted to stay. Jon was fine with that arrangement at the time because he wholeheartedly believed she would choose him. She was his little girl, his best friend, his confidant, his baby. It wasn't until the tables turned on him that he had a problem with that clause in our agreement. He couldn't understand why she chose to stay with me and reduce her interaction with him. Instead of choosing to look within himself and reflect on his own actions, he chose his typical pattern of behavior... blaming me.

By the following month, we had settled into a routine of managing the kids and weekly exchanges of Max. Jasmine committed to a college for volleyball and Elijah decided to take a year off from college. I didn't expect to have two kids with me full-time so soon, making the tiny apartment even smaller for four people to live in every other week.

I decided waiting on the model townhome to come up for sale was too risky and opted instead to build a house in a new home development. They were running a special on premium lots for the holidays. I took advantage of the offer. It wasn't until Jon found out I put a down payment on a new home that he flipped back into his typical degrading behavior; instead of the helpful partner/husband he was pretending to be. All of a sudden, he didn't have time to take phone calls and had a problem with everything in regards to the children.

During my custodial weeks with Max, he would Facetime him every morning before school and every night. When he wasn't Facetiming with him, he was texting him. One late night, Max was up playing a video game with his friends. Jon called me.

"Max just Facetimed me, crying, and wants to come back to my house," Jon said.

I could see clearly from one end of my apartment to the next. Max had been playing his video game for the past hour during this so-called tearful plea to see his dad, and was in the process of playing the game when Jon called. ▶

"Jon, I've been watching Max for the past hour and he's been playing video games with his friends the entire time."

"He just Facetimed me."

"Jon, this is my week. I'd appreciate it if you would stop trying to get Max back during my time."

"He reached out to me!" Jon stated.

"Ok Jon, he's fine now. He will speak with you tomorrow," I calmly responded, hanging up the phone.

This was typical Jon behavior. He was home alone, stewing in his own thoughts and no one was there to give him his supply of admiration and validation that he so desperately needed. Therefore, he resorted to lying to find a way to get the one person he knew would supply it for him, back in the house until he found another unsuspecting female to supply his needs.

Jon also wasted no time putting up his profile on every dating site available and found my replacement within two weeks of posting. During his two weeks of dating, a friend of mine saw Jon out a few times with Max on his dates. I can only assume this was to display how he was a great father and had a cute kid that every woman would love. ▶

## CHRISTMAS DISASTER

As Christmas approached, Jon's mother invited me to her annual Christmas Eve dinner. I grappled with the decision to attend or not, so I asked my cousin to come with me to be a buffer. It wasn't until she agreed to attend that I decided to go.

When we arrived, everyone was already in attendance — Jon's brother and his family, as well as Jon. He moped around the house, angry the entire time, making sly comments, while his mom and brother took the opportunity to interrogate me about the home I was building, making me the sole focus of the dinner conversation. *Where are you moving to? When will the house be finished? How many bedrooms? How many floors? Is it brick or siding?* Whenever my cousin attempted to interject to pull the conversation away from me, they dismissed her and continued to question me about my future plans.

As we got ready to leave, Jon's mom gave me a card she claimed her grandson wrote just for me. I grabbed the card bewildered. *I had never received a personal card from the grandson in the past, why am I receiving one now?*

"You had him make that during your weekly volunteer day at the school, didn't you?" Jon grumbled.

"Yes, I did," his mother replied, smiling at me.

"That's what I thought," Jon muttered.

This was one of her many manipulation tactics to make me change my mind on leaving the marriage. I had no desire to go back to what I considered, the *"marriage from hell"*, after dealing with her and Jon for sixteen years.

The following morning, Jon arrived at the apartment to watch the kids open their gifts for Christmas. He requested we spend Christmas together as a final family gathering. The night before, the neighbors above me had a little kid running around all night, making it hard to sleep. When Jon arrived and called for me to buzz him into the complex, I didn't hear the phone. I overslept.

It was twenty minutes before I buzzed him in, explaining that I had overslept and didn't hear the phone. Apparently, he attempted to call the kids and they didn't answer their phones either. By the time he entered the apartment, he was irate with everyone and fussing. "How come no one answered their phones? I've been calling for twenty minutes," Jon yelled, entering the apartment. No one answered or acknowledged Jon's question. No one cared and everyone ignored him. We didn't live with him anymore, so we didn't have to suffer any consequences after he left.

I began to hand each kid their Christmas gift from under the tree. There was an awkward silence the entire time Jon was there. No one wanted him there. He always brought the mood down with his presence. The kids began to open their gifts while sitting in silence. Afterwards, Jon left, to everyone's relief.

"Why was he here?" Elijah asked.

"Yeah," Jasmine said.

"He wanted to do one final Christmas together," I replied.

"Why? We're no longer a family... It was so awkward having him here," Elijah said.

Jon definitely changed the entire mood in the room when he walked in, as he typically did when we were all together. I knew then, we would never get together like that again. It was too hard on the kids and too stressful on me.

The kids and I lived in a tiny space, but we loved it. We felt safe. We felt relaxed. We felt loved. We felt free. We spent more time together as a family, doing activities and having casual conversations than we did in the marital home. We had a special bond. We were the only people who knew what living with Jon was like and how he treated us all; how he inflicted fear and constant turmoil in the home. The kids were no longer retreating to their rooms for hours on end, living in isolation as they did prior to separation. We all felt safe and we all wanted to be together. It wasn't a "forced" closeness as it was with Jon and his family.

In January of the following year, Jon requested I remove all of the remaining items I planned to take from the marital home, citing he was ready to move on and make changes around the house. Prior to my moving, we had agreed that I would get the remainder of my things once I found a permanent residence to move into during the year of separation. As soon as he found and moved my replacement in, all of a sudden, he needed my things out of the house immediately. He texted me right before Martin Luther King weekend and informed me my things had to be out by the end of the weekend. I had no time to plan for or find a suitable mover to gather my things and he refused to negotiate on the matter.

The day I was finally able to gather my things, I was so rushed with him and his family breathing over my shoulder, that I left a number of sentimental items behind that Jon would later inform me he had thrown away.

A week after moving my things, Max sent me a photo through text of the kitchen stovetop with the name "Shayla" etched below the burners. The burners resembled Mickey Mouse ears, so I'm assuming Shayla was assigning her name to Mickey. I asked Max who "Shayla" was and he said it was a friend from school that I hadn't met yet.

## THE NEW TARGETS

I had to travel for work the first weekend in February. Jasmine asked to stay home with Elijah during that time, instead of staying with her father. She was adamant she did not want to spend the night with her father. Jon, on the other hand, was not having it and threw the separation agreement in my face, which cited he had first "right of refusal" if I was unavailable to care for the children.

"Jasmine wants to stay home with Elijah while I'm gone," I informed Jon on the phone while driving home from work.

"I'm not comfortable with that. I don't trust Elijah."

"She doesn't want to stay with you. She was adamant about that. When will you give her the right to choose?" I inquired.

"I don't know. According to our separation agreement, I have the right of first refusal if you are not available to take care of the children during your custodial time. I'm enforcing that right."

"I will let her know. Just so you know, she will be upset."

"That's fine," Jon replied.

Jasmine waited until the very last minute to go to her father's house for the weekend, dreading her stay, trapped in his home until my return. Jon texted me the morning I left to ask when she was coming over and whether or not her brother was coming in the house: "I'm assuming Elijah is dropping her off. If that is the case, he can either drop her off outside or, if he chooses to come in the house, then he must treat me with respect."

> **Domestic Violence by Proxy**: a pattern of behavior when a parent with a history of using domestic violence, or intimidation, uses the child (as a substitute) when she/he does not have access to the former partner. Continuing the cycle of domestic violence, the cycle of Domestic Violence by Proxy starts when the victim leaves the abuser and the abuser learns the easiest way to continue to harm, and control the former partner is through controlling access to the children. Once the abuser has control of the children, they are able to continue stalking, harassing and abusing the former partner even when the abuser has no direct access. Domestic violence can manifest in ways, such as threats to the children if they display a close relationship with the former partner, destroying the children's favorite possessions given by the former partner and emotional abuse. Children are often coached to make false allegations about the parent. Domestic Violence by Proxy is very deliberate and planned. The abusers know what they are doing and choose their controlling, coercive, and illegal behaviors."—www.onemomsbattle.com

I didn't respond to the text. I saw no purpose since Elijah had zero contact with Jon since Christmas. It was crazy for him to believe that Elijah would want to step foot into his home. Instead, I sent an invitation to a parenting app for all communication, to which he ignored.

I arrived safely in Florida and checked into my room. Before I could get settled and decompress from my trip, I was bombarded with texts from Jon.

"Did you know Jasmine was planning on spending Monday night at the apartment? She just informed me," Jon texted.

"Nope."

"She is insistent that you knew. I've informed her that it is not ok with me," Jon replied.

"She told me she was coming there after school Monday, but she said you knew that when I asked her. I assumed you were picking her up on your way from work."

"Nope," I replied.

"Jasmine just informed me that she gets rides home from school from an older guy? I'm not comfortable with that."

"I sent you a link to a co-parenting app that I would like for us to utilize for conversations in regards to the children as opposed to various texts," I replied.

"Ok, I can look at that later. But it does not change the fact that this is something that needs to be addressed now and not later. I care more about Jasmine's safety than what is documented in an app."

"The friend brought her home one time," I responded.

"She said it has been multiple times. Have you met him?"

"He only brought her home one time. I pick her up from school," I replied.

Finally, the texts stopped. I didn't hear from Jon again until the day I was scheduled to fly back home, informing me Jasmine stayed home from school. She began crying when she arrived at school for the day, so he took her back to his house.

"Just FYI, Jasmine didn't feel good this morning, so she is home with me. I will see if she is feeling better by the time she needs to go to volleyball practice and let you know."

"What's wrong??" I inquired.

"She just got sad and was feeling overwhelmed. She seems to be doing much better now." ▶

"Ok," I replied.

"Taking Jasmine to practice now. She has all of her stuff with her."

Elijah picked Jasmine up from volleyball practice that night and brought her back to the apartment. By the time I arrived home, everyone was settled in their rooms watching TV. I walked into Jasmine's room to see how her stay with her father went.

"Hey, how was your stay?"

"Horrible! Dad kept badgering me about my friend bringing me home ONE TIME after school and wouldn't leave me alone about it."

"Sorry to hear that," I said.

"I did not have a good time at all and couldn't wait to leave. I'm so glad Elijah picked me up from practice."

"Well, you are back home now. You can relax."

I walked downstairs to the complex entertainment room to call Marie to catch her up on what occurred over the last week.

"You need to get full custody of the kids. Jon is going to continue to harass you over stupid stuff for no reason," Marie said.

"I don't have the grounds for full custody and it's a lot of work. I looked up the process. I have to basically prove I'm the better parent through a ton of documentation. I have to have a diary of my daily interactions with the kids, testimonials from their schools, and documentation on his unstableness."

"While he was out cheating on his family you had to parent alone. He was lying about working at night," Marie said.

"True. I also have to prove adequate living conditions. I can't do that until May when I close on the house," I replied.

"Well, that will be here before you know it. In the meantime, start tracking intentionally. And we can figure out how to grab notes from the past."

"Ok."

"Go back to the start of your separation or think back as far as you can; while you two were still living together. The shoving with Elijah was crazy, don't forget that; oppressing others in the household, including you. Elijah was a witness and a victim. I'm sure you can think of numerous incidents where he put himself first and his family second."

I nodded, before responding. "I have a diary from the time period during the affair. I could comb through old texts about the drinking incidents and controlling me."

"He had uncontrolled substance use. With full custody, he can still see Max. I am concerned about Max, the most because he is still very impressionable," Marie said.

"Yes, he is. I'll think about it. I just want Jon to leave me alone and move on with his life; stop trying to control me from afar."

I wrapped up my conversation with Marie and returned to my apartment to relax for the evening and contemplate my next steps based on Marie's advice.

The following weekend was Valentine's Day and my girlfriend and I planned a single ladies' date for the evening. We got dressed up and had dinner at a rooftop restaurant downtown. We had the time of our lives celebrating each other. I was so excited to move on with my life and do the things I wanted to do. It felt good to be able to make my own decisions and do what I wanted to do, when I wanted to do it without answering to anyone, but myself. I also hired a business coach during this time to help me think through a business I would enjoy that would also be profitable. Things seemed to be going well until Jasmine's anxiety crept in again.

Jasmine started having a difficult time getting through her school days without having panic attacks. She would text and call me throughout the day, telling me she couldn't do it and needed to come home. She was struggling with terrible social anxiety to the point that it was giving her physical ailments. My heart ached for her. Every morning before school, she was depressed and didn't want to go. Her stomach would be tied in knots and she barely spoke a word. I tried everything to help her — essential oils, positive thinking, relaxation techniques — but nothing worked. I asked her if she was willing to see a therapist and she refused. All of that changed after her travel volleyball tournament weekend in Florida.

We arrived in Orlando on a Thursday prior to the day of the first game. On the first day of the tournament, Jon sent me a text at 7 a.m.

"I wanted to let you know that I was inviting someone to the game." ▶

"Ok," I replied.

It seemed odd. I couldn't figure out why I was finding out the first day of the tournament that a guest was attending. I arrived at the game at 8 a.m. and saw Max sitting with his father. I assumed Max was the surprise guest, since he was supposed to stay in North Carolina to attend school.

"Hey, Max! It's good to see you!" I said while giving Max a huge hug and kissing him on his forehead.

"Hey, Mom! Max replied, hugging me back.

I walked over to the other volleyball parents and found a seat to watch the game. An hour later, a strange woman showed up and sat with Jon and Max. After the game ended, Jon, Max, and the woman got up from their seats to greet Jasmine to tell her how great she played during the game. They then walked in my direction.

Jon, all smiles says, "I want to introduce you to Shayla. I figured it was time you two met."

I reached out to shake Shayla's hand, looking her up and down. Shayla was a Caucasian woman, short and obese with long brown hair. The complete opposite of me. "Nice to meet you," I said, smiling.

"Nice to meet you as well. Jasmine played great, didn't she?" Shayla stated, grinning from ear to ear, proudly displaying her crooked teeth.

"Yes, she did," I replied.

I walked away, wondering why this woman was at my daughter's volleyball tournament, interacting with my children five months after my separation from my husband. Jon had no regard for how bringing this strange woman to Jasmine's volleyball tournament so soon after separation would impact her.

During the break between games, I stepped outside to call my mom and tell her what occurred. As the day progressed, it was quite apparent the new woman had built a relationship with Max, since she played video games with him the majority of the tournament. I, on the other hand, had to answer the slew of questions from the other parents on the team. *Is that Jon's sister? Aren't you guys still married? Why would he do that to your daughter?*

Needless to say, none of them were impressed with Jon's decision to bring his new fling to a travel volleyball tournament while still married, freshly separated, and prancing around in front of his daughter and her friends. I'm sure Jon and Shayla were staying in the same hotel room together with Max. *What kind of example is that for a child his age?*

> **Triangulation**: *A passive-aggressive manipulation tactic used to instill feelings of jealousy and insecurity in victims by introducing a third party into the relationship. A mind game that enables narcissists to gain a sense of power and control over multiple people simultaneously.*

## ANXIETY HITS

By the end of the tournament weekend, the director of the volleyball club commented on Jasmine's positive change in demeanor. She said Jasmine seemed to smile more since the separation. She, too, was shocked by Jon bringing another woman to the tournament, embarrassing his daughter.

However, after the weekend concluded and we all flew back home to prepare for the school and work week, Jasmine sunk further into anxiety and depression. By mid-week, she asked to see a therapist and explicitly told me she did not want her father to attend. I scheduled her first appointment with a child therapist and Jon received the appointment confirmation through email.

"I received a reminder that Jasmine has a counseling appointment on Friday, but it wasn't on my calendar. Did you set this up and do you need help getting her there?"

"Yes, I set it up. I'm good to take her... Thanks."

"Is this her first appointment?"

"Yes."

"Ok, good. Could you please keep me in the loop when it comes to the kids? If they are sick or in therapy, this is really something I should know about."

Jon was upset and felt I was keeping information from him; however, my first priority was my daughter and she had clearly stated that she did not want him there. Him being there when she didn't want him to be defeated the purpose of her feeling safe to open up.

Jon, ironically, was unable to attend the first appointment. After the therapist's assessment, she recommended Jasmine take medication for anxiety to help her deal with her stress levels. She also stated, "Jasmine does not like staying with her father." Something I was already aware of. I informed Jon of the therapist's medication recommendation and he was highly against it. I was surprised by his reaction, since the first time the pediatrician recommended medication, he was all for it.

"Ok, are the meds what she wants or can we continue with sessions? I'm not comfortable putting her on meds again if we can combat it with therapy," Jon sniped.

"The therapist highly recommends medication for the level of stress she's currently under."

"I'm going to call her and discuss it," Jon said.

Jon immediately called Jasmine and expressed his displeasure with her going on medication; informing her he didn't agree with it, making her feel bad for even needing it — a counterintuitive conversation. Next, he called the therapist and bullied and coerced her into retracting her recommendation for medication. The therapist was so rattled by Jon's demeanor on the phone and the conversation that she called me to discuss it.

"Mrs. McAdams?"

"Yes."

"This is Mandy from the Counseling Center. I just got off the phone with your husband and he was rather resolute about not wanting Jasmine to go on medication. I believe he is in complete denial of what Jasmine needs right now. I told him the meds would be temporary and he continued to blow me off. Instead of listening to me, he kept cutting me off to discuss her current living arrangements. Apparently, she never spends overnights with him and that's a problem for him."

"Correct, she lives with me full-time by choice and he refuses to accept it."

"He was pretty aggressive on the phone, making me feel uncomfortable. Well, meet with the pediatrician and see what they recommend for her care."

"Ok, thank you," I replied, hanging up the phone.

Jon attended every appointment thereafter, to my daughter's dismay. He made Jasmine feel uncomfortable and unsafe at her appointments by his mere presence. By Jasmine's second appointment with the therapist, Jon gave his sob story of how much he loved his daughter, and how she refused to spend any time with him or spend nights at his house. The therapist, in turn, told Jasmine to schedule weekly dinners with her dad.

Jasmine despised and dreaded every single dinner. Her entire demeanor would change on the days she had to see her father, and she was in a horrible despondent mood after every dinner, often having nightmares while sleeping at night.

Two weeks after the tournament in Florida, Elijah and Jasmine were invited to a family birthday gathering for Jon's brother. The kids informed me after they arrived home about their evening.

"Dad sat over on the couch the entire time, barely talking to anyone. After we cut the cake, he left with Max." Jasmine said.

"Did he say goodbye or try to give you a hug?"

"Nope, he just walked out with Max."

"On our way out of the door, Grandma stopped me and asked if I was coming to Dad's birthday party next week. She told me I would be an awful person if I didn't come," Jasmine stated.

"What? That was inappropriate and you can make your own decisions on whether or not you wish to attend," I stated.

Prior to the brother's birthday party, Elijah informed me Grandma called Jasmine, crying all the time, asking her to come around more. *No wonder why the girl was so stressed out! She was being hit up by the entire family through all modes of communication.* I made numerous attempts to have Jon cut back on his phone calls and texts, pressuring Jasmine to come around more, to no avail. I knew speaking with his mother would be fruitless as well. Therefore, I sought the assistance of Jon's brother.

"Hey, are you busy?"

"No, what's up?" The brother replied.

"I need your help. Jasmine is feeling a ton of stress right now and your mother and Jon are not helping with the pressure they put on her to come around all the time."

"Really, I'm confused. Jasmine seems so happy when she's here. Jon says she is happy when she's around him, so I'm getting mixed signals."

"Well, she's stressed and she's expressed to Elijah how she doesn't like the calls and texts from everyone."

"Ok, I'll see what I can do."

I don't know if Jon's brother said anything to Jon and his mom or not, but to Jasmine's dismay, the calls and texts continued. While driving home after picking her up from school two days later, Jon called. I do not know the context of the conversation; however, Jasmine got mad and told her dad, "STOP." Apparently, Jon did not stop because she continued to listen on the phone upset, eyes tearing up the entire time until she hung up. I felt sorry for her and helpless.

Ever since Jon found my replacement in Shayla, co-parenting with him became very challenging, as he often condemned and criticized my parental actions in a very superior, entitled, and authoritative manner. I started to mentally seep back into fight or flight mode, having difficulty sleeping at night again, unable to calm my nervous system down. I dreaded every text, email, and phone call I received from him. Each interaction caused my heart to pound, my blood pressure to rise, and my hands to shake, anticipating the confrontation. Seeing him face-to-face was even worse, and I was forced to sit with him every week in the waiting room while Jasmine was in therapy. He went from a father who didn't have time to take off work to take the children to doctor's appointments while we were married, to a parent who attended everything including dental cleanings. All of a sudden, he could magically take off work whenever he needed to.

With Jon's change in attitude toward me, I no longer wanted him stepping foot anywhere near my apartment; I would meet him in the apartment lobby to exchange Max on Sundays. On one particular Sunday, I was on the phone conducting a business call and couldn't get downstairs when Max arrived. I asked Jasmine and Elijah to go down, but no one wanted to see or interact with Jon, so I ended up ending my business call early to retrieve Max from him in the lobby. It was also around this time that Jon started requesting Max back sooner than our agreed upon custodial time every week. This was a pattern of behavior that exponentially got worse over time.

Once she stopped spending overnights with Jon, Jasmine was not entirely prepared to live in my home full-time. She had a number of items at his house that she wanted to collect, so she scheduled time with him to pick up her things after volleyball practice one day. Once we arrived at the home, Jasmine went to her room and gathered her things, placing them in a laundry basket she had brought from my place.

As she approached the front door to leave, Jon jumped in front of the door, blocking her exit, making her feel trapped and uncomfortable. ▶He questioned her about when she was going to spend the night with him and why she no longer wanted to rotate weeks with Max. Jasmine said she informed her father, "I feel more comfortable at Mom's and it's closer to school." She said at that moment, the dogs ran down the stairs, distracting him so he stepped away from the door. Jasmine quickly picked up her things and walked out the door to my car. She was clearly anxious and scared when she got in... relieved to be out of his presence.

The next day, Jasmine received the following text from Jon:

> "I love you very much Jasmine. You may hear things said about me over the next few days, but they do not concern you in any way. Please remember who I am as a person and that my intentions are always good and meant to protect the ones I love. You are one of the people I am trying to protect right now; I love you more than words can say..."

Jon continued to reach out to Jasmine by phone, calling and texting her, trying to get her to spend nights with him as the weeks progressed. Jasmine would occasionally send me screenshots of the messages that bothered her the most. Somehow, he knew every time she sent me something through text, since he asked her why she was sending stuff to me. He told her their conversations were private and not to be shared with me. Little did he know, she was telling me everything, including the pressure he constantly put on her to spend time with him.

It was also during this time that Jon's mother's birthday was coming up and the family was getting together for a birthday celebration. Jon's family invited Elijah and Jasmine, yet Jon abruptly disinvited Elijah, texting:

> *"Elijah, I understand you are wanting to attend another McAdams family function. As I have mentioned before, our relationship needs to be repaired through a discussion face-to-face. You are still welcome to call me anytime to set that up. Thank you."*

Based on the text Elijah received, Elijah chose not to attend the party and neither did his sister. Jon took it upon himself to call Jasmine and tell her Elijah was not permitted to come to the party, to which Jasmine replied she was not going to attend either. Jon, of course, didn't inform his family that he was the cause of the kids not attending and his family assumed I had something to do with it.

A week after the birthday party fiasco, Jasmine started having issues with her cell phone and asked if she could get it replaced. Prior to my move, all of our cell phones were on a family plan under Jon's name. I removed my line and Elijah's line from his plan and left Jasmine's. Every month, Jon would complain about paying her phone bill. When Jasmine's phone began to act up, I decided to eliminate that conversation by porting her number over to my plan. I asked Jon to release her number from his plan and he ignored my emails. Jasmine's phone continued to be an issue until she couldn't take it anymore.

"Mom, can we please get me a new phone?"

"We can, but we will have to change your number if I put you on my plan. Are you ok with that?" I asked.

"Yes, let's go today, PLEASE?" Jasmine answered.

I got Jasmine set up on a new mobile plan with a new provider that evening and informed her she needed to notify every one of her new number. By 11 a.m. the following day, I began receiving numerous texts from Jon stating he was calling and texting Jasmine and not receiving a reply.

"Do you know if Jasmine's phone is working? I haven't been able to get in touch with her both yesterday and this morning."

"She got a new phone and phone number. She's going to text you," I replied.

"I thought we discussed that I was going to upgrade her and leave her on my plan. Why the sudden need to switch her over?"

"She had been asking for weeks to replace her phone because her old one was acting up."

"Monday was the first day she mentioned it to me and I let her know then that we would upgrade it. I have been trying to get in touch with her to set a night to do it. Again, we had an agreed upon arrangement and it was communicated clearly. I don't understand why you couldn't work with me on this?"

"What agreed upon arrangement? You were only communicating with Jasmine. You ignored my original email for a week and then decided to respond after I followed up on the original email and say you'll keep her on your plan. We already had a new phone by then. What is the big deal about switching her phone over? Especially when you requested I pay half the bill two months ago," I inquired.

"Do you have time to chat?"

"I'm on a call right now. I can call after."

"Ok, thanks," Jon replied.

A short while later, I stepped outside of my office to call Jon. "What is it you wish to discuss? I only have a short break before the next meeting.

"Why did you get her a new phone?" Jon asked.

"One, she told me a number of times her phone was acting up and she needed a phone. I, in turn, informed you and asked if you could port her number over to my plan to remove the expense from you. Two, you were repeatedly complaining about the cost of her cell phone, so I figured I would put her on my plan to ease your burden. Since you wouldn't release her phone number, she had to change her number with the new phone," I stated.

"I just don't understand why you would get her a new phone."

"I just explained to you, her phone was acting up and she needed a phone."

"I just don't understand why you got her a new phone when we had an agreement," Jon questioned.

"Jon, I'm working. I've explained to you more than once the situation with the phone. Unless you have something else you need to discuss, I'm hanging up."

Furious, Jon hung up on me. Later that evening, I asked Jasmine if she gave her dad and his family her new phone number.

"No," she replied. "I'm enjoying the peace and quiet while I can." Her reply spoke volumes to how she felt about them.

While Jon was concerned about a phone being removed from his control, Max, on the other hand, had mysterious bumps on his face that would not go away. I noticed the bumps in a prior custodial visit and asked Jon about them.

"I noticed them too. They have been there," Jon said. "I just told him to wash his face better."

*Hmmm, a ten-year-old child should not have acne.* You would think that would be a red flag for him, but it was not. By the next custodial visit, I noticed the bumps were still there and Max had a crusty patch developing in his scalp. I immediately scheduled an appointment with the pediatrician to have it looked at.

"It improved a lot this week with some polysporin. I have been having him wash his face extra every morning and night. He has been wrapping himself up in his covers while sleeping again and has gotten really sweaty when he sleeps. I've been monitoring him throughout the night and doing additional washing of his face. Please let me know if Dr. Johnson recommends anything," Jon stated.

Jon decided to attend the doctor appointment with us. At the appointment, Max informed the doctor the lady who cut his hair noticed the spot in his head two months ago and told Jon about it. The doctor and I both turned to look at Jon, who sat there dumbfounded. What a nightmare and gross neglect on Jon's part. The spot by his left temple had been there for three to four weeks. Of course, Jon did nothing about it. Max was diagnosed with Impetigo and needed to be on medication for three months to clear it up.

## And Yet He Persisted

Prior to a therapy session in April, Jon asked Jasmine if he could take her to lunch and then take her to her therapy appointment after. Jasmine begrudgingly agreed. Instead of picking her up during the agreed upon time for lunch, he picked her up two hours earlier and took her to his house to "talk." He always wanted to get her alone; something Jasmine did not want to do. Jasmine would later inform me she felt uncomfortable the entire time as he probed her repeatedly with questions on why she didn't spend more time with him and why she never spent the night at his house. He also asked her to stay an extra night with him in Florida in June, when we traveled for her final volleyball tournament for the season. He wanted to do a mini vacation with Shayla and the kids.

When it was finally time for lunch, they picked up Jon's mother and went to a Mexican restaurant. Jon's mother is ten times worse than him when it comes to crossing boundaries and manipulating people into doing what she wants. Her common manipulation tactics were tears and arm twisting until you gave in to what she wanted. She, too, probed Jasmine on the lack of time she spent with the family and how it made them sad and unloved; laying on the guilt trip the entire time. Jasmine's young mind was no match for these professional controlling, skilled manipulators.

By the time Jasmine got to therapy later that day, I could tell something was wrong. She looked out of sorts and upset. Jon came into the waiting room, visibly angry, and plopped down right next to me. Jasmine left to put some things her grandmother gave her in my car. As soon as she left, Jon started in on me. I knew as soon as he sat down beside me, I was in for it. He never sat near me during appointments.

The waiting room was quite busy with patients and parents talking and waiting. Jon looked at me with a stern angry look on his face and said,

"I picked up Jasmine's medicine from Target," Jon said, incessantly tapping his foot on the floor.

"Not a good idea, she needs to increase her dose based on her last appointment," I replied.

Jon bucked toward me with his fists clenched, seething, "Why didn't you tell me?!"

In that moment, I mentally froze and went back to that terrified woman living under the same roof during one of Jon's rages. I began shaking, became sweaty and nauseous, and felt like I couldn't breathe.

"You knew she had a follow-up appointment tomorrow to discuss dosage with the doctor," I whispered, trying to diffuse the situation in the busy waiting room.

He briefly looked away from me, paused, and then sternly replied, "I want to keep Jasmine an extra night while in Florida in June."

"She already has a return plane ticket with her club team just like the other tournaments," I replied.

Jon flipped out again. "Why would you do that without discussing it with me!?" Jon said, slightly raising his voice, bucking at me again as he spoke. "You want me to communicate with you, but you don't communicate with me!"

One of the children in the waiting room looked over to see what was going on. Trying to diffuse the situation quickly and stop Jon from making a scene, "Never mind, we will just get reimbursed from the volleyball club," I mumbled.

Jon calmed down while continuing to incessantly tap his foot on the floor. "Well, she hasn't decided yet," Jon seethed, sliding slightly back in his seat, still tapping his foot incessantly as he stared at the floor in anger.

Jasmine returned from putting her things in the car and Jon completely sat back in his seat and sat up straight, leaving me alone.

Not long after, Jasmine's therapist came to get her from the waiting room, I asked to speak to the therapist in private. The therapist took me back to her office. I explained what happened in the waiting room and how uncomfortable it made me feel. She told me Jon's behavior was unacceptable and walked to the waiting room to get him. He sat down, glaring at me.

"Mr. McAdams, your wife informed me you were verbally aggressive with her in the waiting room. That type of behavior is unacceptable. You can trigger patients with that type of aggression. You cannot behave that way in a mental health facility," the therapist told him.

"Well, I didn't raise my voice," Jon replied.

"But you were still confrontational and tense in our waiting room and it's not appropriate. People have mental triggers here that you can ignite," the therapist replied.

"I agree. I was just frustrated," he declared.

The same lame excuse he typically gave for bad behavior. As I got up to leave the room, he asked to speak with the therapist in private.

Meanwhile, I went back to the waiting room and packed up my things. I walked to my car and immediately burst into tears; a complete mess. He had triggered me. I called Marie to calm me down because the last thing I wanted to do was have my daughter see me in distress and trigger her.

"What's wrong?! Marie said.

I immediately burst into tears again, barely able to speak. "Jon just attacked me in the waiting room of Jasmine's therapist's office over medicine and a trip to Florida," I sniffled. "It was so stupid."

"Are you ok? Marie asked.

"I'll be ok. I just need to calm myself down," I replied. "I don't want Jasmine to see me crying. The last thing she needs is to see me in pain and trigger her."

Meanwhile, the therapist decided to take Jasmine for a walk during their session. Jasmine informed her that she didn't want to spend any nights with her dad and she didn't want to stay with him in Florida. She told the therapist she was too scared to tell him because of how he reacts when he doesn't get his way. As they began walking back to the building, the therapist approached my car and asked Jasmine to go into her office. I rolled down the window, still choking back tears and told my girlfriend I'd call her back.

"So, your husband wanted to speak with me after our meeting to tell me, "See how she blows things out of proportion?"

I just shook my head.

"He doesn't need to come to the appointments because Jasmine hates him being here. Can you talk to him and ask him not to come?" she asked.

"He won't listen to me," I replied. "I'm the last person he will listen to."

"Ok, I'll send him an email," she responded. "I don't want to talk to him on the phone or in person."

Based on her prior tense interactions with Jon over Jasmine's therapy approach, she didn't want to verbally interact with him one-on-one either. He had intimidated her to the point that she was seeking assistance from me; the emotionally abused mother battling PTSD.

After she walked back into the building, I called Marie back to tell her what happened. We decided to meet at Starbucks later that night so she could check on me to make sure I was alright. I scared her to death with my hysterical phone call.

Later that night, I wrote an email to the therapist, informing her I would no longer sit in the waiting room of the facility if Jon continued to attend appointments.

Hi Mandy,

Jon made a point yesterday of stating he didn't raise his voice while he was speaking. This is partially true. Yet, his tone and body language showed the highlighted signs below. I'm going to sit in my car if he continues to show up to Jasmine's appointments. [I attached a link to a website, highlighting the signs of aggressive body language.]

**Aggressive Body Language**
- Pupil contraction
- Direct stare can be hostile and aggressive

> - *Redness in the face*
> - *Rapid speech*
> - *Tense behavior*
> - *Intense Glare*
> - *Stiff, rigid posture*

I also began preparing my phone to record whenever I had one-on-one interactions with Jon, from that point forward, in case I had to file charges against him.

A week after Jasmine's therapy session, Jon's brother invited the kids over to see his kids. Not only did he ambush them with the kid's grandparents, who they did not want to see, but he also lectured the kids for one and a half hours on how they should try harder with their father — the narcissistic father that had mentally battered them for years. Jasmine broke down in tears while being chastised by her uncle, while Elijah stayed strong and simply replied, "I don't see the purpose."

Once Elijah was tired of listening, he grabbed Jasmine and walked out of the home.

As the weeks progressed, Jasmine decided therapy wasn't working for her and requested to stop seeing the child therapist. She also hated the fact that Jon showed up and wanted to talk to her every appointment. One night after a therapy session, we walked back to our car and got in. He walked over to my car on the passenger side.

"Why is he coming over here?" Jasmine questioned, looking at her father through her window, never attempting to put the window down. She simply stared at him through the glass until he tapped on the window. Slowly rolling the window down, she said, "Yes."

"I just wanted to say hello," Jon said, smiling.

"Ok," Jasmine replied blankly, staring at him.

Jon stood there for a few moments and then walked to his car.

"Hurry up and pull off before he comes back," Jasmine said.

I started up the car and drove out of the parking lot, headed for home.

My house was finished by the first week of May. We moved out of the apartment and into the house seven months after I left Jon. Two weeks later, I received a letter from Jon's mother with my birthday card. Below is an excerpt:

> "I know it's probably the farthest thing from your mind right now, but I truly hope you find someone, when you are ready, that treats you like you want to be treated. Jon never expected to find someone to date as quickly as he did, but under different circumstances, I think you'd like her. Especially for the way she treats the kids. They are just lucky to have two great women that care about them and want to spend time with them. God knows if it will work out for them, but she is treating the kids well and is mature enough to never say a bad word about you." ▶

After reading her joke of a letter, I thought to myself, *first of all, don't write to me, trying to convince me that Jon's new fling, who obviously has no moral compass, is a great woman. She moved in with a man newly separated and is prancing around the nation to his daughter's volleyball tournaments, in addition to having Max call her "mom." Second of all, he fully intended to find the next victim "immediately" when he got on every dating site available, as soon as he found out I was building a house. Please!*

We settled in to the new house within a month and got into a routine. I purposely built a home with cameras and a security system. Jon was so volatile and unstable that no one in the home felt safe; you never knew when he was going to snap. It took us two weeks to manage the security system and to remember to shut it off prior to opening external doors in the morning. It wasn't long before I received an email from Jon stating the following:

> "I would like to work with you on something. Max is still not doing very well with going back and forth between the houses and continues to request if he can stop doing this. I have asked him to speak to you directly, but he is too nervous to do so. While I believe it is important for all of the children to get exposure to both parents, I also want them to be happy. This has been difficult for me to do with Jasmine, but I have continued to honor her wishes. I believe we should revisit the parenting plan as it relates to Max as it is a weekly topic with him.
>
> I am open to any suggestions you may have and I have some ideas of my own as well. Again, I think we can work together on this for Max's best interest."

I chose not to respond to the email and consulted with an attorney who informed me I was not violating any orders since we had a signed separation agreement that covered child custody arrangements.

By June, it was time for Jasmine to upgrade her license to be able to drive alone without another licensed driver in the car. Jon wanted to be present; however, it was difficult to sync up schedules due to work. We planned to take Jasmine on a Wednesday morning. I couldn't commit to a time since my workday was erratic. I targeted

11 a.m. to get to the licensing office, but Jasmine overslept and my meetings ran long without a break in between. I informed Jon that we would call him when we were ready, but for some reason, he was stuck on that time and called me, furious when we did not arrive.

"I thought we were meeting at 11 a.m.?!" Jon sniped on the phone.

"Jon, I told you I couldn't commit to a time and that my meeting schedule was erratic. Also, Jasmine overslept."

"WHAT?!," Jon yelled through the phone so loud I had to pull the phone away from my ear. "Why didn't you wake her up?"

"I've been on calls all morning for work. I have not had a break."

"Typical," Jon sniped. "It's your job to wake her up! You're such a bad mother! Why can't..." Jon yelled.

I hung up the phone. He proceeded to call me back and I did not answer. This was typical behavior for him since I had left the house. He would attempt to control and condemn me over the phone, but now I had the power of hanging up without having consequences later. I now had the power.

Jasmine and I picked another day and time for her to get her license. She informed Jon she did not want him present, but needed her insurance information. Jon dropped it off for her late one night, without informing anyone that he was coming. Jasmine found out when he texted her, letting her know he had placed her insurance card under the front doormat. It came as a surprise to us that he wasn't picked up by the cameras. *How did he manage to evade the cameras?* Eerie feelings came over us both and we once again felt unsafe in our home.

## REFLECTION

Once Jasmine moved away from her father and spent less and less time with him, the bond of emotional incest began to break down and she started to become lost. Emotional incest leads to a child having a scattered sense of identity. Their parent's thoughts and feelings become their own, interfering with the child's proper development of self. The parent expects the child to mirror all of their traits, and the child, wanting to please the parent, follows suit. The child has difficulty with their own thoughts, feelings, and opinions and typically has difficulty thinking for themselves.

As a result, the child struggles with boundaries. Since the parent has no boundaries with the child, the child either grows up with zero boundaries and gets taken advantage of by others, or has such strong boundaries that they don't let anyone in. Jasmine and Max created false identities since they didn't have the opportunity to develop their own sense of "self."

Siblings in a narcissistic family identified as the *Golden Child/ Conforming Child* (Jasmine) and *Scapegoat/Trash Bin of Blame* (Elijah) are bonded by emotional trauma. They experience psychological warfare that most people wouldn't understand or believe based on the covertness of the narcissist. Their sense of self-worth is psychologically beaten out of them. The covert narcissistic parent is subtle in their emotional abuse of children, using insinuations and subtle daggers difficult for the child to recognize. Children are left with the impression that they are not good enough because they aren't doing whatever it is the narcissistic parent is visualizing in their head. The children end up confused from the gaslighting, making them feel like a failure or inadequate, needing to strive harder to earn the love and approval of the narcissistic parent, and often develop anxiety anticipating the next narcissistic rage and wanting to avoid it at all costs, trying to conform to whatever the narcissist wants or needs.

The Golden Child and the Scapegoat lack self-esteem from the constant criticism, demeaning remarks, and subliminal messages thrown at them from the narcissistic parent.

> *"As children, we want our parents to love us and take care of us. When our parents don't do this, we try to become the kind of child we think they'll love. Burying feelings that might get in the way of us getting our needs met, we create a false self—the person we present to the world. When we bury our emotions, we lose touch with who we really are, because our feelings are an integral part of us. We live our lives terrified that if we let the mask drop, we'll no longer be cared for, loved, or accepted."*[1]

My emotional reaction to Jon's attack in the therapist's waiting room would later be diagnosed as Post Traumatic Stress Disorder (PTSD). Jon triggered me. Experiencing multiple traumas impacts the body and mind over time. Certain parts of the brain become sensitive, keeping the brain on high alert to perceived threats making victims jumpy and anxious. The part of the brain associated with memory can actually shrink, making it difficult to form new memories. Repetitive stress affects mood, leads to anxiety disorders, and can lead to chronic pain and our ability to control food intake. The energy of the trauma lives in body tissue (primarily muscles and fascia) until it can be released through energy releasing techniques, such as Tai Chi. Stored trauma typically leads to pain and progressively degrades health.

---

1    *4 Ways Childhood Emotional Trauma Impacts Us As Adults, July 13, 2017 | Haven Staff*

*Chapter 10*

# POST SEPARATION
# ABUSE

In the spring of 2019, I planned a surprise vacation for the kids. I put aside money for three months to take them to Hawaii for a much-needed summer vacation. The kids had never traveled to Hawaii before; therefore, it was a new adventure for them. It was the perfect time, with everything they went through the prior year, and were currently experiencing. I didn't inform the kids of where we were going to keep it a surprise.

The night before we were scheduled to leave, Jasmine picked up Max from Jon's house. According to Jasmine, Jon informed her that Max did not want to go on vacation ▶ Jasmine, puzzled, asked Max why he didn't want to go, since he didn't know where we were going to form an opinion. Max had no response. It was obvious Jon was projecting his own feelings about our vacation onto Max and Jasmine immediately noticed that.

When the kids arrived at my house, Jasmine told me what occurred at Jon's. I asked Max if he was excited to go on vacation and he said, "Oh yeah," with a huge smile on his face. We left for Hawaii the next day and the kids enjoyed new cuisine, multiple beaches, parasailing and paddle boarding. Max never asked to call Jon the entire trip, nor did he mention missing his father. He had a great time, as did Jasmine and Elijah.

When we returned home from a very relaxing and mind-resetting trip, I had no idea the rest of 2019 would be a nightmare that would have me fighting to protect my children at all costs. I had just started the process of healing from years of emotional and verbal abuse, only to return back to fight or flight survival mode with high levels of stress, lack of sleep, hair and weight loss. Once again, my Hawaii vacation was marred by Jon's narcissism.

Around mid-summer, Jasmine started to complain about her medication not doing anything to help with her anxiety. Her pediatrician recommended she see a psychiatrist for alternatives. I spoke to my therapist about recommendations for someone who worked well with teenagers. She informed me of a woman she used to work with who was good with teenagers and used alternative methods of treatment. I informed Jon and after a brief discussion, we decided to schedule an appointment to see if she was a good fit for Jasmine.

Rachel was a Psychiatric-Mental Health Nurse Practitioner. She performed a series of social tests with Jasmine to determine her level of anxiety and briefly met with us to discuss possible treatment plans that did not involve medication. She noted Jasmine's anxiety was extreme, yet, believed that she could help her. The next day after meeting Rachel, I received the following texts from Jon.

"What were yours and Jasmine's thoughts on Rachel yesterday? I thought she was really good."

"Jasmine loved her. I thought she was great and I like the fact that she is not all about meds, but also healing from within. She also gave Jasmine full access to her and is monitoring how she's responding to the medication," I replied.

"Fantastic, I'm glad we are all on the same page. I truly hope that this is the blessing Jasmine has been waiting for," Jon texted in his most convincing tone as a concerned parent.

Jasmine decided she no longer wanted to attend talk therapy since it was doing nothing for her. She switched from seeing a talk therapist to seeing Rachel exclusively. After Jasmine's negative experience with her talk therapist, it took her awhile to feel comfortable opening up to Rachel. Jasmine had absolutely no faith in medical professionals at this time, since they had failed her every step of the way. They continued to overlook and expose her to the very person who was causing her significant angst... her father. However, Rachel was different. She had a very different approach to treatment for her patients and she believed in alternative methods as opposed to strict medicinal regimes. She thoroughly took the time to get to know Jasmine — her fears, her goals, her overall mental state. She was, by far, the most thorough practitioner we worked with and Jasmine liked her.

After our initial meeting with Rachel, we met with two psychologists recommended by Jasmine's talk therapist to conduct a personality test. At first glance, the psychologists' believed Jasmine was autistic due to her demeanor. She was very shy and despondent, looked at the floor a lot and barely spoke. After a brief conversation, one of the psychologist's walked Jasmine into another room to take her computer test. Jon and I stayed with the second psychologist to chat about our family dynamics.

"We are currently in the middle of a separation. Our youngest son, Max, rotates from home to home every week and Jasmine lives with her (Jon looked in my direction). We also have an older son who lives with her full-time as well," Jon stated.

"How are the kids doing with the separation?" The psychologist asked.

"Max is not doing well and is exhibiting separation anxiety." ▶

"Not true, he's seen a therapist twice who said he is not experiencing separation anxiety," I retorted.

Jon paused, looked down at the floor and then continued. "Our oldest is a college dropout and a bad influence on the two younger kids." ▶

I looked at Jon in shock. He completely threw Elijah under the bus for no reason.

## THE CONTINUED SMEAR CAMPAIGN

Jasmine concluded her test and walked back into the room. As we prepared to leave, Jon asked to speak to both psychologists privately. This was his opportunity to assassinate my character and play victim, similar to how he portrayed himself to Jasmine's talk therapist earlier in the year. ▶ I told Jon whatever he needed to communicate to the psychologists he could say with me in the room. He refused and didn't say a word until I got up to leave with Jasmine.

After Jasmine's test results came back, the psychologists' diagnosed her with severe anxiety and depression. They recommended outpatient care. I sent the report to Rachel for her records.

By mid-summer, I received an email from Jon, requesting the development of a parenting plan. An odd request, considering we already had an agreed upon parenting plan and custody agreement in our separation agreement. Jasmine wasn't spending time with Jon and it irritated him to his core. Therefore, he wanted to change our agreement to suit his needs. Of course, Jon being Jon, he gave me ten days to respond to his email. Bullying tactics were back in play. ▶

I consulted with two attorneys on Jon's email and asked their advice. Since we had an agreed upon plan in place and we were both adhering to it, they told me not to worry about Jon's email from a legal perspective. Ten days later, I received a civil summons in the mail for Temporary Child Custody citing Parental Alienation. I called Jon after I received the summons to have a discussion. He didn't answer my call. He replied through email and informed me he wanted to handle everything through attorneys; ▶ therefore, I hired my own attorney — the same woman I consulted with during Jon's affair. I needed the big guns for this battle. I also began to research parental alienation.

> **Parental Alienation:** is a controversial issue both in the legal and psychiatric fields. It is often used as a weapon against healthy parents in a custodial battle with narcissists, a common weapon of choice. First coined in 1985, it describes a process through which a child becomes estranged from a parent as the result of the psychological manipulation of another parent.

How he planned to prove I was alienating him from his children was yet to be seen. Based on our separation agreement, I was adhering to schedule in regards to the children and communicating with Jon on the children's needs and status. Jon was furious Jasmine refused to spend time with him; therefore, he wanted to force her into a defined schedule. Since I wouldn't play nicely with him and force Jasmine to see him, he resulted in using the legal system, also known as post-separation legal abuse.

I absolutely refused to let Jon bully me into anything anymore. I was prepared to fight with any means necessary — even if that meant losing every asset I had. Jon, on the other hand, fully expected me to cave with the delivery of the court documents. He provided me an out... *private mediation.* Since we couldn't agree to mediate among ourselves, I saw no point in paying lawyers to mediate for us. Let the judge decide, was my thought process. No judge would force a sixteen-year-old girl into a custodial schedule; therefore, I began to prepare for my legal battle.

I attended court-ordered mediation orientation one month later and started gathering documentation for my case. Guess who didn't attend mediation orientation? Jon, the person who filed the civil summons. I'm sure he thought we would never go to court, so why attend.

A week after receiving the civil summons, Elijah informed me that he had seen Jon at a stoplight, while on his lunch break from work. He just happened to pull up next to Jon and Shayla in the car next to him.

"Guess who I saw today?"

"Who?"

"Dad and Shayla. They were next to me at a traffic light."

"Did they wave?"

"No."

"Did they see you?"

"Yeah, Dad looked dead in my eyes and turned away," Elijah said, laughing.

I found Elijah's story interesting. The civil summons I received from Jon's lawyer also included a letter stating I couldn't discuss the case with Elijah, even though Elijah was legally an adult. The reason being, "Jon wanted to rebuild their father/son relationship." Yet, Jon couldn't even wave at his "son" at a traffic light. Now, if Jon's family was around, it would have been a different story. The same man I watched talk negatively about Elijah to all medical professionals, therapists, psychiatrists, and psychologists would attempt to hug and tell Elijah how much he loved him if his family was around. It was all a game to him. The kids were pawns in his game to exert control, manipulate and win.

Now that Jon sought legal action, he ramped up his requests to get Max back earlier during my custodial visits. Every week I had Max, I received texts from Jon requesting to get Max back early "because Max wanted to come home," Jon would say.

Max never informed me of wanting to leave and always had fun on our visits. He was excited to see and spend time with his siblings. To add insult to injury for Jon, Jasmine removed all of her belongings from Jon's home during this time and transferred everything to my house, to Jon's dismay. She put a stake in the ground that she would never live in his home again —finally coming to a point where she could confidently take a stand.

Jasmine had regular visits with Rachel throughout the summer and seemed to be stabilizing. As we got closer to the beginning of the school year, you could see her carefree spirit begin to diminish. School began the second week of August and so did volleyball. Still, Jasmine's first week of school did not go well. Her anxiety went into overdrive and began to affect her performance in volleyball, as well as school. Thankfully, Jasmine had a great support system in her coaches for school and travel volleyball. They truly cared for her and her well-being, so by the second week of school, one of the coaches reached out to me to talk.

"Every break Jasmine has during the day, she comes to the gym to hang out with us," her coach stated. "You may want to talk to the school counselor about alternative learning; such as homeschool, or concurrent education."

"Ok, I will look into it with her father."

"Also, Jasmine said she doesn't like her father coming to her games; he stresses her out. She said Grandma also stresses her out, putting pressure on her to spend more time with her dad. She said she doesn't like it."

"I'm aware of the situation," I replied, shaking my head up and down. "I've tried asking them to back off. It doesn't seem to be working. Thank you for looking out for her. I really appreciate it."

"You're welcome. She's a really sweet girl. Please keep me posted."

"I sure will," I replied, walking out of the gym.

## A FATHER SCORNED

Jon and I spoke with the school counselor a few days later. She suggested Jasmine's medical provider would be a more suitable person to have the discussion with since she knew Jasmine the best, so we scheduled a phone call with Rachel to discuss moving Jasmine to online learning to help with her school anxiety.

Instead of focusing on the subject at hand, Jon continued to beeline the conversation to his needs and the fact that Jasmine didn't spend any time with him. By the third time he brought this up in conversation, Rachel said, "You sound resentful that Jasmine has chosen not to spend more time with you. As her father, have you asked yourself why?"

"No, I don't know why," Jon responded.

"Why don't you know why? You're her father," Rachel said.

(Silence)

"Ok, so let's get back to the focus of the discussion," Rachel replied.

We discussed the pros and cons of moving Jasmine from traditional school to online learning, and concluded that online learning was the best option for her, considering her anxiety levels and the current complexity of life with travel volleyball.

Jon, unhappy with this suggestion, reached out to Jasmine's school principal for advice without consulting me first. The principal suggested a two-week intensive therapy program to help with

Jasmine's anxiety. This piqued Jon's interest and was a quick fix. He emailed Rachel to obtain her thoughts, copying me on the email.

Rachel replied with, based on her assessment of Jasmine, in-patient care would do more harm than good. Jasmine needed to feel safe and relieve stress. In-patient care would do the complete opposite, in her opinion. I also did not believe Jasmine needed in-patient therapy and expressed that to Jon as well. As long as she had zero interaction with him, she was fine.

It had become quite apparent to Rachel, through her discussions with Jasmine, that Jasmine had significant issues with her father. Jasmine had nightmares of her father harming her. One particular nightmare involved Jon sitting on top of Jasmine, choking her. She feared his rages. So, Rachel scheduled a session between Jon and Jasmine for her to talk about her feelings in a safe environment.

In preparation for the session, Jasmine had to fill out a "feelings" sheet. I walked her through the sheet and asked her what she wanted her relationship with her father to look like and what makes her feel sad. Jasmine immediately became overwhelmed and shut down; tears began to stream down her face and she could no longer talk. She became despondent. I left her alone to calm down and regain her composure. It took her two hours to get back to talking and interacting again. When she did, she filled out the sheet, selecting her father made her feel "uncomfortable", "uneasy", "scared", "mistrustful", "panicked", "nervous", "restless", "stressed", "ashamed", "afraid" and "anxious". All major red flags.

The following week, Jon and Jasmine met for their appointment with Rachel. After her appointment, Jasmine and I discussed what occurred during the ride home.

"I told Rachel I feel like I can't make any decisions about my life. I also told her I used to think about hurting myself earlier this year."

"Do you still have suicidal thoughts?" I inquired.

"Not anymore. A lot of my stress has been removed."

My heart broke for her. My sixteen-year-old daughter was really struggling with life. I instantly felt guilty for staying in an abusive relationship for as long as I did. It obviously impacted her significantly. I thought I was doing the right thing by keeping the family intact and listening to others who encouraged me to stay, when in fact, it was more detrimental to my children's mental health. It was clear that Jon's impact and the years of abuse and control was still affecting the kids even though we were no longer in the same home.

"I also told her I don't want to have a closer connection with Dad and how he and his family stress me out."

"What did Rachel say," I inquired.

"Rachel suggested no contact from Dad or his family for two weeks to give me some time to think and have a break."

"How did Daddy respond?"

"He was emotionless the entire time and agreed to no contact for two weeks."

I was extremely surprised he didn't balk at that. No control over how Jasmine lived her life for two weeks? He's going crazy in his head right now, I thought to myself.

During the two-week time span, Jasmine enrolled in online school and appeared to be less stressed. As I was reviewing her therapy notes at the kitchen table from her talk therapy sessions with Rachel, Jasmine walked into the kitchen.

"Do I have to attend Friday night dinner with Dad?" Jasmine asked, with a look of pure fear on her face.

"No, honey, it falls during your two-week time span of no contact."

"Thank God," Jasmine replied, a sigh of relief coming over her face.

As I read through Jasmine's therapy notes, I noticed it was documented several times that Jasmine did not like spending time with her dad. She didn't like how her dad had treated Elijah over the years, especially the physical assault that occurred prior to me moving out, and she stated it had a huge impact on her. Yet, the talk therapist still forced Jasmine into spending time with her father. I guess the therapist's own fear of Jon impacted her ability to provide safety for Jasmine.

Rachel had a scheduled vacation on the books. She didn't want to interrupt Jasmine's schedule of visits; therefore, she established a consultation with the psychiatrist in her office for a second opinion during her absence. Jon, Jasmine and I sat down with Rachel's colleague to discuss Jasmine's symptoms and what steps we had taken thus far. The psychiatrist provided a few suggestions he would discuss with Rachel upon her return. As we were preparing to leave, the psychiatrist asked if we had any questions.

"No, thank you for your time," I replied as I got up to leave.

"Yes, I'm just so worried about my daughter and I'm scared I'm going to get a call that she killed herself!" Jon said and immediately burst into tears.

I mean . . . this guy went full out. It was an Oscar-worthy performance. Jasmine and I both looked at him like he was crazy.

"She lives with me full-time and I have zero concerns for her safety. We spend a significant amount of time together," I replied. "In fact, she has gotten better and better every day."

"But she told me she was going to kill herself!" Jon blurted. ▶

"Jon, that was months ago when she had thoughts of hurting herself and she didn't tell that specifically to YOU. She has come a long way since then. Rachel told us both she did not believe Jasmine was a harm to herself and that in-patient therapy was a bad idea."

In an attempt to appease Jon, the psychiatrist suggested Jasmine be assessed at a mental health facility an hour away. Jon's ears perked up by the suggestion. His eyes sparkled in anticipation and his tears instantly dried up. He had achieved his goal.

"I'm free now," Jon jubilantly said. "Are you free?" Jon asked, looking in my direction with anticipation of the answer.

"Yes," I replied, rolling my eyes.

We left the psychiatric office and headed to the mental health facility. Jasmine, wondering what all the fuss was about, was confused as to why we were doing this. She had gone into a dissociative state while we were in the psychiatric office.

"Daddy expressed concerns about your well-being to the psychiatrist, so we have to get you assessed."

"Really?" Jasmine questioned, frustrated by the entire situation.

"Yes," I replied.

## DESPERATION SETS IN

*The following section of this chapter includes a detailed sequence of events I sent to my attorney to show what happened to my daughter over several days, and the lengths this man went to in order to make it happen:*

Once we arrived at the facility, they informed us it was a two-hour wait. After two hours of waiting, Jasmine was finally seen. They went over a series of questions with Jasmine and determined she was "no risk." They suggested outpatient therapy just as Rachel had suggested and the two psychologists we had visited in the past.

As the Nurse Practitioner told us her assessment, Jon became visibly angry. His face turned red, he pursed his lips, and he began looking at the floor. As the staff walked us out, Jon didn't say a word. Not even a "thank you" to the staff. He was furious. Walking back to our cars, he was speechless. I knew, then, this wasn't over... and I was right.

The next day, the Friday prior to Labor Day weekend, I received a phone call from him wanting to have Jasmine assessed at another facility; this time, a facility specifically for adolescents and teenagers.

"Jon, we already had her assessed and they said no risk. Rachel said Jasmine does not need in-patient care. Why are you still putting her through this?

"She told me she was going to hurt herself."

"Again, Jon, she did not tell YOU that. She mentioned that in a session you attended months ago. She had those thoughts at one time, but not any longer."

"Well, I can't sleep at night. I need her to have another assessment. Plus, she's open to being admitted."

"No, she's not, Jon. Jasmine does not want to be in a facility. I'm really not comfortable doing anything until Rachel returns from vacation."

"I spoke with the psychiatrist in Rachel's office again today, and he agreed she should be reassessed," Jon said.

"He only met Jasmine one time. Rachel is more familiar with Jasmine's needs and she explicitly said in-patient would do more harm than good," I restated.

With the child custody lawsuit looming over my head and not wanting to appear as if I was being difficult to a Judge, I agreed to have Jasmine assessed for a second time, buckling under the pressure from Jon, who kept texting and calling me nonstop. She had been assessed and sent home the night before; this should be a quick in and out process, I thought.

"Fine, Jon, she has plans to go to a football game tonight with her friends. We will have her assessed prior to the game."

We arrived at the facility and Jon filled out the paperwork. They called us back into a tiny room with a camera overhead. They ran through a series of questions with Jasmine, just like the facility the prior night. During this process, however, Jasmine was brought a plate of food. Odd, but okay... that was nice of them. As Jasmine answered questions, Jon jumped in and added his tidbits of inaccurate information.

"She has active thoughts of suicide," Jon blurted out to the assessor.

Jasmine and I look over at him in astonishment. ▶

"No, I don't," Jasmine sternly replied.

"She does not have active thoughts of suicide, Jon," I stated, staring at Jon with an intense gaze.

However, the assessor wrote down what Jon said.

"Sir, we went to another facility last night and Jasmine was sent home "no risk." She is currently under a psychiatrist's care for outpatient therapy."

The assessor nodded his head in acknowledgment, got up and left the room to consult with the staff physician. They both returned within ten minutes.

The physician looked at Jasmine and stated,

"You need to be admitted."

"What!" I blurted out in surprise. I was shocked! Jasmine's eyes widened in fear.

The assessor looked at Jasmine while expanding his chest, "You can do this voluntarily or involuntarily. It's easier if you do this voluntarily because if you don't, we will force you involuntarily."

Jasmine immediately bursts into tears. Jon sat there stone-faced and silent. *What kind of man does this to their own child?*

"I want you to speak to Rachel immediately. Jasmine is under psychiatric care and has a treatment plan. She does not need your services. We went to another facility last night and she was assessed "no risk." Jasmine said she's removed two stressors from her life, school and volleyball and she's in the process of starting online school."

The physician didn't care about any of it and never called Rachel.

"What options do we have," I asked.

"Voluntary or involuntary admission. You can get her out in three days."

I looked over at Jasmine, who was completely distraught by this point. I gave her a hug and tried to console her while her father signed the consent forms. I did not sign a thing, which seemed odd. How could a facility admit a child in a shared custody situation with one signature? We sat five hours waiting for her to be admitted. Jasmine had on shorts and a t-shirt and the room was freezing. I briefly walked out of the room to get a blanket while we waited. As I walked back into the room, I could see Jon talking to Jasmine and then stopping when I came in. Jasmine was clearly irritated by what he said.

During intake, a nurse came into the room. "Did you bring an overnight bag?"

"No, I didn't plan on staying," Jasmine snapped back.

I found it quite odd the nurse asked if she had an overnight bag. Based on the plate of food and the question on the bag, it would appear that Jon fully intended on admitting Jasmine to the facility and had set everything up prior to our arrival.

I said my goodbyes to Jasmine and walked out the door in tears. I was devastated. How could he do that to his own daughter? I came home and called Elijah to tell him what happened. He was out of town for the night, but drove home to be with me and see his sister during visiting hours the next day. I cried all night long and got zero sleep. I had to find a way to get my daughter out of that awful facility.

Elijah and I visited Jasmine during visiting hours the next morning. When we saw her, we both gave her a huge hug. She looked good considering her circumstances.

"I was worried about you, Mom. You had to stay in the house by yourself last night," Jasmine said.

Here I am worried to death about her and she's worried about me.

"Dad called me this morning to check on me. The nurse handed me the phone and I hung up on him. The nurse asked me why I hung up and I said, "because he's the one that put me here!"

Jon arrived fifteen minutes later and tried to talk to Jasmine. She gave him one-word responses, never looking in his direction.

"There's a girl in my wing that wants to fight me."

"What?" I replied, fearing for her safety.

"Yeah, she said it in front of two nurses and the nurses did nothing."

"I'm furious," Elijah said. "You're supposed to be in here for *safety*, but you have to fear for your life while you're in here. What sense does that make?"

We all turned and looked at Jon, who was speechless with a dumbfounded look on his face.

"Oh yeah, they moved me to the step-down wing. Why? Surprise, surprise... they determined I'm NOT SUICIDAL," Jasmine said sternly, looking at Jon.

We finished up our visit with Jasmine and headed back home. Later in the afternoon, Jasmine called me in tears and was very upset.

"Mom!"

"What's wrong, honey!?"

"The therapist said I'm staying seven to fourteen days!"

"What?! I'm doing everything in my power to get you out quickly. Let me make some calls."

After I hung up the phone with Jasmine, the facility called me. "Mrs. McAdams, I called to go over the program Jasmine is in. It's a seven to fourteen day program.

"I'm confused. When Jasmine was admitted, the physician said she could come home in three days."

"Well, I have here she's enrolled in our seven to fourteen day program."

"I want my daughter discharged immediately. What are the steps to begin the process?"

"Your husband has to agree, since you share custody and it also requires a physician's signature. I'll call Jon to get his thoughts on discharge."

"Thank you," I replied.

Five minutes later the nurse called me back. "Mrs. McAdams, your husband said he will think about it. I will have the nurse supervisor call you both on a conference call tomorrow morning to discuss."

I immediately texted the following to Jon, *"Staying as an in-patient for seven to fourteen days with a girl trying to fight Jasmine the entire time is not solving anything. She can do the same program as an outpatient."*

Jon ignored my text and never responded. ▶

By Sunday morning, Jasmine was still in the facility, two days later, still being threatened by another girl and Jon was not budging. I hadn't slept in two nights and my mind was in overdrive on how to get my baby out of that godforsaken facility that I wouldn't even admit my dog to. It had the worst reviews and was known for keeping kids for insurance money. I reached out to everyone I knew for advice. Finally, a friend of mine familiar with mental health facilities and their practices, told me to discharge Jasmine on an AMA (Against Medical Advice).

I visited Jasmine during visiting hours Sunday morning. Jon was there as well. Jasmine began to tell us about her stay.

"The girl who wants to fight me threatened me again late Saturday. I had to sit by her during group therapy."

Furious, I shook my head, glaring at Jon.

"I feel so bad for the other girls here. They are treated so badly. It's not good. I just really feel bad for them," Jasmine said, scratching her leg.

"I spoke to the therapist and she told me I was going to be here seven to fourteen days. I told her I was told I could get out in three days."

*That's my girl. She is on it and knows her stuff,* I thought to myself.

While looking at Jon, Jasmine sarcastically said, "The therapist told me if I get out early, my FATHER will find another place to admit me for seven to fourteen days."

Jon sat emotionless, and expressionless. He didn't say a word in response.

"Look at my wristband. It says, 'low risk.'" Jasmine held her wrist in Jon's face, practically hitting his nose in the process.

"We can actually discharge you anytime because you are here through voluntary admission. *Both parents just need to sign,*" I told Jasmine, looking at Jon.

"I don't know when you will be discharged. Make the most of your time here," Jon responded.

Jasmine rolled her eyes at her dad and looked away.

Jon knew when the facility would discharge her, since he arranged her visit; however, he pretended to be clueless.

After visiting hours ended, I waited for Jon to leave and requested to see the nurse supervisor. The nurse supervisor came out and the first question she asked was,

"Do you have a complaint?"

"No, I simply want to discharge my daughter," I replied.

She took me back to the assessment room to discuss. I immediately felt uncomfortable, since it was the same room we sat in waiting for Jasmine's admission. It gave me the creeps.

The therapist arrived shortly thereafter.

"I want to discharge my daughter.

"Have you spoken to Jon? Did he agree?"

"I consulted with my lawyer. I am within my right to discharge my daughter without Jon's consent."

"You're right, we can discharge her to you. The physician wants to keep Jasmine and they may do an involuntary hold."

"On what grounds?" I questioned.

"Let me grab Jasmine's paperwork."

The therapist returned, fiddling with her paperwork and informed me Jasmine was admitted on active suicidal thoughts and having a plan to commit suicide.

"As I stated the night of her admission, Jasmine's father made those statements, not Jasmine."

"Were you present during admission?

"Yes, I was and she never said that she had active suicidal thoughts. Nothing she said that night should have led to her admission. She was admitted based on her father's lies about her."

"Who does Jasmine live with?"

"Me, full-time."

"How often does she see her father?"

"Rarely, by her own choice. We do not need your services. Jasmine has a psychiatrist and a treatment plan. She's also signing up for additional outpatient therapy. I want to discharge Jasmine on an AMA."

The therapist looked shocked, got up and immediately went to grab the physician. The physician arrived and reviewed the risks of an AMA with me. I agreed to the risks.

"You know, Jasmine is not acutely suicidal as documented in her admission notes," the physician said.

"I know. I knew that when she was admitted," I replied.

I signed the papers and they prepared Jasmine for discharge. My baby was finally coming home! I was elated and a huge feeling of relief overwhelmed my body. I couldn't wait to tell everyone, I finally got her out. So many of our friends and family were worried about her, including her volleyball coaches who had reached out to me each day for updates.

When I saw my baby girl come through the facility doors, I was jumping for joy. I finally got her out! She was so excited to see me. As we were getting into the car, she said,

"The therapist told me you were here to get me out and you were "aggressive." They didn't want to deal with you, so they just went ahead and did the discharge."

"Ha! Aggressive?" I laughed. "Determined, armed with facts and my rights, yes, but in no way aggressive. I never raised my voice or got angry."

"What did Daddy say to you the night you were admitted, and I went to get you a blanket?"

"Oh, he asked if I knew why I was there and I said, yes, because of YOU. He said, it's your mom's fault because she drove you here." ▶

In true narcissistic fashion, Jon had shifted all blame to me for his actions. He cited me for parental alienation in his child custody filing when in reality, the alienator was him; another tool from the narcissistic toolbox.

The weekend was so emotional and stressful; we were both drained. By Monday morning, I had composed an email to my lawyer, informing her of the weekend's events. I also told her my daughter and I feared for our safety. We already had a security system installed at our home, but didn't feel safe. Jon was so unpredictable; you just never knew what he was capable of or would do next. All of my children had seen Jon angry and no one wanted to be near him when he was in that state of mind.

Would he get a 5150 hold *(5150 is the number of the section of the Welfare and Institutions Code, which allows a person with a mental illness to be involuntarily detained for a seventy-two-hour psychiatric hospitalization)*? Would Child Protective Services show up to my door? Would he try to harm either of us? All of these thoughts and more ran through our minds. Jon was on a mission to win a court case by any means necessary, even if that meant sacrificing his own children.

We were terrified and living in fear.

## FROM BAD TO WORSE

I emailed my lawyer the timeline of events, along with this note:

> *This weekend's events have caused my daughter and I emotional stress. This man is on a mission to build a case against me to the extent of sacrificing his daughter. I fear for the safety of myself and my children. I do not know what this man will do next; if he will try to put my daughter on a 5150 hold, or come after me or my children to get his way. I want to stop him in his tracks. Please advise on the best course of action, whether that is a restraining order or lawsuit.*

## HE HAS NO LIMITS

I was concerned with how Jasmine would do returning home after being in the facility over the weekend. Would she have nightmares? What additional trauma did she experience by being ripped away from the people she loved the most?

To my surprise, she seemed to adjust fine to being back home. However, she was done with her dad and wanted nothing to do with him. She had a scheduled therapy appointment with Rachel the Thursday after her release from the mental health facility.

Jon attended the session. Still, he was not remorseful, nor did he apologize for admitting his daughter, knowing she was being threatened her entire stay and the facility labeled her low risk.

After the session was over, we all walked to the elevator to leave. On the ride down, Jasmine said, "I'm going no contact for one month. No texts, phone calls or emails. This is not Rachel's request; this is all me."

Jon began biting his lip in disgust, but agreed to her request.

On our way to the car, Jon attempted to give Jasmine a hug and she pushed him away. She was done with her father and he knew it.

Now that she was no longer in his clutches, he began to focus on Max. Every custodial weekend, I began to receive texts requesting to get Max back early.

> 9/5/2019
> Jon: Max has asked to come home. ▶
> Me: I just spoke with him and he said he's fine.
>
> 9/7/2019
> Jon: Can Max come home tonight? I'm getting the impression he wants to come home. I can pick him up. ▶

In September, Jasmine and I went on a weekend trip to Williamsburg, VA to visit with my parents. Jasmine became ill with nausea and headaches over the weekend, but we thought she had a brief virus. I bought her over-the-counter meds to make her comfortable throughout the trip. By the time we returned home the following Sunday, Jasmine took a turn for the worse. She spiked a fever and was vomiting. I took her to the pediatrician the next day, who immediately suggested she go to the ER to have her appendix looked at. I called Jon on the drive to the ER to inform him.

Jasmine was admitted for appendicitis and they scheduled emergency surgery. I notified Elijah and Jon informed his family. We all sat in the waiting room waiting for the doctor to tell us she made it through surgery without any issues.

Jon's mom, who I had not seen in months, took it upon herself to sit by me in the waiting room.

"So, what happened?" she inquired.

"She wasn't feeling well all weekend. I took her to the doctor this morning and he said to immediately bring her to the ER. She complained of nausea and headaches all weekend."

"Ohhhh, that's odd."

I had no desire to talk to Jon's mom and her mere presence made me uncomfortable. I had been informed by mutual friends of her racist comments about me and my lack of parental skills, so I moved next to Elijah while Max spoke to his grandmother. Jon's mother was clear from the beginning of our relationship that she didn't want him marrying a black woman; therefore, it was no surprise to me in hearing she was making racial comments about me.

Jasmine successfully made it out of surgery. She was required to spend one night in the hospital. As we settled into her room for the night, the nurse asked her a series of intake questions. She rattled off her answers until the nurse asked, "Do you feel safe?"

Jasmine paused. She thought for a moment, looked over at her dad and her grandparents prior to answering.

"Yes," Jasmine replied with a despondent look on her face.

It was my custodial week with Max and I planned to stay with Jasmine in the hospital. I asked Elijah to take care of Max for the evening and get him to school the next day. Jon immediately had an issue with that.

"I think Max should stay with my parents tonight."

"Max, do you want to stay with your grandparents or Elijah tonight?"

"I want to stay with Elijah," Max replied with a huge smile on his face.

Jon bit his upper lip in disgust, staring at the floor. "I'm not comfortable with that," he stated.

"Ok, you saw me ask Max his preference. He clearly doesn't want to stay with your parents."

"I'm not comfortable with Max staying with Elijah."

"Ok, well he doesn't want to stay with your parents, so he's staying with Elijah. It's one night. He will be fine."

I walked away to check on Jasmine while Jon stewed in his anger. Jon's parents got up from the couch they were sitting on to leave for the evening. They said their goodbyes to Jasmine and attempted to give Max a hug. Max was completely oblivious to their presence and left with Elijah, saying goodbye as he went out the doorway without giving them hugs.

Jasmine was discharged from the hospital the next day. I gave her meds throughout the day and she never seemed to get comfortable.

By 7 p.m. that night, Max ran to get me yelling, "Mom, Jasmine can't breathe!

"What?!"

I immediately ran into Jasmine's room where she was struggling to clear her lungs to obtain air. All I could hear were wheezes. I called the ER to ask what to do. They told me to immediately bring her in. I called Jon on the way and we met at the hospital. The hospital assessed and diagnosed her with pneumonia. She was admitted and taken to the PICU.

I called my mom to let her know what was going on, and she flew out the next day to help me with Max while I stayed with Jasmine. Jon and I remained in the hospital room with Jasmine her entire stay. Jon barely spoke to me unless he absolutely had to and only spoke to Jasmine when I stepped out of the room. The second day of her stay, Jon left for a couple of hours to take a shower and change clothes.

As soon as he left, Jasmine turned to me in desperation and said, "Mom, don't leave me alone with him. When you leave the room, he attacks me."

"Ok, honey. I won't leave you alone with him again."

Later that day, Jon returned and his parents came to visit Jasmine. She was tired and uncomfortable. She really didn't want any company and it showed in her demeanor. Jon's mother went home upset and immediately began texting her.

> *Jasmine's grandmother: It breaks our heart you and your mom don't care about us anymore. What did we do?*
>
> *Jasmine: No response.*
>
> The next morning Jasmine received another text from her grandmother.
>
> *Jasmine's grandmother: What?!*

I took the phone from Jasmine and typed, "I'm in the hospital in pain. I can't talk right now."

"She's got three other grandchildren. She's always worried about someone not liking her," Jasmine said in disgust.

Jasmine's grandmother continued to text her.

> Jasmine's grandmother: "I'm so sorry your pain came back, honey. Please rest. But please explain things to me when your pain is gone. I just don't understand what we did or what you were told we did. We've also loved you and been there for you. Pops is really hurt, too."
>
> Jasmine: "I haven't been told anything."
>
> Jasmine's grandmother: "I really didn't think so, I was just so upset, I cried all the way home and couldn't sleep last night. I knew I hadn't seen you to offend you. Just never been ignored like that by either one of you in all of your years. I love you with all of my heart and love to talk to you in person when you are feeling better. But for now, please briefly explain to me what I or Pops has done."

The fact that Jasmine and I weren't actively engaging her grandmother in conversation during her hospital visit, bothered Jasmine's grandmother to the core. Jasmine stopped responding to her texts.

On Jasmine's final night in the hospital, Jon left for three hours. We couldn't figure out where he had gone. He returned saying to Jasmine, "I just spent two hours talking about you," as he leaned over to give Jasmine a kiss. Jasmine jerked away terrified. Her lips began to tremble as she slowly raised her head up from the bed. She feared Jon and it showed. She looked over at me in despair.

During our hospital stay, Jon's nephew had a birthday party. Elijah volunteered to take Max to his cousin's party for me, since I was not leaving the hospital. He had just finished dropping Max off when he called to inform me about a conversation he had with his grandmother, Jon's mom.

"Mom! Let me tell you about my convo with Grandma! She came up to me crying, talking about the family not being a unit and Jasmine not wanting to talk to her yesterday."

What?"

"Yes! I told her she better stop texting Jasmine that crazy stuff or she will be on "no contact" like Dad. Then she brought up the mental health facility."

"Oh Lord," I responded.

"I said don't bring that up. He put her in jail! She said, well he thought he was doing the right thing. ▶ I said, by putting her in jail where someone wanted to beat her up every day!? She said, well I didn't know that. I said of course not! He's not going to tell you that! He tells you what he wants you to hear. I just shook my head. I couldn't take her anymore. I just walked away and got in my car," Elijah said.

"O-M-G. She's a trip. I'm in the room with Jasmine and Dad. Let's catch up tomorrow," I replied.

Jasmine was released from the hospital after seven days. We returned home and she continued to rest, glad to be away from seeing her father on a daily basis. In the days that followed, she showed no signs of lung injury from her pneumonia.

## SPINNING A WEB OF LIES

In the state of North Carolina, you are required to attend family court mediation in an attempt to resolve your child custody issues, eliminating the need for a court proceeding. Jon and I had scheduled mediation two days after Jasmine was released from the hospital. I was a nervous wreck. I got two hours of sleep the night before. I hated having to ever be in the same room with him, and I had no idea what direction the session would go in.

The mediator began by asking Jon why he felt the current child custody agreement in the separation agreement wasn't working.

"I don't get to see Jasmine, and I used to see her all the time until my girlfriend came to her volleyball game in Florida. When Jasmine gave my girlfriend a hug, her mother had an upset look on her face and ever since then, Jasmine doesn't want to see me." ▶

"Maybe it's because you brought your girlfriend to her travel volleyball tournament in front of all of her friends and their parents and she was embarrassed," I replied.

The mediator agreed and asked if he would honor not bringing the girlfriend to events if asked. Jon agreed.

Jon then turned to me and asked, "Would you be willing to set a schedule for Jasmine?"

"No, I would not. If you repaired the issue Jasmine has with you, there wouldn't be a need for a schedule to see her. She would want to spend time with you without it being required," I replied.

"The judge will not enforce a schedule at her age," the mediator replied. "Let's focus on Max and what you want, Jon."

"I want a 70/30 split of time with Max."

"Based on what justification?" the mediator questioned.

"Separation anxiety." ▶

"Max has seen a therapist twice and she found no signs of separation anxiety," I countered.

"You will have a difficult time with that request unless you can prove your wife is a drug addict or an alcoholic," the mediator replied.

"Max said the older kids don't want to be around him when he's with his mother. He never likes going to her house," Jon blurted out.

"Teenager sibling rivalry," the mediator responded.

"Elijah is a threat to the younger two kids' safety," Jon stated.

"Max is nothing but smiles when he comes over. The first thing he does every Sunday is run up to me and give me a hug."

"The older kids vape in front of Max," Jon blurted.

"No they do not, Jon," I responded.

"Vaping is not against the law. You do realize that?" the mediator responded.

"Max is scared to talk to me when his mother is around."

The mediator, visibly frustrated, sighed, turned to Jon and said, "You are not working in the best interest of the kids. I suggest family counseling."

I also informed the mediator how Jon consistently infringed on my custodial time, trying to get Max back.

The mediator looked at Jon and said, "You can't force someone to be around you."

Mic drop! Yes! The mediator was my new best friend. I don't know how many times I told Jon the same thing. She gets it! Thank you for seeing through his BS. I was jumping for joy on the inside, trying my hardest to contain it and not revel in my win.

"Well, we're definitely not going to come to an agreement today. You can schedule another session at a later date or continue on with your court date in December," the mediator stated.

I gathered my things and immediately walked to the bathroom, so I wouldn't have to ride the elevator with Jon. I was so excited!

## SWITCHING TARGETS

Jon's case against me was in shambles and he was grasping at straws. Everyone he contacted for information on me to use in his case refused. I am a damn good mother and everyone who knew me and my kids knew that. So, what did Jon do? He began to hone in on Max. Constantly texting and emailing, requesting to get Max back early every week that I had him and getting angry when I refused. He began to tell Max all the things he was getting ready to do while Max was at my house, leaving Max feeling guilty for having to spend time with me.

The worst example was Monday night football. Jon sent me numerous texts requesting to keep Max an extra night so that he could watch Monday night football with him and his father. When I refused, he insisted I was being outrageous and going against my son's wishes.

9/15/19, 12:07 P.M.
Jon: Max has asked to stay longer so that he can watch the Browns on Monday Night Football with the family.

9/15/19, 1:36 P.M.
Me: I'll still get him tonight. You can pick him up from school tomorrow and take him to watch the game and then bring him back Monday night.
Jon: Ok, he wishes to stay here. Are you saying no?
Me: I will get Max tonight as scheduled and you can pick him up from school if he wishes to watch the game tomorrow. Thanks. You can drop him off by 6.
Jon: Will do.
Jon: Max asked if he can stay for the week.
Me: To keep a consistent schedule with Max and create stabilization, I will be keeping Max the entire week. I'll watch football with him tomorrow night if that is the activity he chooses. Thanks.

9/16/2019, 7:36 A.M.
Jon: Max was so excited to get to watch the Browns with me and Grandpa tonight. I don't think it will harm any stabilization to allow him to attend; it is what he wants. ▶

Jon dropped Max off at my home, as scheduled, Sunday night and picked him up from school the next day. He brought Max back to my house prior to the football game. Max arrived at my home super happy to see me and his siblings as usual.

"Hey buddy! How are you?"

"Good," Max replied.

"Did you want to stay with Dad tonight to watch Monday night football?"

"Not really. Daddy told me to ask you if I could stay an extra night to watch. He told me he wished I could stay to watch football or have a movie night, but I had to go to *Mom's house.*" ▶

"Oh, ok. Well, if you want to see the game, we can watch it later."

"Thanks, Mom."

Max went into his room to play Xbox with his friends.

Two weeks later, at the start of my next custodial week, Jon called me from his car, in front of my house, during drop off time.

"Max is crying hysterically and doesn't want to come in. Can Max stay with me an extra night? ▶

"No, Jon," I replied.

"Ok," he said, hanging up the phone and sending Max in.

Max came into the house excited to see me as usual — no tears, no red face, no swollen eyes, and completely elated for his visit.

Later that night, I decided to question Max on how he felt prior to his visit. This time I recorded the interaction for my attorney. "Hey buddy, were you sad and crying on the way to my house today?"

"No."

"Ok, bud. I don't ever want you to be sad to visit. You let me know if you're sad, ok?"

"Ok, Mom," Max said, giving me a huge hug.

Fall arrived and we were two months away from our court date. My lawyer filed my answer to the civil summons, a child support order and a deposition for Jon's girlfriend. Since she was living with Jon and interacting with my children, my lawyer suggested finding out what this woman was all about.

Shayla dodged the delivery of the deposition for two weeks, until the processor finally served her at her job. She immediately filed a motion to quash her deposition, citing the processor was aggressive and threw the deposition at her during a meeting with her boss and other executives, even though video evidence proved that was a lie. She also claimed my lawyer was aggressive, and I was a pathological liar. I knew all I needed to know about her from that point on. She and Jon were two peas in a pod and perfect for each other. Two pathological liars. My lawyer immediately issued a motion to compel, forcing her to appear based on her evasiveness to be served.

Meanwhile, travel volleyball tryouts were right around the corner and Jasmine decided to try out for different clubs. Jon was completely against this. He didn't understand why she would leave the club she had been playing with for two years and refused to pay any of the registration fees for tryouts. I kept a log of his emails since the separation agreement stated we would split all expenses for the children, and I paid the registration fees on my own.

Jasmine was hitting a turning point in her therapy. She was building her self-confidence, gaining autonomy, and making her own decisions. Now, it was time to face her father and tell him how she felt about him. Rachel scheduled a group session with Jon and Jasmine. Jasmine got everything off of her chest that had been eating her up inside. She told me about the session on our drive home.

"I told Dad how he made me feel, witnessing the abuse he did to Elijah during our childhoods. I told him how I was terrified of him and often had nightmares about him. I told him how I felt about him admitting me to the "psych ward" and how I've done so much better without him in my life. I told him how scared I was in the hospital when he returned one night and said he just finished up a two-hour conversation about me. I didn't sleep all night, scared he was going to admit me somewhere again. I told him I was tired of being forced into things and not having a voice."

"How did Daddy respond?"

"He sat there speechless and emotionless. It was like talking to a wall. I was in tears."

"Well, I'm glad you were finally able to get that off your chest and express your feelings. You should feel like a huge weight was lifted from your shoulders."

"It feels sooo good to get it out," Jasmine said, relieved.

## THE DARKNESS COMES TO LIGHT

Two days later after Jon and Jasmine's session, I received a settlement offer from Jon's lawyer, continuing to request a 70/30 split of time for Max and threatening to depose Elijah, if I didn't accept the offer within seven days. I didn't accept. Anything less than 50/50 was not an acceptable offer. Jón was continuing his attempts to exert control and punish me for leaving.

Within seven days, a process server appeared at my door to serve Elijah; such a great father. Elijah was confused as to why he was even brought into the battle, especially since the original letter I received from Jon's lawyer explicitly stated that I could not discuss the proceedings with Elijah.

Elijah was the last person he needed to depose for a child custody case because boy, oh boy did Elijah have a story to tell and it was NOT going to be in Jon's favor. In preparing Elijah for his deposition, Elijah shared incidences of abuse I was unaware of and incidents between his sister and Jon as well. When Elijah and I got home that night, I sat them both down at the table and had them tell me their stories. It was during this time that I learned the true extent of Jon's mistreatment of the kids, and discovered that not only was he abusive to me, but to the children as well. I was devastated and felt extremely guilty for putting my children through a tortured childhood. My children literally lived in fear when they were alone with Jon.

Elijah shared how he watched TV shows to see what a normal family was like. He shared how Jon repeatedly physically assaulted him in anger, beginning at a very young age. With every revelation, a piece of my heart broke into tiny pieces as my eyes welled with tears. *Why didn't I know this was going on? Why didn't I leave sooner?* The reality was, I was caught up in my own survival and didn't recognize the signs of abuse happening to my own children.

My son shared a very disturbing incident that occurred while being dropped off at school one day during his second-grade year. Jon was upset with him on the ride to school for not wanting to have a conversation during the trip. That was a requirement. You couldn't just ride in the car and listen to the radio. You had to appease Jon with conversation. Once they arrived at school, Jon got out of the car with my son, began yelling at him and shoved him into the car door. My son began crying and walked into school to tell the teacher. As tears rolled down his face, he told the teacher how his father had just shoved him into the car. The teacher listened and told Elijah there was no need to tell me since I wouldn't do anything about it. My heart sank. As a school teacher trained to recognize the signs of child abuse, how could she tell my child not to tell me?

Elijah continued with story after story of numerous incidents in which Jon raged at him and sometimes Jasmine; coming into his room, making a demand of him, and when he didn't move quick enough for Jon, he was shoved into furniture and walls. Even Jasmine felt the wrath, his pride and joy. Elijah told me about an incident where he and Jasmine were fighting over the TV remote.

Jon stormed downstairs and told them to shut up. Elijah attempted to explain what was going on when Jon pushed him down on the couch. As Jasmine stood up for her brother and told him to stop, Jon shoved her down as well.

Listening to each and every incident, I became more and more distressed and remorseful. I felt like a failure as a mother and it began to weigh heavily on my heart. I always taught my kids to tell someone when they were being hurt by an adult; what I didn't take into consideration was my children being hurt in their own home by someone who vowed to love and care for them. This caused my kids to suffer in silence, as they had been conditioned to not tell what occurred within the confines of the family. Speaking out meant disrespecting the family because that was the unspoken rule of the home that we all lived by.

My daughter began to chime in as well with each incident she witnessed. "Mom, Dad would go into Elijah's room every night and yell at him for no reason," she said.

"Every night?" I asked.

"Yes, every night."

"I heard him from my room, he was so loud," she replied.

## WHAT YOU CANNOT SEE, EVEN WITH YOUR EYES OPEN

*Where was I?* I thought to myself. The only time I could think these incidents occurred was when I was not home or in the shower. He knew when to cross the line and when to stay in his lane. My children were terrified of Jon and I had no idea. I thought I was doing the right thing by trying to keep the family unit when, in actuality, I kept us all in danger. I was trying to survive myself and didn't even realize my children were suffering right along with me. Guilt began to overcome my mind and body. My mind began racing and my heart was pounding. *How could I bring this man into my life? How did I not see what he was doing to my kids? I should have left the marriage sooner.*

But then I realized, I went through years of sleep deprivation, degradation, emotional and psychological abuse. I couldn't think clearly. I wasn't eating properly. I was mentally confused. I was in constant fight or flight mode, trying to survive and keep my family together. I cried myself to sleep that night in shame and guilt for the suffering of my children.

Jasmine ultimately decided to stay with her current travel volleyball club and signing night was approaching. It was a beautiful November evening when I picked her up after work, and we headed over to the club for the event. Twenty minutes after we arrived, we saw Jon walk in with Max. Max ran over to Jasmine and I and gave us both huge hugs. He was so excited to see us.

After the event was over, Jon pulled me to the side and asked if I was willing to chat. It was the night before my lawyer was going to depose his girlfriend, so I knew what the conversation was going to entail.

"I wanted to know if you would consider dropping the legal proceedings."

"I didn't start the proceedings, Jon, you did. I have spent thousands of dollars to defend myself over something that could have been a discussion."

"When Jasmine and I met with Rachel to discuss her feelings, I was shocked she felt that way about me. I had no idea," Jon replied.

"No, because you'd rather blame me than believe your daughter has her own issues with you."

Jon stood there speechless, not saying a word, looking across the gym floor. "Write up your offer and send it to me to review with my lawyer."

"I am not interested in revisiting the conversation a year from now because something didn't go your way. I need legal documentation and I want to recoup legal fees. I am not accepting less than 50% time with Max and I will not force Jasmine into a schedule."

"You didn't offer to negotiate on anything my lawyer sent over," Jon said.

"Your lawyer sent ultimatums and never moved from me having Max 30% of the time. I will never agree to that and I refuse to be bullied into it."

Silence.

"Talk it over with your lawyer and send me your offer. Based on the offer, I'll decide whether or not we will stop the deposition tomorrow," I concluded.

We walked over to Jasmine and Max, who were patiently waiting for us to leave. Jon leaned in to give Jasmine a hug as she stood there void of emotion and motionless.

Later in the evening, I receive a call from Jon. He was unable to get in touch with his lawyer to write up the agreement. "Can you call off the 10 a.m. deposition tomorrow, since we already agreed to settle?"

"I'm not calling off anything until I have a signed agreement in hand. I suggest you get your lawyer to write it up now."

"My lawyer said we can call off the deposition since we agreed to negotiate."

"Again, I'm not calling off anything without a signed agreement. I didn't start this fight, you did."

"But you filed for child support."

"I sure did, as a part of my answer to your lawsuit for child custody."

"You're a part of the problem," ▶ Jon replied.

"Jasmine lives with me 100% of the time. I wouldn't have filed if you didn't try to use the legal system to infringe on my time with my children. We had an agreed upon signed separation agreement in place."

"I may not be able to afford my mortgage and Max won't have a place to stay."

"I lived in an apartment for six months. The kids don't care where they stay. They loved that tiny apartment."

Jon sat on the phone, speechless.

"I suggest you get your lawyer to write something up tonight. Otherwise, I'll see you and the girlfriend at 10 a.m. tomorrow for the deposition."

Needless to say, Jon's lawyer never wrote up the agreement the night before the deposition. My lawyer, having no faith in Jon's lawyer based on prior experience with her, started a draft for review. I arrived at my lawyer's office at 8:30 a.m. to review the draft and make revisions. Jon and his lawyer showed up at 9 a.m. to review it. By noon, we had not reached an agreement. I informed my lawyer to proceed with the deposition.

After four hours of letting Jon's girlfriend dig herself into a hole that she was having difficulty digging herself out of, I looked over at Jon and asked if he wanted to try to negotiate again. He agreed and we finally reached a settlement.

I called all of my close friends and family to let them know it was finally over. Although, I didn't feel victorious. I didn't sleep the entire night, worried that it wasn't actually over; that Jon in his twisted, sadistic mind would attempt to come after me again. We had an agreement in place prior to his filing the Civil Summons and he still came after me. When would he stop and just leave me alone? Or, would he never stop...

## REFLECTION

Narcissists will attempt to control the narrative in regards to their self-image. They do not want people to see them for the vulnerable shell of a person they truly are. They will recruit therapists, family members, friends, coaches, teachers and anyone else involved in their intimate partner's lives, as well as their children, to believe their false sense of truth to obtain empathy and gain allies in their campaign of destruction.

It has been three years since I left my husband to start a new life. The harassment, abuse, counter parenting, and intimidation thrown my way for so many years built up my strength. I stepped into post separation abuse since leaving Jon, continuing to experience legal and financial abuse in regards to my children. I refuse to be broken by a person who thrives off of abusing others. I will protect my children by any means necessary, even if that means losing everything I own to keep them safe.

My kids and I finally feel like a family. One that loves, nourishes and supports one another. Something we never had with their father. I finally got to be a mom to my daughter and teach her about womanhood. Elijah finally had a safe haven free of ridicule, harassment and abuse. We are all broken in our own ways, yet we accept that fact, work on healing every day and still continue to thrive. I'm not entirely free from Jon's narcissistic tactics, since Max is still a minor that we currently parallel parent.

I take each day one day at a time. Although I received EMDR therapy to treat my Post Traumatic Stress Disorder (PTSD), I still have the occasional triggers and break down in tears when my ex stirs the pot of drama.

I refused to date for two years after leaving Jon, fearful of meeting the same type of man. I chose to work on myself and implemented self care. Rebuilding myself was of utmost importance. When I felt I was strong enough to date again, my fears were confirmed with the first man I dated. He was a full- blown narcissist. He began to gaslight, blame shift and project his inappropriate behavior onto me. This time I saw the red flags and stopped seeing him. Convinced I would not meet anyone of interest who would meet my standards, and I would, therefore, be alone for the rest of my life, I gave up and accepted my fate.

While vacationing with a friend in early 2021, I met a man who would prove me wrong. A man who was different from anyone I had dated. A man who treated me with respect, valued my intelligence, listened to me when I spoke, and cared about my feelings. After sixteen years of abuse, I didn't know how to accept his kindness and see him for the genuine person he truly is. I call him my "unicorn" because he's a rare find in my mind. A true "giver" when the majority of my life, I dated "takers" — men interested in what I could provide them and what they could take from me, whether that be emotional, physical or monetary support. I don't know what our future holds, but I know my life is brighter with him in it, and I feel safe with him.

Elijah and Jasmine are both adults now and have ceased all contact with their father. The abuse they endured and continued to endure after leaving the marital home was enough to break all ties with Jon and his enabling family, who continue to support him and his ways. Jasmine continues to heal from her anxiety, childhood trauma and PTSD. She, as well as the rest of us, are triggered whenever we see a car that resembles Jon's around town, fearful that we have to come into contact with him. Elijah has moved out of town to get away from Jon and his family. He keeps in touch with his sister and me and visits on occasion.

Max is now a teenager with a strong affinity for his father. He has blocked the traumatic memories of the physical assaults and emotional abuse he repeatedly witnessed in the family home. My only hope is that one day he will be open to therapy as a coping mechanism for when those memories return.

Narcissists damage their children during their developmental years. It's mentally exhausting to deal with a narcissist as an adult with life experience in dealing with high conflict people. Children have zero life experience and do not know how to counteract narcissistic abuse; therefore, they internalize their pain until it exhibits itself in the form of anxiety and depression. I still feel guilty at times for putting my children through the trauma of my marriage, but I can't kick myself forever. I, too, was trying to survive in a relationship that society feels is normal. If you aren't being physically abused, society downplays your trauma, normalizing verbal and emotional abuse as if it is something you should accept and learn to live with in an intimate relationship.

> *"The typical adult from a narcissistic family is filled with unacknowledged anger, feels like a hollow person, feels inadequate and defective, suffers from periodic anxiety and depression, and has no clue about how he or she got that way." —Pressman and Pressman, The Narcissistic Family (reference addition)*
>
> **EMDR Therapy:** *- Eye Movement Desensitization and Reprocessing (EMDR) therapy is an integrative psychotherapy extensively researched and proven effective for the treatment of trauma. It enables people to heal from the symptoms and emotional distress that are the result of disturbing life experiences.*

# RESOURCES

## CHARACTERISTICS OF A COVERT NARCISSIST

Narcissistic Personality Disorder (NPD) is a diagnosis obtained from a licensed medical professional; however, an individual can exhibit recognizable narcissistic traits without a diagnosis.

1. Does your partner excessively attention seek — requiring your attention day in and day out?
2. Does your partner throw temper tantrums when they do not get their way?
3. Did your partner appear to be the perfect mate in early dating; telling you what you wanted to hear, having the same exact likes and dislikes, enjoying the same hobbies, meeting all of your expectations and desires in a partner?
4. Is your partner possessive and controlling; expressing dismay or anger when you spend time with others or enjoy activities without them?
5. Does your partner constantly complain that you are not meeting their needs or providing them enough attention, no matter what you do or say to meet their needs? (They

typically require you to say things in a very specific way to be acknowledged by them or else the effort is discounted.)

6. Does your partner make you feel crazy at times; starting arguments over the most benign things that don't make sense, continuously looping the conversation no matter how you respond and never end the argument with any resolution?

7. Does your partner violently explode in an argument, verbally and emotionally abusing you and acting as if nothing ever happened the next day?

8. Does your partner refuse to take accountability for their behavior or make changes to their behavior, even though you've expressed how hurt they make you feel?

9. Does your partner constantly make you feel like their insane behavior is all your fault?

10. Does your partner constantly forget incidents of verbal and emotional abuse and deny they ever occurred?

11. When you reach your breaking point and finally take a stand for yourself against your partner, does your partner play victim and cry or appear hurt as if you did them wrong?

12. When you try to express things to your partner, does that make you feel upset or uneasy; does your partner immediately reply back with, "Well, you did this to me" instead of acknowledging the behavior?

13. Does your partner often interrupt you while speaking to say, "Can I finish, or you didn't let me finish what I was saying?"

14. Does your partner often accuse you of trying to be in control of the relationship with comments similar to "It always has to be your way"?

15. Does your partner often want you to quickly get over a traumatic event they have put you through; such as physical or

mental abuse with comments similar to "Why can't you just get over it?" or "How many times do I have to apologize?"

16. Does your partner have a distorted negative view of events you recall completely differently?

17. Does your partner accuse you of flirting with people you regularly interact with, regardless of how innocent the interaction is?

18. Does your partner consistently behave as if they found evidence of your wrongdoing when you have done nothing wrong?

Covert narcissists are master manipulators. They will often use "gaslighting" to make you seem crazy. They instill confusion through projection and inaccuracies in events to make you feel crazy and believe their false truths.

## COGNITIVE DISSONANCE

According to cognitive dissonance theory, individuals seek consistency in their beliefs and actions. We seek a balance of beliefs. When a person has two or more conflicting thoughts at the same time or engages in behavior that conflicts with their beliefs, they feel a sense of mental discomfort. This is known as cognitive dissonance. When in a state of dissonance, a person feels a need to resolve it and restore balance.

## COGNITIVE DISSONANCE AND THE NARCISSIST

Narcissists are masters at creating dissonance in their relationships. They often use manipulative tactics — intimidation, emotional, physical, financial, and sexual abuse, social isolation, sleep deprivation, and more to maintain power and control over their victims.

The threat of abuse is always present and usually becomes more frequent with time.

Victims of narcissists doubt their gut reactions and continue to cling to their narcissistic partner, despite walking on eggshells daily and living in fear of what will happen next, "Will he be a loving partner today, or start an argument over nothing and demean me?" This keeps the victim torn between believing what they want to believe about their partners – *the partner is capable of changing into someone who can really love me if I pay more attention to them and show them how much I care* — versus the reality that the narcissist's behavior is anything but loving and will never change, regardless of what the victim says or does. The narcissist will continue to shame, belittle, criticize and punish the victim, creating extreme dissonance.

There are three ways to relieve cognitive dissonance:

- Change your behavior.
- Change your beliefs.
- Justify your beliefs and behavior.

Victims often choose to change their behavior to please the narcissist and try to restore balance.

*For example:*

> Narcissist: "You're selfish."
> Victim Response: Will try their hardest to be giving and kind to the narcissist

> Narcissist: "You're mean," or "If you hadn't said this or did this, I wouldn't have…"
> Victim Response: Will go out of their way to show the narcissist how caring and loving they are, often without reciprocation.

For a victim in a narcissistic relationship, finding ways to reduce cognitive dissonance is a primary defense mechanism. It is the path of least resistance that the victim believes will keep them safe. For example, the victim may justify the situation by lying to themselves, *"he loves me, and everything will go back to how it was while we were dating, as soon as I...".* However, every time the narcissist abuses, the victim continues to experience the stress of cognitive dissonance.

When nothing changes regardless of the victim's changes in behavior, the victim begins to doubt their own self-perception. Prior to meeting the narcissist, the victim typically has strong self-perception. They see themselves as competent, caring, giving, generous, independent, loving people. They are effective outside of the home and get along with just about everyone. However, in the home, the narcissist repeatedly calls the victim selfish, uncaring, mean and thoughtless.

The narcissist wants the victim to think and act like them and will consistently attempt to make the victim conform. The narcissist uses fear, obligation, and guilt (FOG) to manipulate the victim. When the victim resists, they are plummeted with verbal attacks of being selfish, uncaring, mean and thoughtless. The victim tries time and time again to convince the narcissist of their point of view; however, their attempt falls upon deaf ears.

The victim, in turn, becomes a full-time caregiver who nurtures, listens, cares for and takes responsibility for the uncomfortable negative feelings of the narcissist; trying to fix what cannot be fixed. The victim begins to lose themselves, resulting in depression, anxiety, frustration, confusion, guilt, low self-esteem and physical stress symptoms. They lose sight of who they are, what they want, and their own interests, feelings and needs. They adapt to the narcissists highly emotional, tense, traumatic and chaotic environment.

Victims of narcissistic abuse who have lived with cognitive disso-nance for long periods of time, experience brain changes similar to those in people with PTSD. They also develop a series of physical symptoms often manifested in the form of autoimmune disorders and can even suffer brain disorders. Victims literally can't think straight. This makes it difficult for them to change their situation and move on from the narcissist. Techniques such as Eye Movement Desensitization and Reprocessing (EMDR) Therapy and Tapping can help the victim with the healing process after they leave the relationship.

## WORD SALAD

A "Word Salad" is a combination of manipulative conversational techniques designed to frustrate, confuse, and poke holes at the sanity of the victim. This leads the victim to question their recol-lection of events, as well as their own judgment in general. Word salad commonly happens when the victim confronts the narcissist about their behavior. However, it is also used as a gaslighting tech-nique on a regular basis.

The six most common techniques of word salad are:

1.  *Denying Bad Behavior.* Narcissists will often deny their own bad behavior and focus on the victim's. Here's an example:

    *Victim: "You told the therapist you were going to stop insulting me."*

    *Narcissist: "You told the therapist you would show me more attention."*

    *Victim: "How are the two equal?"*

*Narcissist: "I told you what my needs are, and you consistently do not meet them. You're probably cheating on me with your boss and that's why you don't show me any attention."*

2. *Circular Conversations.* Conversations that are repetitive, circular, and never resolved, regardless of the compromises made with the narcissist. When confronted with their bad behavior, the narcissist becomes defensive, denies the behavior, denies previous conversations about the behavior, and brings up other unrelated topics and spins those topics endlessly.

3. *Condescending & Patronizing Tone.* The narcissist will provoke the victim into an intense emotional reaction, regardless of the victim's warnings that they are becoming upset. The narcissist's non-emotional response comes across as insulting, condescending and patronizing. This tone is often used by a narcissist during the "discard" phase of the relationship or during a smear campaign. The narcissist has already told friends and family that the narcissist is leaving because the victim is crazy and has an awful temper, even though the narcissist provokes the victim to prove their point.

4. *Projection.* Accusing the victim of doing things that they are doing. During a confrontation, a narcissist will often "project" or accuse the victim of the exact thing that they are doing themselves, whether that be cheating, displaying possessiveness and/or jealous behavior, etc.

5. *Multiple Masks.* Whenever a narcissist feels like they are losing control of a situation, they will begin to use every manipulation technique and mask they have in an effort

to regain control. The victim might see masks such as the "caring emotional mask" (I love you), "the abusing mask" (it's all your fault), and "the self-pity mask" (pity ploy). A narcissist trying to regain lost control is one of the craziest interactions ever witnessed. They try any and every attempt to regain control over the victim.

6. *The Eternal Victim.* The root cause of the narcissist's cheating and deceitfulness is always some perceived issue the narcissist has with the victim, the kids, or work. The victim, showing empathy, feels bad for the narcissist and believes things will get better when, in reality, things continue to stay the same. Narcissists always claim they are the victim, when in reality, it is those closest to them that are continually victimized by the narcissist.

## WARNING SIGNS FOR FRIENDS AND FAMILY

A victim in the middle of the narcissistic abuse cycle often does not realize it. Since they do not realize they are being abused by their partner, they are unable to properly reach out for help.

Here are some early warning signs that someone you know may be experiencing abuse:

- They limit or stop spending time with family and friends.
- They become obsessed with time and frequently check in with their partner.
- Their partner insists on accompanying them everywhere, including events at which their attendance is inappropriate.
- They are always worried about their abuser's mood or upsetting them (walking on eggshells).
- They are typically outgoing and cheerful but have become quiet and withdrawn.

- They stop participating in activities they would usually enjoy.
- They may reveal that the partner is mean when drinking alcohol.
- They begin to exhibit low self-esteem, which is not their typical personality.
- They develop a drug or alcohol problem.
- They are sleep-deprived or always tired.
- They talk about or attempt suicide.
- They have to ask permission to go anywhere or to meet and socialize with other people.
- They may refer to their partner as jealous or possessive.
- They may say their partner accuses them of having affairs.
- Their partner constantly calls or texts them, wanting to know where they are, what they are doing, and who they are with. The partner may even follow the victim to check up on them.
- They make excuses for their partner's behavior.
- They appear to be depressed, anxious, or exhibit other changes in their personality.

How can you help family and friends subjected to abuse?

- Be a listening ear when they need one.
- Let them know you love and care for them.
- Let them know you are there for support when they need you.

## VERBAL AND EMOTIONAL ABUSE NEUROLOGICAL AND PHYSICAL EFFECTS

*Fight or Flight Response:* Constant verbal and emotional abuse cause the victim's sympathetic nervous system to constantly invoke the "fight or flight" response. Victims often express symptoms of:

- Excessive tiredness
- Hair Loss
- Irritability
- Insomnia
- Headaches
- Chest pain, heart palpitations
- Fatigue
- Lack of sex drive
- Gastrointestinal Issues – bloating, gas, nausea, SIBO

*C-PTSD:* Complex Post-Traumatic Stress Disorder (C-PTSD) is the brain's response to a traumatic event. Verbal and emotional abuse can often lead to (C-PTSD). Here are the signs and symptoms:

- Intrusive thoughts or memories, flashbacks
- Physical-emotional reactions to reminders of trauma
- Nightmares or insomnia
- Severe anxiety, guilt, or loneliness
- Distorted sense of self related to trauma
- Detachment or isolation from other people
- Hyper-vigilance, irritability, hostility

Unfortunately, C-PTSD in women is often undiagnosed or misdiagnosed by health professionals, due to a lack of training. Also, many women who are victims of C-PTSD do not even realize they have the disorder and suffer in silence.

# NARCISSISTIC ABUSE CYCLE

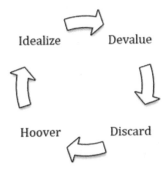

Idealize     Devalue

Hoover     Discard

The narcissistic abuse cycle is manipulation through the phases of Idealization, Devaluation, Discarding and Hoover.

- *Idealization (Love bomb)* - constant attention, gifts, and immense flattery at the beginning of the relationship
- *Devalue* - verbal abuse, name calling, condescending comments
- *Discard* - abandonment (new love interest or "shiny toy")
- *Hoover* - attempts to "suck" the victim back into a severed relationship and pull them back through the cycle of abuse

In the midst of an ongoing abuse cycle, it's difficult for victims to verbalize what they are experiencing. Abusers twist and turn reality to suit their own needs, idealize their victims over and over after abusive incidents, and convince their victims that they are the ones who are the abusers.

Victims of narcissistic abuse often feel mentally exhausted, depressed, controlled and constantly on edge in a "fight or flight" mode. Although there are no physical scars for this type of abuse, psychological and verbal abuse affects the brain the same way as physical abuse. A punch to the face and a verbal attack are perceived the same way in the brain. Both experiences can lead to and often do lead to Complex – Post Traumatic Stress Disorder (C-PTSD).

## ARE YOU A VICTIM OF VERBAL AND EMOTIONAL ABUSE?

*Does your partner...*

1. Blame you for how he or she feels or acts?
2. Pressure you sexually for things you don't want to do or force you to do sexual acts against your will?
3. Make you feel guilty for not having sex with them?
4. Prevent you from doing things physically or psychologically — like spending time with friends or family?
5. Shame you about qualities or traits you have that they once praised?
6. Shut down conversations about their behavior before the conversation begins?
7. Call you names when he or she doesn't get their way?
8. Frequently compare you to others in a demeaning way in terms of appearance, personality, success or any other aspect of yourself they like to criticize?
9. Have frequent rage attacks when their ego is threatened?
10. Discourage you from pursuing dreams or goals that would make you independent of them?
11. Treat you affectionately one minute and coldly the next?
12. Make you feel sorry for them after mistreating you?
13. Make you feel guilty for voicing your concerns in the relationship?
14. Make you doubt things that you know for a fact your partner has said or done?
15. Punish you for making choices independent of their opinion?

16. Make you feel ashamed about qualities and accomplishments you used to be proud of?
17. Accuse you of having flaws that they themselves possess?
18. Constantly call or text you to "check in" when you're not with them?
19. Keep you up all night or wake you up in the middle of the night to argue?

*Do you...*

1. Sometimes feel scared of how your partner will act?
2. Believe that you can help your partner change if you changed something about yourself?
3. Try not to do anything that would cause conflict or make your partner angry?
4. Always do what your partner wants you to do, instead of what you want?
5. Stay with your partner because you are afraid of what your partner would do if you broke up?
6. Feel tense around your significant other?
7. Constantly take the abuse, get frustrated, explode and then feel guilty after your partner plays victim to your attack?
8. Wish for a peaceful, calm life that is supportive, friendly and easygoing?
9. Feel tired, overwhelmed and alone in your relationship?
10. Feel guilty and confused when thinking about your life?
11. Find that the way your partner treated you in the beginning of the relationship is unrecognizable from the way your partner treats you now?
12. Find yourself questioning your own reality on a daily basis?

13. Feel like your accomplishments are belittled, ignored or minimized by your partner?
14. Feel like you're always walking on eggshells around your partner, constantly thinking about what to say or do just to avoid "offending" them?
15. Find yourself apologizing for things you're not at fault for in the relationship?
16. Find yourself apologizing for the mistakes that your partner made but refuses to own up to?
17. Feel anxious when you think about how your partner treats you?
18. Feel you have to ask permission from your partner before you do something?

*Self-Reflection...*

1. Are you afraid to express your true feelings around your partner because of the way they've reacted to you in the past?
2. If you call out your partner's behavior, do they become excessively angry?
3. How many ways have you wasted time trying to please your partner, only to learn that they are never satisfied with anything you do?
4. When your partner is acting kind, does it seem out of place with the way they usually act?

## THE RED FLAGS

Covert narcissists can be hard to spot at first glance because they're extremely charismatic. Here are some common red flags for awareness.

▶ Grandiose sense of self-importance

- Preoccupation with fantasies of unlimited success, power, brilliance, beauty, or ideal love
- Belief they're special and unique and can only be understood by, or should associate with, other special or high-status people or institutions
- Need for excessive admiration
- Sense of entitlement
- Interpersonally exploitative behavior
- Lack of empathy
- Envy of others or a belief that others are envious of them
- Demonstrates arrogant and haughty behaviors or attitude
- Their behavior flips after you commit to the relationship, becoming less attentive, outwardly self-centered, and inconsistent.
- You feel controlled, as if you can't speak your mind without jeopardizing the relationship.
- You make excuses for their behavior.
- The relationship moves quickly.
- They really need you.
- They don't have close friends.
- They have little to no sense of humor.
- They gaslight you.
- They rarely speak about themselves during the love bombing stage.

## PREPARING TO LEAVE A NARCISSISTIC RELATIONSHIP

Starting over is a scary thing and you may say to yourself, *"I can't leave my partner; I need him/her financially,"* or *"There's no way I can manage being a single parent."* These are called excuses. Your mental health and peace of mind are more important than staying with your abuser. Free yourself from the traumatic bond that binds you. Where there is a will there is a way.

When you mentally prepare to leave your abuser, devise an action plan to leave. First and foremost, inform family and friends of your decision for awareness and personal safety. Here are some items to include in your action plan:

- Financial Plan (budget, income, expenses)
- Legal Resources
- Abuse Documentation
- Housing Options
- Home Essentials (furniture, kitchen essentials)

*Financial Plan*

Depending on your circumstances, you may or may not have ever had to manage your finances. In either case, it's always best to have a budget and additional income sources when you move out on your own. A minimum of one month prior to leaving your significant other, do the following:

- Prepare a budget, documenting current income and future expenses. This will give you an idea of housing you can afford.
- Obtain a lockbox and keep it at a friend or family member's home for copies of important documents; such as pay stubs, bank statements, loan statements, life insurance, tax returns, cash, mortgage documents, medical insurance documentation, green card or immigration papers, passports, birth certificates (you and your children) deeds, car title, registration and insurance and anything else of joint ownership.
- Make copies or take photos of your spouse's pay stubs, bank statements, investment statements, 401k statements, life insurance.

- Make copies of credit cards, front and back and credit card statements
- Document passwords for all online accounts that are held jointly
- Take inventory of what is in the current home and what you want to remove. Document and take photos.
- With every shopping trip (Target, Walmart or the grocery store), purchase one item each trip to store at a friend's house:
  - ✓ Toilet paper
  - ✓ Paper towels
  - ✓ Shampoo/Conditioner
  - ✓ Body wash
  - ✓ Toothpaste
  - ✓ Hair styling products and tools
  - ✓ Towels/Washcloths
  - ✓ Visa gift cards, food gift cards, gas gift cards
- When paying for your groceries with a debit card, select the "cash back" option and siphon off an extra $20 plus dollars with each trip.

### Legal Resources

Seek the guidance of a high conflict attorney if you are married and leaving the marital home. Contact your local domestic violence shelter or utilize the resources below:

- Legal Aid - offers legal services to low-income families
- Avvo.com - offers legal guides for domestic violence survivors.
- Womenslaw.org - has a wealth of information on legal issues pertaining to domestic violence survivors.

Interview lawyers and determine the best fit for your case. Ask each lawyer if they are familiar with the study "Confronting the Challenges of the High-Conflict Personality in Family Court", located at https://www.npdandlaw.com.

## *Abuse Documentation*

It is imperative that you document your abuse for legal reasons. If you wish to file an order off protection, you'll need evidence of abuse, whether that's in the form of police reports or personal documentation. If you are married and filing for divorce and are seeking full custody of the kids for their own protection, you'll need evidence of abuse.

- Document exact days and frequency of abuse.
- Journal incidents of abuse with dates, times, and witnesses utilizing audio recordings on your phone, a phone diary app, phone notes app, google docs or simply keep a physical journal with you. Keep it factual, avoid hearsay.
- Record arguments and tense conversations.
- Document abusive patterns of behavior and categorize themes such as incidents or rage, substance abuse or inability to co-parent.
- Visit your doctor and obtain a medical report of stress-related diagnoses.
- Call the police and obtain police reports during incidents of physical abuse or when an imminent threat to your personal safety is felt.
- Store all emails, texts and/or social media messages from your abuser.
- Save all abusive voicemails on your phone.

### Housing Options

The quickest way to remove yourself from an abusive environment is to move in with family or friends. It is also the least expensive. If this is not an option, research affordable housing with your local domestic violence center and on the internet. Some additional options are:

- Apartments.com
- hudexchange.info
- Craigslist.org (House Rentals)
- Realtor.com (House Rentals)
- Zillow.com (House Rentals)

### Home Essentials

Starting over is not cheap and there will be a number of items you'll need to get back on your feet. Here are a few ideas:

- Ask family and friends for kitchen and bath essentials they no longer use as well as furniture.
- Reach out to your local domestic violence centers for information on their furniture programs.
- Check craigslist.org for free or inexpensive items.
- Visit your local thrift stores for inexpensive household items.

## SAMPLE PLAN

Here are the steps I followed to leave. While this may not apply to everyone's situation, it offers a useful guide.

- Created a plan to leave
- Created a financial budget documenting income and expenses

- Informed family and friends of my decision to leave for awareness and safety
- Consulted with a lawyer about a separation agreement
- Created a draft separation agreement for negotiation with my husband
- Researched and visited potential places to stay
- Re-routed my paychecks to my personal bank account
- Changed beneficiaries on my life insurance
- Finalized the separation agreement and legalized it with my lawyer
- Signed a lease on an apartment
- Packed up my things, hired movers and moved out
- Limited contact with my husband
- Immediately started a healing plan for personal recovery from the abuse

The most important aspect of your plan is your safety, and if you have children, their safety and well-being as well.

## BARRIERS TO LEAVING ABUSIVE RELATIONSHIPS

Victims of verbal and emotional abuse stay in abusive relationships for many reasons. The average person typically asks, "Why don't they just leave?" It's not easy to leave someone you love. You've seen the softer side of that person and you wait in hopes that the person you fell in love with will appear again. The brain is rewired after long-term exposure to abuse, rendering the victim incapable of pulling themselves out.

If a victim does find the strength to say enough is enough, they are often pulled back in by the abuser through manipulation, guilt or promises that things will change. Victims often say:

I didn't know it was abuse.

I was scared to be without him/her.

I had no support.

I had abuse amnesia.

I thought the abuse was all in my head.

I had high anxiety about leaving.

I thought everything was my fault.

I was trauma bonded.

I thought it was my job to love and serve them.

I didn't know where to get help.

I thought it was my fate.

I was financially dependent.

I was scared of further abuse if I tried to leave.

I didn't think anyone would believe me.

I wanted to please him/her by taking the abuse.

I was afraid he/she would kill me.

I thought he/she would change.

In addition to the victim's personal hindrances to leaving an abusive relationship, family, friends, and society in general, present barriers to leaving. These include:

- A victim's fear of being charged with abandonment, losing custody of children, or losing joint assets
- Anxiety about a decline in living standards for themselves and their children
- Spiritual counselors' encouragement of "saving" a couple's relationship at all costs
- Religious and cultural practices that stress divorce is forbidden
- Failure to maintain the relationship equals failure as a person

- Isolation from friends and families due to feeling "ashamed" of the abuse
- The rationalization that their abuser's behavior is caused by stress, alcohol, problems at work, unemployment, or other factors
- Societal factors that teach women their identities and feelings of self-worth are contingent upon getting and keeping a man
- Inconsistency of abuse; during non-violent phases, the abuser may fulfill the victim's sense of romantic love

## THINGS TO EXPECT FROM THE NARCISSIST WHEN YOU LEAVE

- Blame
- Guilt-tripping
- Attention demands
- Social attacks, gossip
- Using the children as pawns
- Continued abuse of the children
- The creation of chaos and discord with medical professionals, coaches and teachers
- An unrelenting display of "involvement" and "concern" for the children that did not exist before
- Playing the suffering victim and the problem being you
- Long drawn out divorce or child custody battles

Narcissists are skilled at destroying their partner's social circles and relationships with family members. The prospect of leaving may equate to a feeling of being truly alone; fear of reprisals — The narcissist may have created a culture of fear and anxiety in their partner's life. Thus, the act of leaving is not as simple as outside observers would assume. Additionally, to the outside observers and those aligned with the narcissist, you are the one that needs to be left, the one causing grief and pain.

Here are a few things you can do to make your exit less stressful:

- Join an abuse support group, locate a trauma therapist, and lean on sympathetic friends
- Become more autonomous. Create a life aside from your relationship that includes friends, hobbies, work, and other interests. Whether you stay or leave, you need a fulfilling life to supplement or replace your relationship.
- Build your self-esteem. Learn to value yourself and honor your needs and feelings. Develop trust in your perceptions and overcome self-doubt and guilt.
- Learn how to be assertive and set boundaries.
- Learn how to nurture yourself.
- Identify your triggers.
- If you're physically threatened or harmed, immediately seek shelter.
- Don't make empty threats. When you decide to leave, be certain you're ready to end the relationship and not be lured back.
- If you decide to leave, find an experienced high conflict attorney. Mediation is not a viable option when there is a history of abuse. Narcissists refuse to negotiate and collaborate. They would rather run up your legal fees.
- Whether you leave or are left, allow yourself time to grieve, build resilience, and recover from the breakup.
- Maintain strict no contact, or only minimally necessary, impersonal contact that's required for co-parenting in accordance with a formal custody-visitation agreement

## THERAPEUTIC HEALING

A victim goes through a series of grieving or healing stages while in an abusive relationship. Although these stages may be difficult at times, they are necessary to bring clarity and healing to the situation.

### Denial

Denial is a defense mechanism against painful emotional experiences that are difficult to accept. For example, you may know that you're in a bad situation with your narcissistic partner, but you have difficulty taking the proper steps to leave the narcissist and move on with your life.

### Anger

Anger follows the denial stage. It typically shows up when the narcissist is inflicting hostility towards their victim. You're angry the narcissist continues to exhibit behavior that hurts you and you do not understand why they do not change. Anger also arises within you when you realize the abuse cycle you've been in.

### Bargaining

You begin to make changes to your behavior or initiate changes in the relationship in an effort to make life with the narcissist better. You may take a family vacation to re-bond with the narcissist, buy a new house, have another child, or initiate a separation to give each other space. You try numerous things to make the relationship fulfilling for you as well as the narcissist.

You'll cycle through the phases of denial, anger, and bargaining over time.

### Depression

Depression is unexpressed anger turned inward on the self. You've tried everything and nothing seems to work in the relationship. Logical solutions fail and the numerous changes you've made have done nothing to fix the relationship. Although this is a low point, it actually signifies you are experiencing relationship awareness and realize there's nothing you can do to change and/or satisfy the narcissist.

Depression appears as someone experiences a loss of self-worth. This is the most difficult stage to be in, and it makes one feel withdrawn and exhausted. Passive anger needs to be converted into expressive activity to see things more objectively.

### Acceptance

Acceptance is when you realize you are powerless to change the narcissist. The relationship with the narcissist can never be normal. The phase brings a sense of relief when you finally realize it's not you! You no longer need to give in, placate, or satisfy the narcissist's ridiculous demands. You begin to take back your own power.

You will move through these phases in different ways. One phase may dominate while others may merge together. Whatever your personal process, a full experience is necessary to help you recognize and release your attachment to the narcissist.

Once you finally accept the fact that the narcissist will never change and your attempts to have a normal, loving relationship will never materialize, you can begin to take steps to move on and heal your mind and body after your traumatic experience.

*sur—Prefix meaning "over, above"*
*Thrive—Verb meaning to "prosper, flourish"*

### Forgive

You will probably never forget the abuse you endured at the hands of your partner, but you have to learn to forgive your partner for the abuse. You are probably angry with yourself for staying in such an abusive relationship for so long. To your defense, you were bonded to the abuser through the traumatic bond.

Forgive yourself... forgive your abuser and end the cycle of negativity to allow yourself to grow and heal. Holding onto the pain of abuse will leave you in emotional turmoil and affect your health. Forgiveness is linked to lower mortality rates, cholesterol, blood pressure, and cortisol (the stress chemical in our brains) and a lower likelihood of developing cardiovascular disease. Therefore, there are physical as well as psychological benefits to forgiving. Free your mind to focus on positivity and to move into the future.

> *"Suddenly, the fight-or-flight response of vengeance is replaced by the calming green pastures and still waters of peace."* —George Vaillant, MD

## Journaling

Therapeutic journaling is the process of writing down your innermost thoughts and feelings about your personal traumatic experience. It validates experiences and provides mental and emotional clarity. It is especially therapeutic when healing from narcissistic abuse. Some tips for therapeutic journaling:

- **Time Yourself:** Timed writing exercises help you tap into relevant unconscious material.
- **Write Freely and Openly:** You are writing for you and your healing. Silence your inner critic.
- **Be Genuine:** Honor your thoughts, feelings, and experiences with authenticity.

Write down your experience, process it, and understand it. Journal your lessons learned and how you changed from the experience. I spoke to therapists off and on during my healing journey without any impact. The biggest impact to my healing was through journaling my experience. It was a very liberating and uplifting experience to release the negativity I held within for so long. Below, you will find a Therapeutic Writing Exercise you can use to prompt your journaling:

1.  How has your partner used your own insecurities against you? How will you improve on those insecurities to take away their power of being used as a weapon?

2. How did being in an abusive relationship change you?
3. What early warning signs did you miss that you now realize are red flags?
4. Looking back on your relationship, what would you have done differently?
5. What are the positive aspects of enduring and surviving your abusive relationship?
6. What did you learn about yourself after leaving the relationship?
7. What are you going to do or what have you done to heal from the abuse you have endured?

## *Meditation*

Research has scientifically proven that meditation is a safe and simple way to balance your physical, emotional, and mental state. It has been practiced for thousands of years. More doctors are promoting the practice of meditation to cure many stress-related illnesses.

When you slow down your brain rhythm through meditation, your heart rate, metabolism, and breathing rate slows down, which lowers your blood pressure. Endorphins (natural painkillers) are released into your system, giving a sense of calm.

Below are some of the benefits of meditation:

- Reduced anxiety
- Increased self-confidence
- Lower cortisol levels (stress chemical)
- Increased serotonin (low levels of serotonin are associated with depression, headaches, and insomnia)
- Enhanced energy
- Normalized blood pressure

- Reduced stress and tension
- Increased concentration and strengthening of the mind

### Affirmations

Affirming is the practice of positive thinking. Reciting daily affirmations is attributed to changing your mood, a habit, and mitigating stress. You've lived in negativity, now it's time to live in positivity. Rebuild and retrain your mind to be positive.

Affirmations are carefully constructed, positive statements and phrases. They are exercises for your mind; a tool for positivity. Repeat them daily and believe in them for these positive mental repetitions can reprogram your thinking patterns and influence how you think, act, and feel.

**Step 1:** Look at yourself in the mirror

**Step 2:** Recite the following statements out loud every day for a minimum of thirty days:

- I am confident.
- I am beautiful.
- I am loved.
- I am worthy.
- I am happy.
- I am courageous.
- I am good enough.

**Step 3:** Write your own healing affirmations

### Healthy Lifestyle

Since you have endured mental and physical stress over a period of time, it is likely your body is displaying signs of stress. It's time to rebuild your temple and get yourself back in good health.

1. Build Your Social Network: It's time to lean on the support of family and friends. You've probably kept the extent of the abuse away from them, due to guilt or fear. Now is the time to open up and let them support you. If you're not comfortable opening up to those closest to you, locate a local narcissist abuse support group and/or social network group to express your feelings and work through your emotions.

2. Get Your Body Moving: Exercise is a powerful way to eliminate stress and heal the mind. Take an exercise class, lift weights, do Pilates, or join a boot camp.

3. Load up on the Nutrition: Clean up your diet by limiting caffeine, alcohol, and refined sugars. Increase your intake of fruits, vegetables, and healthy protein.

4. Take Supplements: Take a multivitamin and supplements to balance the stress response; such as vitamin C, B-complex vitamins, zinc, and magnesium (the relaxation mineral). Drink Holy Basil tea to relieve stress and energize.

5. Learn to Relax: Go to the spa, get a massage, take a yoga class, read books, or any relaxing exercise to ease your mind.

*"Ninety-five percent of all illness is caused or worsened by stress."* —Mark Hyman, MD

## AFTER LEAVING YOUR ABUSER

Post Separation Abuse:
Domestic violence (DV) is more than just physical abuse. During the relationship, domestic violence can be physical abuse, verbal abuse, emotional abuse, psychological abuse, sexual abuse, and financial

abuse. When the relationship ends, the abuse does not stop, it just transitions to a new form of abuse referred to as post-separation abuse.

> *Post-separation abuse continues to escalate, and often, far surpasses the DV that victims are subjected to while under the same roof as their abuser. After the relationship ends, the perpetrator sets their sights on the child(ren) to exert control and, to terrorize the healthy parent. Every high-conflict custody battle has three basic narratives: the abuser's need for control, the abuser's need to "win" and, the abuser's desire to hurt or punish the healthy parent.*
>
> *While there are many resources available to victims of DV during the relationship, the only resource available to victims of post-separation abuse is the Family Court System itself (judges, mediators, minor's counsel, custody evaluators, therapists, co-parenting counselors, parenting coordinators and attorneys). It is so important for those in the family court system to be educated on post-separation abuse and to recognize it in high-conflict divorces, custody battles and paternity cases.*
>
> –www.onemomsbattle.com

## POST SEPARATION ABUSE WHEEL

After leaving your abuser, you'll go through a series of emotions. You may feel sad, you may feel excited, or you may feel scared. You're taking on full responsibility of your own life and the life of your children if they are a factor. You need to begin to provide for yourself and your family while healing from the abuse you have endured. Here are a few action items to get you started:

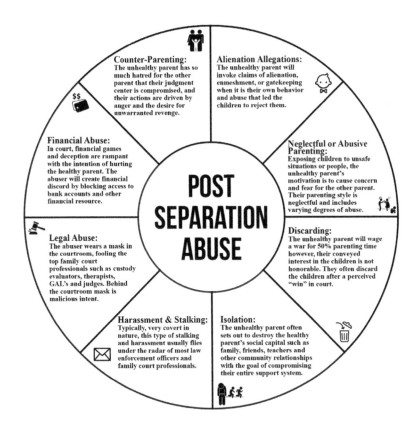

## POST SEPARATION ABUSE

**Counter-Parenting:**
The unhealthy parent has so much hatred for the other parent that their judgment center is compromised, and their actions are driven by anger and the desire for unwarranted revenge.

**Alienation Allegations:**
The unhealthy parent will invoke claims of alienation, enmeshment, or gatekeeping when it is their own behavior and abuse that led the children to reject them.

**Financial Abuse:**
In court, financial games and deception are rampant with the intention of hurting the healthy parent. The abuser will create financial discord by blocking access to bank accounts and other financial resource.

**Neglectful or Abusive Parenting:**
Exposing children to unsafe situations or people, the unhealthy parent's motivation is to cause concern and fear for the other parent. Their parenting style is neglectful and includes varying degrees of abuse.

**Legal Abuse:**
The abuser wears a mask in the courtroom, fooling the top family court professionals such as custody evaluators, therapists, GAL's and judges. Behind the courtroom mask is malicious intent.

**Discarding:**
The unhealthy parent will wage a war for 50% parenting time however, their conveyed interest in the children is not honorable. They often discard the children after a perceived "win" in court.

**Harassment & Stalking:**
Typically, very covert in nature, this type of stalking and harassment usually flies under the radar of most law enforcement officers and family court professionals.

**Isolation:**
The unhealthy parent often sets out to destroy the healthy parent's social capital such as family, friends, teachers and other community relationships with the goal of compromising their entire support system.

1. Obtain therapy for yourself and your children. Your children have experienced the abuse alongside you. They need healing as well.

2. If you have children, notify their schools, coaches, etc. of your separation for their awareness.

3. Obtain a new cell phone plan in your name or buy a prepaid phone for yourself and your children.

4. Have your electronics analyzed for spyware (phones, laptops, ipads, chromebooks, etc.).

5. Search your car for a tracking device.

6. Reset ALL of your passwords.

7. Forward your mail to your new address.

8. Get your résumé in order if you are seeking employment.

9. Create new bank accounts and re-route your paychecks.

10. Change beneficiaries on your life insurance and 401k plans.

11. To minimize expenses, downsize your lifestyle. Trade in your car for a less expensive one, minimize eating out, and avoid costly activities. Use free activities for entertainment.

12. Use coupons to save money on groceries.

13. Start building your credit if you have none.

14. Sell items you no longer need in a yard sale or on eBay, Craigslist, Facebook, etc.

15. Seek post-separation support, alimony or child support if your children move in with you full-time and your spouse's income is higher than yours.

16. Research additional income sources to utilize after your move. Do you have a skill you can use for freelance work; such as writing, virtual assistance, PowerPoint presentation development, logo development, etc.? Check out these work-from-home sites:

   - Fiverr.com
   - Upwork.com
   - Guru.com
   - Craigslist.org
   - More traditional sources of income:

      ✓ Obtain a part-time job
      ✓ Work for Amazon Mechanical Turk
      ✓ Work through a temporary employment agency

   - Drive for Door Dash, Grub Hub, Uber, Lyft, etc.

If you have an immediate need for cash, ask family and/or friends for a short-term loan. If you are in debt, devise a plan to pay your debt down slowly over time. You won't be able to do this immediately after leaving, but it is essential for your own financial security.

*Additional Resources*

- **www.freefrom.org**

The FreeFrom mission is to create pathways to financial security and long-term safety that support survivors of gender-based violence.

- **wispinc.org**

Provides educational scholarships to women survivors of intimate partner abuse.

- **www.modestneeds.org**

Provides short-term financial assistance to individuals and families in temporary crisis who are ineligible for most types of conventional social assistance.

- **www.facebook.com/groups/SurThriveTribe/**

The SurThrive Tribe is a community of survivors THRIVING after abuse. It is also an educational resource for those beginning their journey to THRIVE. Starting over can be scary and overwhelming. Our goal is to lessen your fears and provide resources and support to help you regain your life with confidence. THRIVE with renewed hope and enthusiasm for life.

## HELP IS AVAILABLE

I am a Certified High Conflict Divorce and Child Custody Consultant. I help individuals in High Conflict Divorce and Child Custody battles to strategize, establish evidentiary documentation (incidents of emotional, verbal and physical abuse) for their legal battles, and strategically communicate with their ex during the legal process and beyond. I also serve as a support person and shoulder to cry on when needed.

If you're interested in learning more about my consulting, and how I can assist you in your High Conflict Divorce or Child Custody legal battle, read more about my services and what I have to offer on my website: www.surthrivetribe.com

Let's stay connected:

Follow me on Instagram @alanasharps and @surthrivetribe
Follow me on Facebook SurThrive Tribe

Here are some additional support resources for you:

WomensLaw.org
**www.womenslaw.org**

The National Domestic Violence Hotline
**www.thehotline.org**

National Coalition Against Domestic Violence
**www.ncadv.org**

Office of Women's Health
**www.womenshealth.gov**

Dr. Ramani: Narcissism Expert, Licensed Clinical Psychologist, Best-Selling Author, Professor of Psychology, Distinguished Speaker, & Workplace Consultant: **www.doctor-ramani.com**

World Narcissistic Abuse Awareness Day
**www.wnaad.com**

Love is Respect
**www.loveisrespect.org**

Purple Purse
**www.purplepurse.com**

## BOOKS

Arabi, S. *Becoming the Narcissist's Nightmare: How to Devalue and Discard the Narcissist While Supplying Yourself.* New York: SCW Archer Publishing, 2016.

Fjelstad, M. (2013). *Stop Caretaking the Borderline or Narcissist: How to End the Drama and Get On with Life.* Lanham: Rowman and Littlefield Publishers, Inc.

Forward, S. Frazier, D. (1998). *Emotional Blackmail: When the People in Your Life Use Fear, Obligation, and Guilt to Manipulate You.* New York: Harper Collins

Bessel van der Kolk M.D., *The Body Keeps the Score: Brain, Mind, and Body in the Healing of Trauma,* New York: Penguin Books, 2015.

Made in the USA
Columbia, SC
07 December 2021